KU-737-589

ZERO
HURRICANE & P-38

Stewart Wilson

Original illustrations
by
Juanita Franzi and Dennis Newton

INTRODUCTION

Welcome to the fourth in our *Legends of the Air* series, this one dealing with three of the leading fighters of World War II, the Hawker Hurricane, Lockheed P-38 Lightning and Mitsubishi A6M Zero. Each was revolutionary in its own way, offering new features and new levels of capability for its time and each played a crucial role in the air battles of the 1939-45 war.

The Hurricane was one of the outstandingly versatile combat aircraft of the war, earning immortality in the summer of 1940 during the Battle of Britain when it and its counterpart, the Supermarine Spitfire, turned back Germany's *Luftwaffe* in the skies over Britain. Because it was available in sufficient numbers – just – it is not unreasonable to suggest that without the Hurricane, the Battle of Britain would have been lost and the course of history changed forever.

Despite being the RAF's first monoplane and eight gun fighter, the Hurricane was half a generation behind most of its contemporaries in terms of structural and aerodynamic design and was therefore quickly superseded in its original role as an interceptor fighter. From 1941 it began a new and hugely successful career as a ground attack fighter-bomber capable of carrying bombs, rockets and large calibre anti tank guns.

In this role, Sydney Camm's sturdy design served on all fronts, particularly making its mark in North Africa, the Mediterranean and India/Burma. The Hurricane also found useful employment as a night fighter and naval fighter, production continuing in quantity until late 1944 by which time about 14,500 had been built in Britain and Canada.

The Lockheed P-38 represented a radical departure for the USAAF, not only due to its then unique twin boom configuration but also because it was the service's first twin engined single seat fighter, the first with tricycle undercarriage and the first with turbocharged engines. Numerous other technical innovations were a feature of its design.

The P-38's career got off to an unfortunate start when the prototype crashed just two weeks after its first flight, but by then its potential had already been demonstrated and interest aroused. Its major attributes – firepower, speed and range – made the P-38 an ideal choice for long range escort missions over Europe and in the Pacific campaign. Although quickly replaced as an escort fighter in Europe by the remarkable P-51 Mustang, the Lightning really shone in the Pacific where the USAAF's two leading aces of the war – Majors Richard Bong and Thomas McGuire – scored their victories in the aircraft the Germans called 'The Fork Tailed Devil'.

The P-38 remained in production until the end of the war, by which time just over 10,000 had been built. Like most successful combat aircraft, the P-38 was versatile and used for a variety of roles during its career, photo-reconnaissance, night fighting and ground attack among them.

Japan's best known combat aircraft of World War II, the Zero (or *Zeke* as the Allies called it) provided an unexpected shock for its opponents when it first appeared, offering high performance, an extraordinary range capability and unmatched manoeuvrability in a light and relatively low powered airframe. To achieve all this in a fighter designed for carrier operations was in itself a considerable feat. Early models fought against China in 1940 and subsequently against the Allied forces in the Pacific, debuting in that theatre on the raid against Pearl Harbour.

The Zero came to be regarded as just about invincible by the Japanese and held sway in the Pacific during 1942. After that, the myth of invincibility was exploded as it became outclassed by new American naval fighters such as the Grumman Hellcat and Vought Corsair. Attempts to improve the Zero were generally unsuccessful, a lack of power providing ongoing problems.

Japan's failure to properly develop a successor meant the Zero had to soldier on, and by the time a notably more powerful version was built it was too late with Japan's forces in retreat and its industry in ruin. Like many other Japanese combat aircraft of the time, the Zero's swansong was as a *Kamikaze* suicide bomber.

As always, there are several friends to thank for there assistance in compiling this book, and to them my gratitude: Jim Thorn, Gerard Frawley, Ian Hewitt, Juanita Franzi, Dennis Newton, Mike Kerr, Neil MacKenzie and Philip J Birtles. I'd like to give special thanks to production manager Maria Davey. This is the 20th book she's put together for me over the years and despite the numerous problems I continually burden her with, she still talks to me – most of the time!

Stewart Wilson
Buckingham 1996

Published by Aerospace Publications Pty Ltd (ACN: 001 570 458), PO Box 1777, Fyshwick ACT 2609, publishers of monthly *Australian Aviation* magazine.
Production Manager: Maria Davey

ISBN 1 875671 24 2

All rights reserved. No part of this book may be reproduced or transmitted in any form or by any means, electronic or mechanical including photocopying, recording or by any information storage and retrieval system, without permission from the publisher in writing.

Copyright © 1996 Stewart Wilson and Aerospace Publications Pty Limited

Proudly printed in Australia by Pirie Printers Pty Ltd, 140 Gladstone Street, Fyshwick 2609
Distributed throughout Australia by Network Distribution, 54 Park Street, Sydney 2000. Fax (02) 264 3278
Distribution in North America by Motorbooks International, 729 Prospect Ave, Osceola, Wisconsin 54020, USA. Fax: (715) 294 4448. Distribution throughout Europe and the UK by Airlife Publishing Ltd, 101 Longden Rd, Shrewsbury SY3 9EB, Shropshire, UK, Fax (743) 23 2944.

CONTENTS

Front cover (top to bottom): A6M5 Model 52 Zero of Genzan Naval Air Corps, Wonson Korea 1944; P-38J-15 Lightning 43-28420 of 55th FS USAAF, UK 1944; Hurricane IIC Z3069/QO-F of 3 Sqdn RAF 1942. *(not to scale)*

HAWKER HURRICANE

An aggressive portrait of Hurricane IIC HL844, one of the three 'MacRobert' Hurricanes operated by the RAF in the Middle East and named after three brothers, all of whom lost their lives in the war. (via Neil Mackenzie)

THE EIGHT GUN FIGHTER

Simultaneously revolutionary and evolutionary, the Hawker Hurricane's place in aviation history is assured as one of the great fighter aircraft of World War II.

It was a revolutionary aircraft as it was the first eight gun fighter, the first monoplane fighter to join the Royal Air Force and that service's first aircraft capable of exceeding 300mph (483km/h) in level flight. The design of the Hurricane was nevertheless evolutionary and in many ways cautious despite its advanced features for the time, evolving from a long and noble line of biplane fighters, light bombers, naval interceptors, army co-operation and general purpose aircraft designed by Hawker's chief designer Sydney Camm from the late 1920s. For Camm, a monoplane fighter was the logical next step in meeting his perception of the RAF's future needs, incorporating state-of-the-art innovations with tried and tested principles.

It's interesting to note that although Camm has traditionally been regarded by many as a designer who rarely strayed from the idea of cautious evolution, and logical series of design development can be seen in his work, the end result was often advanced and usually classic aircraft. One design which owed little or nothing to previous concepts resulted in one of the most revolutionary aircraft of all time, the vertical takeoff and landing (VTOL) P.1127 and its production development, the Harrier.

While the Hurricane's immortality resulted from the crucial role it played in the Battle of Britain, its story does not end there, as it went on to become one of the most versatile single engined fighters of the 1939-45 war, capable of operating as a night fighter, fighter-bomber, tank buster and naval fighter with equal aplomb.

It would be fair to say the Hurricane was obsolescent as a pure day fighter by the end of 1940 with other types of more modern design leaving it well behind in terms of performance and general technical development. It was in the ground attack role that the aircraft began a second and most rewarding career, carrying bombs, rockets and substantial guns against the enemy in Europe, the Far East, North Africa, the Mediterranean and elsewhere.

Much has been written about the Hurricane by way of comparison with its even more famous British contemporary, the Supermarine Spitfire. Such comparisons are a very dangerous practice for any aviation writer to indulge in as we are talking about two very great aircraft, but for often different reasons. It is a fact that even though the two fighters recorded their first flights only four months apart they were separated by half a generation in terms of aerodynamic and structural design.

The more advanced Spitfire was able to be developed into a multitude of versions which offered vastly superior performance and in the later models, a shape and specification which bore minimal similarities to earlier aircraft. By contrast, the last Hurricane looked pretty much like the first.

The Hurricane's relatively conservative design also brought some advantages. It was easier to build than the Spitfire, easier to repair and easier for inexperienced pilots to manage, particularly on the ground. These characteristics all proved vital during the Battle of Britain, as did its ability to absorb tremendous punishment, provide a steady gun platform and outturn any contemporary monoplane fighter.

As far as that pivotal battle is concerned, and the contribution of both aircraft, it's not unreasonable to suggest that without the Hawker aircraft, the outcome would have been entirely different. Of its many virtues, perhaps the Hurricane's greatest during the summer of 1940 was that it was available in sufficient numbers – just – to thwart the *Luftwaffe*.

The first prototype Hurricane was flown in November 1935 and the final example rolled out in August 1944. In between, production amounted to about 14,500 aircraft in Britain and Canada and a small number assembled under licence in Yugoslavia and Belgium. It served with the air forces (and navies) of some 19 nations during World War II and others afterwards, gaining a deserved reputation as a solid, reliable and adaptable workhorse, lacking only the 'newsworthiness' of some of its more glamorous counterparts.

Tropicalised Hurricane I V7476, the only Hurricane delivered to the Royal Australian Air Force 'at home'. RAAF squadrons flew Hurricanes overseas under RAF control, while many Australian pilots flew them in RAF squadrons. (Defence PR)

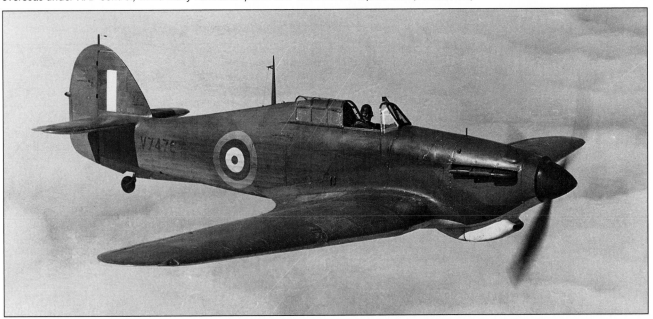

The Hawker Heritage

The H G Hawker Engineering Company Ltd was established in November 1920 largely to replace Sopwith Aviation, the company which had provided some of the Great War's most notable fighter aircraft but had folded earlier in 1920 after the British Treasury had served an enormous claim for Excess War Profits Duty.

Hawker took over Sopwith's premises at Canbury Park Road, Kingston-upon-Thames, in the south-west part of the Greater London area.

The company was named after the Australian pilot Harry Hawker, who had joined Sopwith in 1912 as a test pilot and who subsequently achieved fame as a pioneer. Hawker was appointed one of the original directors of the company which bore his name, but his life ended tragically in July 1921 when the Nieuport Goshawk he was testing for a race crashed, the result of Hawker suffering a haemorrhage while pulling heavy 'g' loadings in tight turns. Hawker was 32 years old.

But the company carried on, its golden years occurring during the 1925 to 1959 period when Sir Sydney Camm was the chief designer. The first new design to be launched under Camm's leadership was the Hornbill light fighter of 1926, the ancestor of the family of single engined biplane day bombers, fighter/bombers, army co-operation and general purpose military aircraft beginning with the Hart of 1928 and progressing through the 1930s with the Nimrod, Demon, Osprey, Audux, Hardy, Hind and other variants.

Following the same basic design was the smaller, single seat Fury fighter of 1931. Like its bomber counterparts, the Fury was ordered in quantity for the Royal Air Force and foreign customers.

Hawker became a public company in 1933 and assumed the new title Hawker Aircraft Ltd. On its flotation, the new company took over the assets of the old, which was eventually dissolved.

In 1934, Hawker took over another famous British aviation name, Gloster Aircraft, although the two companies retained separate identities until 1963 when they and other companies – including de Havilland, Armstrong Whitworth, Blackburn, Avro and Folland – were grouped together under the Hawker Siddeley banner.

The Interceptor Monoplane

The 1933-34 period proved to be a significant one for Hawker and what would eventually become the Hurricane. Hawker Aircraft Ltd was formed in May 1933 following a public float of shares of the old H G Hawker Engineering Pty Ltd, Gloster Aircraft was purchased by the new company in February 1934 and at the time, there was a healthy order book for various of Hawker's biplane military aircraft from both home and abroad.

1933 was also significant for other reasons which were eventually connected but would not manifest themselves for another handful of years – in January Adolf Hitler's National Socialist Party came to power in Germany and in August, Hawker's chief designer, Sydney Camm, began work on a new fighter, at that time known as the Fury Monoplane.

The original biplane Fury I had entered service in 1931. Initially powered by a 525hp (390kW) Rolls-Royce Kestrel vee-12 liquid cooled engine, it was capable of a maximum speed of 207mph (333km/h), the fastest in Royal Air Force service at the time. The Fury was subsequently developed into more powerful and refined

versions for the RAF and for export and a total of 276 was eventually manufactured until 1937. The Yugoslav Fury II with a 745hp (555kW) Kestrel, low drag radiator and cantilever undercarriage was the fastest of the series, reaching 242mph (389km/h).

Despite the undoubted merits of the Fury, it was still a biplane with the performance limitations imposed by its configuration and carried the barely adequate armament of two fixed, forward firing machine guns. In these terms, nothing much had changed since World War I except that the speed had increased.

Sydney Camm had in the meantime been looking at improved versions of the Fury, including the PV.3 of 1934 which was basically a slightly larger, heavier and strengthened development of the earlier aircraft. Its armament was doubled to four nose mounted machine guns and the Kestrel engine was replaced by a 700hp (522kW) Rolls-Royce Goshawk engine.

This powerplant was a development of the Kestrel but with an evaporative cooling system in which the coolant was allowed to boil in its jackets, the resultant mixture of water and steam being separated in a header tank and the water returned to the inlet side of a circulating pump, the condensed water returning to the system by another pump.

The system proved troublesome and its unreliability and potential susceptibility to battle damage negated its main intended advantage – reduced airframe drag through the use of smaller external radiators. The result was that the Goshawk was fitted to only a small number of experimental aircraft designed to meet Air Ministry Specification F.7/30 including the Hawker PV.3 and the Supermarine 224, both of them one-offs. The latter

'The Last Of The Many' – Hurricane IIC PZ865, preserved and operated by the Battle of Britain Memorial Flight. (Philip J Birtles)

is often described as being the predecessor of the Spitfire and differed from the other F.7/30 designs in being a monoplane, albeit with fixed undercarriage.

The PV.3 demonstrated no significant performance premium over the Fury and was not developed, its main advantage over the earlier aircraft being its ability to carry four rather than two guns. In revised form, Specification F.7/30 was filled by the RAF's last biplane fighter, the Gloster Gladiator with a Bristol Mercury radial engine.

Developing The Concept

By the second half of 1933 Sydney Camm had realised that the only way to increase fighter performance was to change to a monoplane configuration. He therefore started work on design concepts for a 'Fury Monoplane' and in August of the same year presented his first ideas to the Air Ministry. Camm and senior people within Hawker had a close relationship with the Ministry and the company's chief designer also had a well tuned feel for the commercial aspects of aircraft designing and manufacturing. A look at Hawker's products during the Camm period of influence and the numbers built confirms this.

Two of Hawker's successful biplane designs of the of the 1930s – the Hart day bomber (top) and its close relative, the Demon fighter (bottom). Both were two seaters and part of a family of aircraft covering numerous military roles. (BAe/RAAF).

Hawker trio: designer Sydney Camm, H G Jones and 'George' Bulman, who took the Hurricane prototype into the air for the first time. The aircraft is a Hawker Cygnet, designed by Camm in 1924.

Camm faced several problems when he first approached the Ministry with his 'Fury Monoplane' ideas including the fact that there was still a general distrust of the monoplane within the RAF (the result of structural failures in Royal Flying Corps aircraft before World War I), the general depletion of the RAF due to the effects of the Great Depression and a general philosophy of disarmament within the British Government of Ramsey MacDonald.

These inhibitions were gradually overcome as an increasing number of British politicians (led by Winston Churchill, then a back bencher) started to warn of the perils associated with Hitler's rise in Germany and the massive rearmament programme which quickly followed. Additionally, the idea of monoplane fighters began to gain favour within the RAF hierarchy.

Probably the greatest single event which eventually allowed official backing for the development of monoplane fighters and other modern aircraft designs was the October 1933 withdrawal of Germany from the Disarmament Conference and the League of Nations. It took a while for the message to completely sink in, but by mid 1934 the Disarmament Conference had been adjourned indefinitely and more in Britain began to realise that war with Germany was a possibility in the not too distant future.

The powers-that-be had not quite reached that opinion when Camm first approached them on the subject of a Fury Monoplane in August 1933 and there was a general lack of enthusiasm, an attitude which would shortly begin to change for the better.

The design which Camm initially presented to the Air Ministry looked very much like a 'Fury Monoplane' with a fuselage and tail unit similar to the earlier aircraft in combination with an enclosed cockpit (with rearward sliding canopy), a 660hp (492kW) Goshawk engine, a tapered two spar wing of relatively thick section and fixed, spatted undercarriage similar to that which had been fitted to the Yugoslav Fury.

The traditional Hawker structural design was retained – tubular steel fuselage box structure with external frames covered by metal sheeting forward and fabric aft; and metal wings, tail and control surfaces covered by fabric.

Wing span was 38 feet (11.6m), length 28ft 10in (8.79m), an armament of two Vickers 0.303in machine guns was allowed for and maximum speed was estimated at 280mph (450km/h).

Enter The Merlin

The technical and performance prospects of Camm's concepts received a boost in early 1934 when he was made aware of the development of a new Rolls-Royce engine, the PV.12, later known as the Merlin. Fitted with a single stage supercharger, this conventionally liquid cooled vee-12 of 27 litres capacity promised 40 per cent more takeoff power than the Kestrel and up to 60 per cent more power at medium altitudes, both figures substantially better than that offered by the Goshawk which would soon prove to be troublesome in any case.

Like Camm's new fighter concepts, the PV.12 was very much a private venture by its manufacturer (thus the designation prefix) and was considerably larger and heavier than the Kestrel. It did, however, offer considerable development potential.

The first PV.12 was bench tested in October 1933 and its 100 hour type test was completed in July 1934 at which time the engine was rated at 625hp (466kW) for takeoff and 790hp (589kW) at 12,000 feet (3660m). Despite some ongoing problems during its development, it wasn't long before the promise of 1,000hp (745kW) on production engines was a realistic aim. The first Merlin to fly did so in the front of a Hawker Hart light day bomber in April 1935, complete with the underfuselage radiator which would later become so familiar on the Hurricane.

Encouraged by the potential offered by the PV.12, Camm immediately revised his design to accept the new engine, and from January 1934 the aircraft was known internally as the Hawker High Speed Interceptor Monoplane. The new design was larger than its predecessor, having a wing span of 40 feet (12.2m) and length of 31ft 3in (9.52m). Loaded weight was initially estimated at 4600lb (2086kg) and it was quickly realised that if a retractable undercarriage was incorporated in the design, a maximum speed of over 300mph (483km/h) was entirely possible.

A lineup of Hawker Fury I fighters, which entered service in 1931. At the time it was the fastest aircraft in RAF service.

The decision was therefore taken to include this then very advanced feature, Hawker's first attempt at it. Of great benefit to pilots in the years ahead was the fact that the company decided to incorporate an inwards retracting, wide track undercarriage in the design, making ground handling simpler and operation from rough fields possible.

Coincidental to the decision to incorporate retractable undercarriage came another look at the aircraft's armament. Four machine guns were originally intended to be included (two each in the forward fuselage and wings) but by mid 1934 the possibility of six or even eight guns was being examined.

Work progressed rapidly during the first half of 1934 with stressing calculations beginning in March, the preparation of drawings in May and the building of a one-tenth scale model for wind tunnel testing in June. The completed design was submitted to the Air Ministry in September of the same year.

It's important to note that despite some encouragement from within the Ministry, all the work performed thus far on the Interceptor Monoplane had been at Hawker's own behest and expense. Elsewhere in Britain, Reginald Mitchell and Supermarine were involved in another private venture monoplane fighter design which would later emerge as the Spitfire. Likewise, Rolls-Royce, whose PV.12 Merlin engine had not received official backing as yet.

The Air Ministry and RAF attitude to Hawker's monoplane fighter was still officially lukewarm, even after Germany's threat had been revealed to the world. The problem stemmed from the top, the RAF's Chief of Air Staff from 1933-37, ACM Sir Edward Ellington, believing there would be no war until at least 1942 and that the bomber should receive priority over fighter development, especially monoplanes. After all, new Prime Minister Stanley Baldwin had said "the bomber will always get through"! As a result, bomber development continued to win priority over the new fighters.

Fortunately for Hawker, the RAF and Britain, there were some who thought these new developments in fighter design had some merit. Across the Channel, German designers were facing no serious official obstacles, the *Luftwaffe's* major fighter of World War II, the Messerschmitt Bf 109, flying two months before the prototype Hurricane.

Squadron Leader Ralph Sorley of the Air Ministry's Operational Requirements Branch was one who played a major part in the gaining of acceptance of the monoplane fighter. It has

The Fury II was Hawker's final expression of the biplane fighter concept and appeared after the prototype Hurricane had flown. It was capable of 242mph (389km/h), considerably slower than that promised by the new generation of monoplane fighters.

been said that Sorley launched a one man campaign in favour of the monoplane fighter within the Ministry and that he also fiercely promoted the concept of such a fighter carrying an armament of eight guns and encouraged Camm to incorporate them in his design.

The Rolls-Royce PV.12 engine was meanwhile suffering from some persistent technical problems as it was gradually developed to produce more power. Cylinder jacket cracking and reduction gear failures were common and the engine failed its first attempt at the official 50 hour Civil Type Test. It passed only in December 1935, the month after the prototype Hurricane had flown but by then in its Merlin 'C' guise was producing 955hp (712kW) for takeoff and 1,050hp (783kW) at rated altitude.

The Need Recognised

Official recognition of the need for a new generation of fighters for the RAF came in 1934 when the Air Ministry issued Specification F.5/34 for a single seat, eight gun Fury replacement capable of a maximum speed of at least 280mph (450km/h). This performance capability implied a monoplane with retractable undercarriage and prompted responses from Hawker, Gloster, Bristol, Vickers-Armstrong and Martin-Baker.

Hawker's submission for its Interceptor Monoplane closely matched this specification (with the exception that it still had only four fuselage and wing mounted guns) with the result that after the presentation of its proposals in September 1934, a new specification – F.36/34 – was written around it. Hawker went ahead with detailed drawings and the building of a mockup from October 1934 but it

wasn't until the following February that a single prototype was ordered. Part of that contract was that Hawker should modify its design to accept eight wing mounted machine guns, at least in its production form.

This involved some redesign of the wing structure outboard of the centre section and meant that at first, the prototype would fly unarmed.

The decision to specify eight guns on the F.5/34 came after a lengthy investigation into the merits or otherwise of numerous weapons, including cannon. It was obvious that the old gas operated Vickers 0.303in machine gun – a veteran of World War I – would have to be replaced. The Vickers was prone to jamming, which meant that it virtually had to be mounted in the nose of a fighter so the pilot could have access to its breech in that event.

This meant that if the guns were to be wing mounted in the new fighter, then they would ideally not be Vickers. Wing mounting also meant that the complications of propeller interrupter gear could be avoided. Bear in mind that at this stage, Hawker's proposal still had two Vickers guns in the nose along with a pair of Brownings in the wings.

The American 0.303in Colt-Browning gradually emerged as the favoured weapon despite its rifle calibre providing less 'hitting power' than some of the 0.50in machine gun and 20mm cannon alternatives which were examined. It was a known quantity as far as its reliability was concerned, although its use in wing mounted positions meant that an alternative to the usual Bowden cable operating mechanism had to be developed as this would have incurred an unacceptable time lag between operation of the control and the guns firing. This resulted in the development of a pneumatic firing system by Dunlop, triggered by a button on the control column.

Uncertainty as to the final armament which would be fitted to the Hawker fighter continued until July 1935 when eight wing mounted Vickers or Browning guns was specified, with the older weapon finally eliminated from the equation the same month when the Birmingham Small Arms Co (BSA) concluded a licence production deal with the Colt Automatic Weapon Corporation.

The Browning was modified in British production to take rimmed 0.303in ammunition instead of the American-standard 0.300in rimmed type and the weapon remained a standard fitting in numerous British military types for some years before 20mm cannon gained favour. Hawker completed an eight Browning mockup in August 1935 and this became the standard armament for the production Hurricane Mk.I.

By the time Hawker had been awarded a contract to build a prototype F.36/34 in February 1935, the company's performance estimates for the new fighter showed it would easily beat the figures required by the original specification. They included a maximum speed of 330mph (531km/h) at 15,000ft (4,570m) and a service ceiling of 32,500ft (9,900m). Maximum takeoff weight was put at 4,900lb (2,222kg) although that estimate increased to 5,200lb (2,359kg) when provision was made for eight guns and rose further by the time the prototype was built.

Of interest is the fact that as early as mid 1935, Hawker had begun investigating the installation of metal rather than fabric covered wings on its new fighter. This was prompted by concerns over the fabric's battle worthiness and its suitability for the planned heavier eight gun armament. Due to the delays it would have caused to the production schedule, the metal wing would not appear until 1939, by which time the aircraft was rolling out of the factories in numbers.

From Concept to Hardware

Construction of the prototype F.36/34 (the name 'Hurricane' was not yet bestowed) meanwhile began at Hawker's Experimental Department at its principal factory at Kingston-upon-Thames (the site of Sopwith production in WWI) near London. By August 1935 the airframe was completed and the Merlin C engine of 1,025hp (764kW) at 11,000ft (3,350m) was installed the following month. By now, the aircraft had been allocated the RAF serial number K5083.

The construction of K5083 followed the metal structure with largely fabric covering design tradition established by previous Hawker aircraft and that which was proposed with the response to the original Specification F.5/34.

Notable features included the Dowty hand pump hydraulically operated retractable undercarriage (with retractable tailwheel, a feature unique to the prototype); a thick section wing comprising a flat centre section of parallel chord and thickness to which were attached tapered, two spar outer panels; all metal split flaps

across the rear of the centre section; aft sliding canopy ahead of the now familiar Hurricane upper fuselage 'hump'; two bladed Watts fixed-pitch propeller of 11ft 6in (3.50m) diameter; engine and oil coolant radiators mounted under the fuselage; strut braced tailplane; and fuel tanks in the wing centre section between the spars plus a reserve tank in the upper nose immediately forward of the cockpit. Total capacity was measured at 107.5imp gal (488 litres), some 10imp gal (45 l) more than production aircraft.

In the last week of November 1935, K5083 was transported by road from Kingston to Hawker's flight test facility at Brooklands for assembly and preparation for its first flight. Ballasted for four guns, ammunition and fuel, the aircraft weighed in at 5,416lb (2,457kg) all-up. It is said that the centre of gravity was within half an inch of Sydney Camm's estimate.

The age of the monoplane fighter in RAF service began on the morning of 6 November 1935 when after some exploratory fast taxying runs, chief test pilot P W S 'George' Bulman lifted K5083 from Brooklands' 'soup plate' airfield, contained within the limits imposed by the concrete motor racing track which surrounded it. Bulman left the undercarriage down during this maiden flight as there was uncertainty about the reliability of the hand pumped hydraulic jacks which operated it.

The flight lasted half an hour, and upon taxying in, Bulman quietly said to Camm: "Another winner, I think". He was right, but there was still much to do.

Still to be named 'Hurricane', the prototype Hawker F.36/34 first flew on 6 November 1935. This shot shows the aircraft in its initial guise with strut braced tailplane and lightly framed canopy. Note the retractable tailwheel, a feature unique to the prototype.

Photographed at Duxford in May 1996 are two airworthy Canadian built aircraft, Sea Hurricane I Z7015 (top) and Hurricane XII 'Z7381', actually the former RCAF 5711. (Keith Gaskall)

Another view of the Duxford Hurricane lineup in May 1996 (top) with the Battle of Britain Memorial Flight's Mk.IIC PZ865 in the foreground. The Sea Hurricane Z7015 (bottom) has recently been restored to airworthiness and is the oldest airworthy Hurricane in the world powered by the oldest Merlin. It is operated jointly by the Shuttleworth Trust and the IWM Duxford. (Keith Gaskall/Vance Ingham)

Two views of the BBMF's Hurricane IIC PZ865 'The Last of the Many' in its 1996 colour scheme remembering the Hurricanes used in the defence of Malta. (Philip J Birtles/Paul Merritt)

Hurricane IIC LF363 of the Battle of Britain Memorial flight was badly damaged in a 1991 accident and in 1996 was being rebuilt. It is shown here as 'GN-A' (top) of 249 Squadron and 'VY-X' of 85 Squadron. (Bruce Malcolm)

HURRICANE VARIANTS and DEVELOPMENT

HURRICANE PROTOTYPE

Early flight trials of the as yet unnamed F.36/34 prototype generally reinforced the high expectations which had preceded them, certainly as far as the airframe was concerned, although the Merlin engine – which was still in the early stages of development – did suffer from some ongoing problems which took time to solve.

As first flown from Brooklands on 6 November 1935, the prototype's (K5083) configuration was 990hp (738kW) Merlin C, two bladed Watts fixed pitch wooden propeller, strut braced tailplane, lightly framed canopy, retractable tailwheel and no guns. Empty weight was measured at 4,129lb (1,873kg) ballasted to simulate four guns. Takeoff weight was initially 5,416lb (2,456kg) subsequently rising to 5,672lb (2,573kg).

The prototype had recorded seven flights and about six hours in the air by mid December 1935, although it would shortly be grounded for a period of six weeks while a new engine was installed and other modifications incorporated. These included removing the tailplane struts and the wheel flaps which covered the lower half of the wheels when retracted, fitting additional frames to the cockpit canopy and installing a larger radiator bath to improve engine cooling. Another change which would shortly be incorporated was to fix the centre portion of the wing flap in the up position, as it was thought this was causing engine overheating at low speeds when the flaps were down.

K5083 was fitted with four different Merlin Cs during the first few months of its life as various maladies cropped up, although it had already been decided that production aircraft would be fitted with the improved Merlin F, or Merlin I as it was to be known in its production form. The decision was subsequently made to install a further development, the Merlin G/Merlin II, in production Hurricanes, necessitating a substantial redesign of the aircraft's nose contours.

Official Testing

The prototype was reflown in early February 1936, by which time the RAF was showing some impatience about getting its hands on the new fighter. To date, all test flying had been performed by Hawker's George Bulman and Phi Lucas and they weren't quite ready to hand the aircraft over for official evaluation as a couple of niggling problems with the canopy (which couldn't be opened in flight at anything over moderately low speeds and fell off after one early flight), the undercarriage (which was difficult to retract and lock using the hand pump) and of course the engine.

Despite these misgivings, K5083 was handed over to the Aircraft and Armament Experimental Establishment (A&AEE) at Martlesham Heath in February 1936 for initial service trials. By then, it had flown only ten times and recorded eight hours in the air.

The aircraft remained at Martlesham Heath for just one week but during that brief period impressed all concerned with its performance, handling (both on the ground and in the air) and cockpit layout. The only substantial criticism was of K5083's heavy controls at high speeds but the A&AEE's pilots adapted quickly to its new and advanced features, including the novelty of retractable undercarriage. The reliability of the powerplant continued to cause concern, however.

Performance figures achieved at Martlesham Heath were considered extraordinary for their day: maximum speed 315mph (507km/h) at 16,200ft (4,938m); time to 15,000ft (4,572m) 5.7 minutes, to 20,000ft (6,096m) 8.4 minutes; service ceiling 34,500ft (10,515m).

Production Approved

Encouraged by the success of the A&AEE tests and influenced by the worsening international situation, Hawker's directors in March 1936 took the courageous decision to authorise work to begin on the drawings for production aircraft and to plan the manufacture of 1,000 aircraft, all of this ahead of any official indication that the new fighter would be ordered for the RAF.

This decision would have far reaching effects in that it helped ensure that production of what would shortly be known as the Hurricane would be sufficiently well established by the outbreak of war in 1939 to enable enough aircraft to be in service when they were most needed. The company's well developed commercial instincts also contributed to this decision as a substantial export market was also envisaged for the aircraft.

Three months later, in June 1936, Hawker's confidence in its new product was vindicated when as part of the Air Ministry's Expansion Plan F, 900 monoplane fighters were ordered for the RAF. Of these, 300 were for the recently flown Supermarine Spitfire

The prototype Hurricane in its initial guise with the two bladed Watts fixed-pitch propeller prominent. Note the arrangement of the undercarriage fairings.

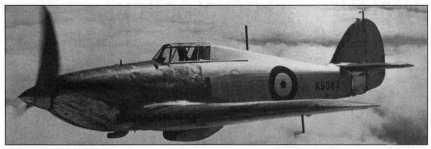

Hurricane prototype K5083 as it appeared in 1937 with the tail bracing struts removed, a radio mast fitted, revised canopy frames and larger underfuselage radiator.

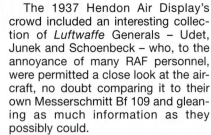

and 600 for the Hawker F.36/34, henceforth known as the Hurricane.

It would be another 16 months before the first production Hurricane I was flown, the sole prototype carrying the burden of development in the meantime. Likewise the prototype Spitfire, which was the only example of type in existence for over two years until the first production aircraft appeared in May 1938.

Development flying with K5083 continued, the most significant further modification appearing in August 1936 when armament was fitted. The cockpit canopy posed ongoing problems, several of them parting company with the aircraft at high speed before redesigns of its framework and mountings finally resulted in a satisfactory installation.

The prototype returned to Martlesham Heath in September and October 1936 for full service handling and performance trials. New tests with a revised Merlin C engine resulted in a maximum speed of 318mph (512km/h) at 15,500ft (4,724m).

The prototype Hurricane was by no means kept way from the public's gaze during its lifetime – if anything its appearance at air shows and displays was encouraged. Its first public appearance was made at the 1936 Hendon Air Display, shortly after the production contract was announced. A routine which has been described as "dazzling" was put on by Sqn Ldr Anderson in front of a large crowd which included representatives of several nations which were potential Hurricane purchasers.

The 1937 Hendon Air Display's crowd included an interesting collection of *Luftwaffe* Generals – Udet, Junek and Schoenbeck – who, to the annoyance of many RAF personnel, were permitted a close look at the aircraft, no doubt comparing it to their own Messerschmitt Bf 109 and gleaning as much information as they possibly could.

The Hurricane prototype appeared at many other similar shows and exhibitions both at home and overseas, the last one in Brussels a matter of weeks before war was declared!

The prototype's ultimate fate is unknown except that it was reported to be in storage at Brooklands shortly after war was declared.

HURRICANE I

The June 1936 order for 600 Hurricane Is for the Royal Air Force ensured the future of Hawker's new fighter and was the largest contract placed by Britain for military aircraft since World War I. A further order for 1,000 aircraft was placed in November 1938, necessitating production from two sources – Hawker (from its Brooklands and Langley facilities) and Gloster Aircraft at Brockworth. Of the 3,774 Hurricane Is eventually built in Britain up to 1941, 1,924 were manufactured by the parent company and 1,850 by Gloster, the latter flying its first aircraft (P2535) in October 1939.

Early production Hurricane Is differed from the prototype in several important ways, although the fabric covered wings and fuselage was retained. The powerplant was the

Two views of the first production Hurricane I (L1547) on the ground showing its salient features compared with the prototype. Note the revised nose profile, undercarriage covers and the triple ejector 'kidney' exhausts. This aircraft first flew on 12 October 1937. (BAe)

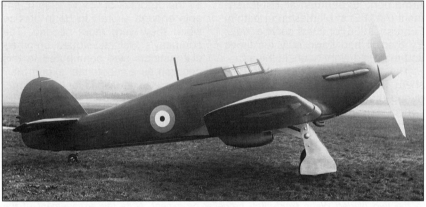

Early production Hurricane Is of 111 Squadron RAF pose for the camera. 'Treble One' was the first squadron to receive the new fighter, in December 1937. (BAe)

Merlin II rated at 1,030hp (768kW) at 16,250ft (4,953m) driving the same fixed-pitch Watts two bladed wooden propeller as the prototype. The Merlin II had a different shape than the earlier model fitted to the prototype (due to inclined rocker box flanges) necessitating a revised nose profile. This change resulted in production being delayed by a few months, the last of the 600 aircraft covered by the initial contract being handed over in October rather than March 1939.

Other external differences included the introduction of triple ejector 'kidney' shaped exhausts, a fixed tailwheel, the larger radiator bath which had been tested on the prototype, increased rudder area and stronger canopy framing. Early aircraft lacked pilot protection armour or a bullet proof windscreen. Armament was eight 0.303in BSA built Browning machine guns each with 334 rounds of ammunition.

The first production Hurricane I (L1547) was flown on 12 October 1937, followed by the second aircraft six days later. Deliveries to the RAF began quickly, with 111 Squadron at Northolt receiving its first aircraft on 15 December 1937. Nos 3 (Kenley) and 56 (North Weald) Squadrons began receiving Hurricanes in March and May 1938, respectively, and by the end of that year a total of 11 RAF Fighter Command squadrons had Hurricanes on strength.

A 111 Squadron Hurricane achieved national fame in February 1938 when the squadron's Commanding Officer, Sqn Ldr John Gillan, flew from Edinburgh to Northolt (near London) in just 48 minutes at the then phenomenal average speed of 408mph

(656km/h). Helped considerably by Mother Nature, the effort captured the public's imagination and Sqn Ldr Gillan immediately acquired the nickname 'Tailwind', something which remained with him throughout his career!

Production built up rapidly during 1938 and 1939, Gloster flying its first aircraft (P2535) in October 1939 and handing over its 1,000th just 14 months later. Between them, Hawker and Gloster achieved an average peak production rate of 236 Hurricanes per month in the first three months of 1940 and sustained that figure for the next three years.

Metal Wings and Other Mods

While the Hurricane retained the fabric covered fuselage and control surfaces during its production life, an early modification was the incorporation of metal covered and strengthened wings. Investigations into this began as early as July 1935 but incorporation of this feature was postponed as it would have caused considerable production delays as Hawker's manufacturing facilities were geared up for the older method of construction.

Development of metal wing skinning for the Hurricane continued despite this and the first Hurricane I so equipped was flown in April 1939. Production metal wings were at first randomly fitted to Hurricanes (the first delivered to the RAF in September 1939), aircraft with either these or fabric wings appearing until March 1940, after which the metal covered item became standard.

Another modification of even greater significance was the replacement of the original Watts fixed-pitch two bladed propeller with three bladed variable-pitch units. The Watts necessarily imposed performance limitations on the Hurricane – in both speed and rate of climb – and as the aircraft's early service continued (and war approached) it became obvious that a change would have to be made. The similarly powered Supermarine Spitfire was also subject to the same modification.

Hurricanes with variable-pitch propellers were powered by Merlin III engines of similar power to the Merlin II, the difference between the two marks being confined to the III's standardised propeller shaft which could accept either de Havilland or Rotol three bladed propellers and the mechanism associated with variable pitch.

The Merlin III first flew in Hawker's civil registered demonstration Hurricane (G-AFKX, ex L1877) in July 1939. By then, both Rotol (a company formed jointly by Rolls-Royce and Bristol) and de Havilland constant-speed propellers were under test but they would not be available for production for some months.

As an interim measure, most Hurricanes built in 1939 were fitted with two speed variable-pitch DH Hydromatic propellers (built under licence from Hamilton Standard) before the constant-speed units became available. A major conversion programme was undertaken in mid 1940 to convert Hurricanes still fitted with the variable-pitch DH prop to constant-speed units.

Operational experience resulted in numerous other modifications being incorporated including the fitting of

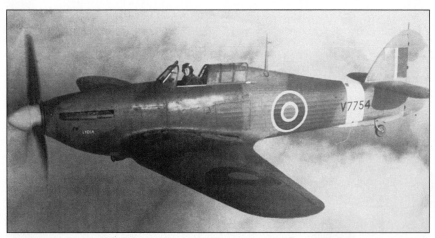

Hurricane I V7754 illustrates the definitive standard for the mark with metal covered wings, three bladed constant-speed propeller and the shallow ventral fin around the tailwheel. (via Neil Mackenzie)

pilot protection armour from February 1940, bulletproof windscreens and reflector gunsights. Externally, all but the earliest production Hurricane Is featured a slightly larger rudder which was lengthened at its base and faired in by a shallow ventral fin which extended from the base of the rudder forward to a point under the rear fuselage, broken only by the tailwheel.

Cannon Experiments

Although no production Hurricane Is were fitted with cannon armament, experiments were carried out with this weapon despite there being in 1940 official reluctance to install it in the Hurricane due to the perception that the all important flow of production would be interrupted.

The first investigations into a cannon armed Hurricane were carried out in 1936 when Hawker responded to Air Ministry Specification F.37/35 for a fighter armed with four 20mm Oerlikon cannon for the purpose of attacking enemy bombers. Hawker's proposal was rejected (and the twin engined Westland Whirlwind accepted) on the grounds that the Hurricane's then fabric covered wings would not be able to withstand the stresses imposed when four cannon were fired and the entirely false premise that 20mm cannon could not be satisfactorily carried by *any* single engined fighter.

Hawker continued its investigations regardless of this and in 1938 a wiser Air Ministry again broached the subject, requesting that two Oerlikons be fitted to a Hurricane. L1750 was the aircraft selected, and a single cannon was installed under each wing with ammunition belt fed from the normal magazines. Trials revealed the guns' low rate of fire and their general inaccuracy, prompting the RAF to discard them in favour of the Hispano 20mm weapon which would become the standard fitting on British fighters.

This decision resulted in the fitting of four 20mm Hispanos to Hurricane I V7260 in July 1940, this aircraft seeing some active service in September 1940 when it briefly flew with 46 Squadron in the Battle of Britain and was responsible for the destruction of a Messerschmitt Bf 109E.

Despite a degradation in performance (top speed was reduced to 304mph/489km/h) the worth of the Hispano armed Hurricane was sufficiently proven to encourage further development, although the belt feed ammunition mechanism in V7620 was unreliable, resulting in the decision to switch to a drum fed Chatellerault system. This in turn necessitated considerable modification to the Hur-

87 Squadron received its first Hurricane Is in July 1938. This posed squadron 'scramble' shows aircraft with both two bladed fixed-pitch and three bladed variable-pitch propellers. (via Neil Mackenzie)

Gloster built Hurricane I Z4251 of 33 Squadron displays the Vokes carburettor intake filter developed for tropical and desert service. The Vokes decreased the aircraft's maximum speed by about 12mph (19km/h) but considerably increased engine life in dusty conditions.

ricane's gun bays and wing structure, changes which would manifest themselves in the following Hurricane II.

Tropical Hurricanes

An important modification applied to many Hurricane Is (and later models) was the Vokes carburettor intake filter under the aircraft's nose. This was originally developed for fitting to aircraft destined for Far and Middle East service and was intended to protect the aircraft's Rolls-Royce Merlin engine from damage caused by the ingestion of sand, dust and various other foreign objects when operating from unprepared airfields.

The Vokes filter considerably changed the Hurricane's nose profile (as it also did to the Spitfire when fitted), reduced the maximum speed by about 12mph (19km/h) but had the desired effect on engine life, increasing the time between overhauls substantially compared with what was being achieved by unprotected engines operating in rough conditions.

The first Hurricane I to fly with the Vokes filter was L1669 in July 1939, quickly followed by two others (L1893 and L1877), the latter featuring a Rolls-Royce designed filter for comparison. L1669 was subsequently sent to Khartoum in September 1939 for trials. These were successful and the Vokes filter was adapted as a standard fitting on Hurricanes destined to serve in the hot and dusty parts of the world.

Export Action

Despite the RAF's need for more fighters in the 1938-40 period, a surprising number of Hurricane Is were delivered to foreign customers during this period, Hawker building on the export successes it had achieved with its biplane military aircraft during the previous decade.

These operators are discussed in more detail in a following chapter, but in summary, deliveries were made to Belgium (20), Yugoslavia (24), Rumania (12), Iran (1), South Africa (6), Turkey (15) and Canada (22), the latter as a prelude to licence production in that country. Canadian production is discussed later in this chapter.

Production licences were also granted to Avions Fairey in Belgium and to Yugoslavia. Eighty aircraft were ordered from Fairey for the *Force Aerienne Belge* in addition to those obtained from Britain, but only three had been built before the German invasion. These were fitted with four heavier calibre 12.65mm Browning machine guns instead of the standard eight 0.303s.

Yugoslavia was the first export customer for the Hurricane I, ordering an initial batch of 12 from Britain, the first of which was delivered in December 1938. Licence production was organised by the Yugoslav Government with plans to produce 40 at the Rogozarski factory and 60 at the Zmaj plant. Production got underway but was permanently interrupted in early April 1941 when Germany attacked. By then, 20 Yugoslav built Hurricanes had flown.

HURRICANE II

Investigations into producing a more powerful and therefore faster Hurricane began during 1939, with Hawker looking at alternative engine installations to improve the aircraft's performance. Among those considered were the Bristol Hercules 14 cylinder radial, the Napier Dagger 24 cylinder 'H' configuration inline, the Rolls-Royce Griffon V12 and more powerful versions of the Merlin.

The problem facing Hawker's designers was that of the limitations imposed by the Hurricane's relatively 'old hat' airframe design, not just in its method of construction, but also due to its thick wing design, something which was always going to limit its performance. No amount of extra power was going to push the Hurricane towards a 400mph (644km/h) maximum speed, something which in 1939 had still not been achieved by any production fighter but was not too far away.

This combination of factors meant that the Hurricane was really obsolescent as a pure day fighter by 1941 and completely outmoded a year later. The creation of what would become the Mk.II with its more powerful Merlin and the ability to carry a wide variety of guns and external offensive stores in its major subvariants resulted in a versatile ground attack aircraft which allowed Camm's design to have a second and highly successful career.

This success is measured by the fact that the Hurricane II models remained in production at a high rate until well into the second half of 1944. Of the approximately 13,000 Hurricanes built in Britain, some 8,400 or

---

HURRICANE I

Powerplant: *One Rolls-Royce Merlin III liquid cooled V12 piston engine with single speed/single stage supercharger rated at 880hp (656kW) for takeoff and 1,030hp (768kW) at 16,250ft (4,953m); three bladed Rotol constant-speed propeller of 10ft 9in (3.28m) diameter. Fuel capacity 97imp gal (441 l) in wing and fuselage tanks, provision for two fixed 44imp gal (200 l) underwing tanks on late aircraft.*

Dimensions: *Wing span 40ft 0in (12.19m); length 31ft 5in (9.58m); height (prop blade vertical) 12ft 11.5in (3.95m); wing area 258sq ft (23.97m²); wheel track 7ft 10in (2.39m); tailplane span 11ft 0in (3.35m).*

Weights: *Empty 4,982lb (2,260kg); normal loaded 6,532lb (2,963kg); max overload 7,490lb (3,397kg).*

Armament: *Eight 0.303in Browning machine guns in wings with 334 rounds per gun.*

Performance: *Max speed 281kt (521km/h) at 16,250ft 221kt (408km/h) at sea level; cruising speed 236kt (438km/h) at 15,000ft; long range cruise 152kt (281km/h) at 15,000ft; initial climb 2,300ft (701m)/min; time to 15,000ft 6.3min, to 20,000ft 9.8min; service ceiling 34,200ft (10,424m); range (at 236kt) 387nm (716km); max range 520nm (965km).*

Notes: *Early aircraft with similarly rated Merlin II and Watts two bladed, fixed-pitch propeller of 11ft 6in (3.50m) diameter. Max speed 276kt (512km/h) at 17,400ft; service ceiling 33,400ft (10,180m). De Havilland two position propeller also fitted to some aircraft.*

HAWKER HURRICANE PROTOTYPE K5083

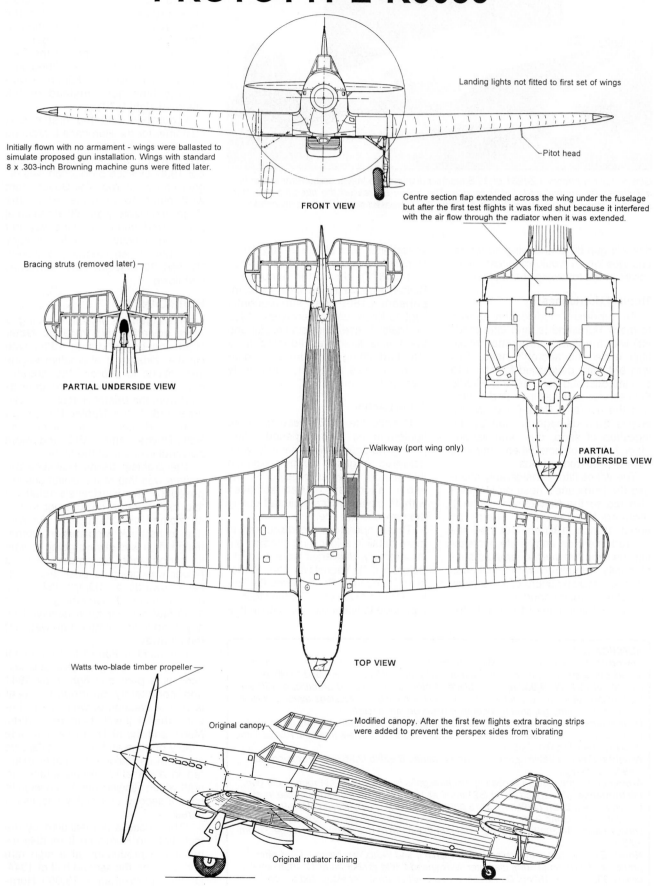

Landing lights not fitted to first set of wings

Initially flown with no armament - wings were ballasted to simulate proposed gun installation. Wings with standard 8 x .303-inch Browning machine guns were fitted later.

Pitot head

FRONT VIEW

Centre section flap extended across the wing under the fuselage but after the first test flights it was fixed shut because it interfered with the air flow through the radiator when it was extended.

Bracing struts (removed later)

PARTIAL UNDERSIDE VIEW

Walkway (port wing only)

PARTIAL UNDERSIDE VIEW

TOP VIEW

Watts two-blade timber propeller

Original canopy

Modified canopy. After the first few flights extra bracing strips were added to prevent the perspex sides from vibrating

Original radiator fairing

SIDE VIEW (PORT)

Dennis Newton

HAWKER HURRICANE Mk.I

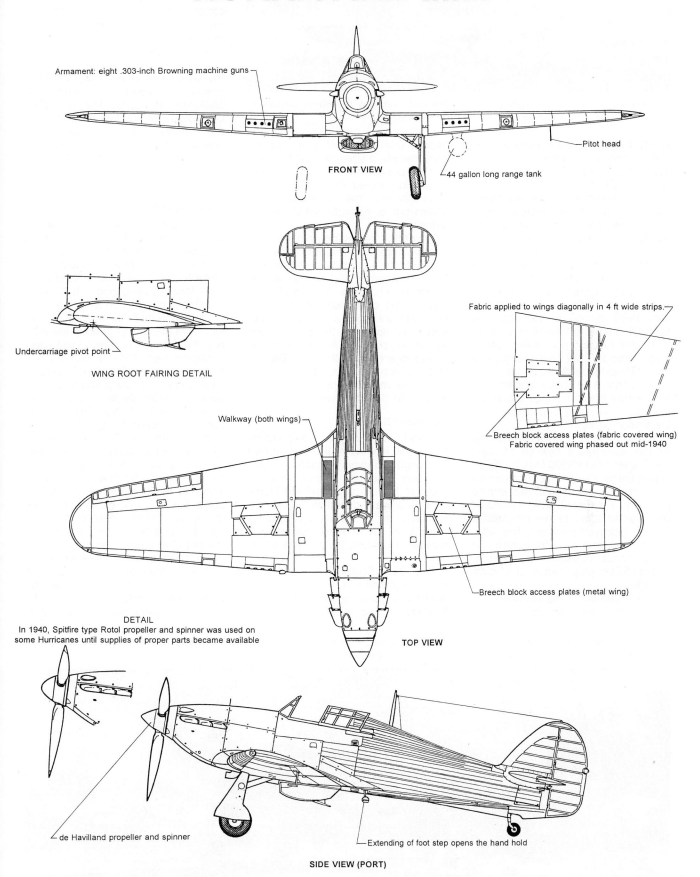

Armament: eight .303-inch Browning machine guns

Pitot head

FRONT VIEW

44 gallon long range tank

WING ROOT FAIRING DETAIL

Undercarriage pivot point

Fabric applied to wings diagonally in 4 ft wide strips.

Walkway (both wings)

Breech block access plates (fabric covered wing)
Fabric covered wing phased out mid-1940

Breech block access plates (metal wing)

TOP VIEW

DETAIL
In 1940, Spitfire type Rotol propeller and spinner was used on some Hurricanes until supplies of proper parts became available

de Havilland propeller and spinner

Extending of foot step opens the hand hold

SIDE VIEW (PORT)

Dennis Newton

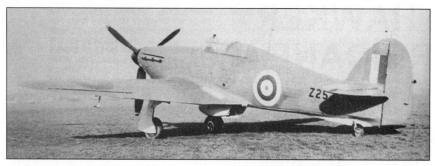

An early Hurricane IIA with eight gun wing. The first Hurricane IIs entered service in September 1940, just as the Battle of Britain was reaching its climax.

nearly two-thirds were Hurricane IIs and that mark provided the basis for most of the 1,451 aircraft built under licence in Canada.

It was decided that for the Hurricane II, installation of a more powerful Merlin was the way to go as this would provide better performance and also be the simplest solution as a minimum of redesign would be required. Several different Merlin variants were tested in Hurricane I airframes including a Merlin VIII in July 1939 (similar to the standard Merlin III but using 100 rather than 80/87 octane fuel and pure water cooling rather than 100 per cent Glycol)) and an 1,175hp (876kW) Merlin XII in the same month. This engine was fitted to the Spitfire II and retained the single speed/single stage supercharger of the earlier marks.

A prototype for what would emerge as the Hurricane II flew on 11 June 1940 when Mk.I P3269 took to the air with a Merlin XX installed. Featuring a two speed supercharger, this engine produced 1,300hp (970kW) for takeoff and was selected as the powerplant for the improved Hawker fighter after testing revealed a useful increase in performance including a maximum speed of 348mph (560km/h) at 17,400ft (5,303m).

Also essential to the Hurricane II's specification was the installation of heavier gun armament in all but the early models, a strengthened fuselage and the provision for a wide variety of underwing stores to be carried. To meet this end, the Hurricane's wing underwent some substantial internal redesign.

The Mk.II was quickly put into production, with Hurricanes delivered from Hawker's Langley assembly line from September 1940 built to this standard, while the Brooklands line and Gloster continued with the Mk.I into 1941 until stocks of the Merlin III were used up. A fourth assembly line was established by Austin Motors at Longbridge to build 300 Mk.IIBs, the first of which was handed over in May 1941. The vast majority of these were sent to the Soviet Union.

Hurricane IIA

Introduced to service in September 1940, the Hurricane IIA was armed with eight Browning machine guns and was produced in two versions. The first 120 out of a total 451 Hurricane IIAs were designated Series 1 and were an interim model featuring the Merlin XX in combination with standard Hurricane I wings and armament.

The Mk.IIA Series 2 followed in October 1940 and was a further interim model incorporating the strengthened fuselage longerons necessary for the fitting of later wings which would have attachment points for external stores. The Series 2 also featured the slightly greater overall length which would characterise subsequent Hurricanes, a few inches being added to the nose. Armament remained as before: eight 0.303in Brownings with 334 rounds per gun.

The Mk.IIA was the fastest of all the production Hurricanes, recording a maximum speed of 342mph (297kt/550km/h) at 22,000 feet (6,705m). Climbing to 20,000 feet (6,096m) took 8.2 minutes and the service ceiling was 37,000 feet (12,777m). The IIA's empty weight was 5,500lb (2,495kg) and maximum loaded weight 7,100lb (3,220kg).

Hurricane IIB

Two types of new wing were designed while the Hurricane II concept was being developed, one internally modified to accept a 12 machine gun armament and the other to accommodate four 20mm cannon. Both were capable of carrying underwing stores.

Hurricane IIs fitted with 12 Browning guns were designated Mk.IIBs, and this model was introduced to production in early 1941, a total of 2,948 being built by Hawker (1,781), Gloster (867) and Austin (300). The first Hurricane IIBs were issued to the squadrons in May 1941, Nos 601 and 605 the first to receive the type.

Early Hurricane IIBs were delivered without the capability to carry external stores but extensive trials were carried out in the first half of 1941 involving the carriage of two 250 or 500lb (113 or 227kg) bombs under the wings. Development of this new fighter-bomber variant resulted in the popular name 'Hurribomber' being applied to what were to be the first examples of many thousands more Hurricanes which would be built to fill this role.

Hurribombers were used opera-

The Battle of Britain Memorial Flight's Hurricane IIC PZ865 on the ground at Biggin Hill in June 1989 during an air show. It carries the markings of No 303 (Polish) Squadron on this occasion. (Vance Ingham)

tionally for the first time in October 1941 against enemy shipping in the English Channel while others appeared in action in the Western Desert, fitted with the Vokes carburettor air intake filter under the nose. This modification was applied to many Hurricane IIs of all marks.

An important part of the Hurricane's career as a ground attack aircraft was the development of the capacity for it to carry underwing 3-inch (7.62cm), 60lb (27kg) rocket projectiles. First trials were conducted in a Hurricane IIA (Z4215) from February 1942 with three launching rails under each wing and the fixed armament of eight machine guns retained. Further testing at the A&AEE resulted in the development of a four rail installation under each wing which was adopted for service.

Many Hurricane IIBs and IICs were subsequently equipped with the rocket launching rails, the cast iron headed projectiles proving effective against vehicles, armour, small vessels and structures. Rocket equipped Hurricane IIs flew against targets in Europe until replaced by similarly armed Typhoons and also found use-

Hurricane IIB BE485/AE-W of 402 (RCAF) Squadron in 'Hurribomber' guise with 250lb (113kg) bombs under the wings. Development of the Hurricane as a ground attack aircraft gave it a second and highly successful career. (via Neil Mackenzie)

ful employment in the Mediterranean and Burma campaigns.

Even though the primary role of the Hurricane was changing from fighter to attack aircraft by the end of 1941, the aircraft still had a role to play as an interceptor and was used extensively as a night fighter in Mk.IIB and IIC (see below) forms during 1941. Completely devoid of any detection equipment (apart from the good old 'Eyeball Mk.1' and some usually vague directions from the ground), the Hurricanes had limited success.

An extension of this was the Turbinlite trials conducted in Britain between September 1942 and January 1943. About a dozen Hurricane squadrons were involved in this unsuccessful experiment which involved a radar and 'Turbinlite' equipped Douglas Havoc light bomber operating in tandem with a Hurricane at night. The theory was that the Havoc detected and tracked an enemy aircraft and then illuminated it with its powerful nose mounted searchlight, allowing the Hurricane to close in for the kill.

Hurricane IIB BD930 of 73 Squadron is dismantled to be taken away for repairs while based in Egypt during 1942. This shot shows some good detail of the wing centre section structure, leading edge fuel tank placement and so on. This aircraft unofficially carries the squadron's pre war markings. (via Neil Mackenzie)

The experiment was not successful and was soon rendered unnecessary with the arrival of more specialised radar equipped night fighters such as certain Bristol Beaufighter and de Havilland Mosquito marks.

Hurricane IIC of 1 Squadron in standard 'temperate' scheme. This photograph was taken in mid 1941, shortly after the squadron began receiving the first IICs off the line.

HURRICANE IIB

Powerplant: One Rolls-Royce Merlin XX V12 piston engine with two speed/ single stage supercharger rated at 1,300hp (970kW) for takeoff and 1,460hp (1,088kW) at 6,250ft (1,905m); Rotol three bladed constant-speed propeller of 11ft 3in (3.43m) diameter. Internal fuel capacity 97imp gal (441 l) in wing and fuselage tanks; provision for two underwing 45imp gal (204 l) drop or 90imp gal (409 l) fixed ferry tanks.

Dimensions: Wing span 40ft 0in (12.19m); length 32ft 3in (9.83m); height (prop blade vertical) 13ft 3in (4.04m); wing area 258sq ft (23.97m²).

Weights: Empty 5,467lb (2,480kg); normal loaded 7,233lb (3,281kg).

Armament: 12 0.303in Browning machine guns in wings with 332 rounds per gun; two 250lb or 500lb (113/ 227kg) underwing bombs or provision for eight 3in/60lb (7.62cm/ 27kg) rocket projectiles.

Performance: Max speed 285kt (528km/h) at 18,000ft (5,486m); long range cruise 154kt (285km/h) at 16,000ft (4,877m); initial climb 2,950ft (899m)/min; time to 15,000ft 5.5min, to 20,000ft 8.4min; service ceiling 36,000ft (10,973m); max range (internal fuel) 404nm (748km), with drop tanks 812nm (1,505km), with ferry tanks 938nm (1,738km).

Hurricane IIB (Tropical) supplementary data: Max speed 269kt (499km/h) at 18,000ft; initial climb 2,800ft (853m)/ min; service ceiling 33,600ft (10,241m); empty weight 5,594lb (2,537kg); normal loaded weight 7,396lb (3,355kg); max overload 7,896lb (3,582kg).

Tropicalised Hurricane IIC HL931 with 45imp gal (205 l) drop tanks under the wings. The IIC was the most numerous of all the Hurricane variants with 4,711 built. (via Neil Mackenzie)

Hurricane IIC

Numerically the most important Hurricane variant with 4,711 built (all by Hawker), the IIC was the cannon armed version of the Hurricane II, fitted with a quartet of 20mm Hispano guns in the wings, each with 90 rounds of ammunition fed by the Chetallerault belt system.

Earlier experiments with cannon armed Hurricanes were described above, these tests and trials culminating in the decision to go ahead with this form of firepower which was capable of inflicting considerably more damage on targets than previous models with rifle calibre machine guns, even the Mk.IIB with 12 on board.

Hurricane IICs began reaching RAF squadrons in May 1941, Nos 1 and 3 Squadrons receiving the first aircraft. All had provision for underwing

Hurricane IICs on Hawker's production line. The rate peaked at about eight per day at Kingston and Langley in 1942-43.

bombs (or fuel tanks) and rocket projectiles later on, and those in combination with the hitting power provided by the four Hispanos resulted in a more than useful ground attack aircraft.

By the time the Mk.IIC entered service the Hurricane was on the way out as a day fighter, but this version and the machine gun armed IIB both found employment on night fighter duties over the United Kingdom. For home based squadrons the main role was offensive sweeps over the French Channel ports until Typhoons began to take over in 1943, and night intruder raids.

Many squadrons served overseas, usually equipped with tropicalised Hurricanes fitted with Vokes filters. By that date Hurricane IICs equipped 10 Squadrons in the Middle East and by 1945 a further 21 Squadrons were flying the aircraft in various parts of South-East Asia, notably the India-Burma theatre of operations. Altogether, Hurricane IICs equipped more than 80 RAF squadrons between 1941 and 1945.

The last Hurricane delivered to the RAF in September 1944 was a Mk.IIC (PZ865, *The Last of the Many*), still flying today with the Battle of Britain Memorial Flight.

Hurricane IIC BD936/ZY-S of 247 Squadron RAF in 1942. 247 used its IICs for intruder missions over north-west France. (via Neil Mackenzie)

> ### HURRICANE IIC
> **Powerplant:** *One Rolls-Royce Merlin XX V12 piston engine rated at 1,300hp (969kW) for takeoff and 1,460hp (1,088kW) at 6,250ft (1,905m); Rotol three bladed constant-speed propeller of 11ft 3in (3.43m) diameter. Fuel capacity 97imp gal (441 l) in wing and fuselage tanks; provision for two underwing 45imp gal (205 l) drop or 90imp gal (409 l) fixed ferry tanks.*
> **Dimensions:** *Wing span 40ft 0in (12.19m); length 32ft 3in (9.83m); height (vertical prop blade) 13ft 3in (4.04m); wing area 258sq ft (23.97m²).*
> **Weights:** *Empty 5,658lb (2,566kg); normal loaded 7,544lb (3,422kg); max overload 8,044lb (3,649kg).*
> **Armament:** *Four 20mm Hispano Mk.I or II cannon with 90 rounds per gun; provision for two underwing 250lb or 500lb (113/227kg) bombs or eight 3in/ 60lb (7.62cm/27kg) rocket projectiles.*
> **Performance:** *Max speed 284kt (526km/h) at 18,000ft (5,486m); range cruise 155kt (286km/h) at 16,000ft (4,880m); initial climb 2,750ft (838m)/ min; time to 15,000ft (4,572m) 6.0min, to 20,000ft (6,096m) 9.1min; service ceiling 35,600ft (10,850m); max range (internal fuel) 400nm (740km), with drop tanks 799nm (1,480km), with ferry tanks 944nm (1,748km).*
> **Hurricane IIC (Tropical) supplementary data:** *Max speed 262kt (484km/h); initial climb 2,400ft (731m)/min; service ceiling 33,200ft (10,119m); range (internal fuel) 370nm (686km); empty weight 5,785lb (2,624kg); normal loaded 7,707lb (3,496kg); max overload 8,207lb (3,723kg).*

HURRICANE IID

As the Hurricane II's role as a ground attack aircraft developed, so did the need to produce more potent and specialised versions. The Mk.IID was the first of them, built as a dedicated anti armour attack aircraft with modified wings capable of carrying a pair of 40mm cannon in underwing fairings plus two 0.303in Browning machine guns internally, the latter firing ball and tracer rounds as a means of sighting the larger weapons.

Both Vickers and Rolls-Royce developed compact 40mm cannon for anti armour use in 1940-41, and in September 1941 a Hurricane II (Z2326) was flown with a pair of Vickers S guns (each with 15 rounds of ammunition) installed. The same aircraft was tested with two Rolls-Royce BH guns in early 1942, by which time design of the new wing capable of mounting these weapons had been completed and production was under way. The Rolls-Royce guns carried 12 rounds each.

Deliveries of the Hurricane IID began in March 1942, early aircraft featuring the Rolls-Royce gun although this was soon replaced by the Vickers S which was lighter, more reliable and carried more ammunition. Early aircraft also featured the same standard of armour protection as the Mk.IIC but

this was soon upgraded by more heavy duty protection for the pilot, radiator and engine which added 368lb (167kg) to the aircraft's empty weight.

With the standard tropical equipment (including Vokes filter) the Hurricane IID was a heavy aircraft, maximum combat weight reaching 8,100lb (3,674kg). This reduced performance substantially, although that was not necessarily a major consideration given the IID's low level ground attack role. At a lower weight, maximum speed was 290mph (252kt/ 467km/h) at 12,000 feet (3,660m) and 316mph (275kt/508km/h) at 19,000 feet (5,795m).

Hawker built 296 Hurricane IIDs, most of which served with RAF squadrons in the Western Desert and India-Burma. The aircraft proved highly effective against Rommel's armour in North Africa, and quickly became known as the 'Tank Buster'.

HURRICANE III

An unused designation intended for application to Hurricanes powered by 1,300hp (969kW) US built Packard Merlin 28 engines. This combination was proposed in late 1941 as insurance against a shortage of Merlin XXs but was not needed. The Packard Merlin was used in the Canadian built Hurricane Mks. X, XI and XII.

The first specialised ground attack Hurricane variant, the Mk.IID. Optimised for anti armour operations, it featured two 40mm Vickers guns under the wings plus two 0.303 machine guns for sighting. Deliveries began in March 1942 and the aircraft was highly effective against Rommel's tanks in North Africa. (via Neil Mackenzie)

HAWKER HURRICANE

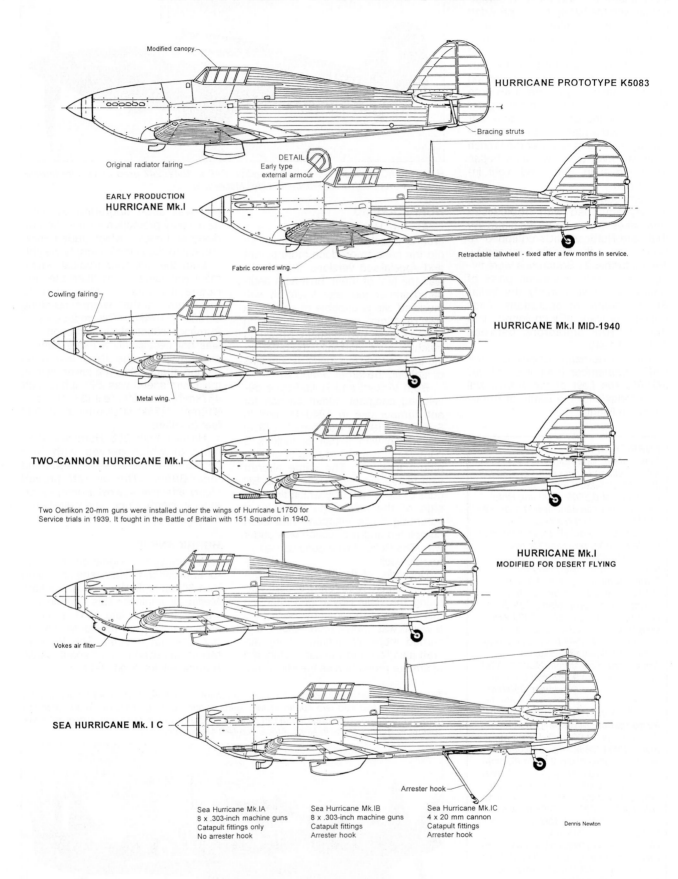

Modified canopy.

HURRICANE PROTOTYPE K5083

Bracing struts

Original radiator fairing

DETAIL
Early type
external armour

EARLY PRODUCTION
HURRICANE Mk.I

Retractable tailwheel - fixed after a few months in service.

Fabric covered wing.

Cowling fairing

HURRICANE Mk.I MID-1940

Metal wing.

TWO-CANNON HURRICANE Mk.I

Two Oerlikon 20-mm guns were installed under the wings of Hurricane L1750 for
Service trials in 1939. It fought in the Battle of Britain with 151 Squadron in 1940.

HURRICANE Mk.I
MODIFIED FOR DESERT FLYING

Vokes air filter

SEA HURRICANE Mk.I C

Arrester hook

Sea Hurricane Mk.IA
8 x .303-inch machine guns
Catapult fittings only
No arrester hook

Sea Hurricane Mk.IB
8 x .303-inch machine guns
Catapult fittings
Arrester hook

Sea Hurricane Mk.IC
4 x 20 mm cannon
Catapult fittings
Arrester hook

Dennis Newton

HAWKER HURRICANE

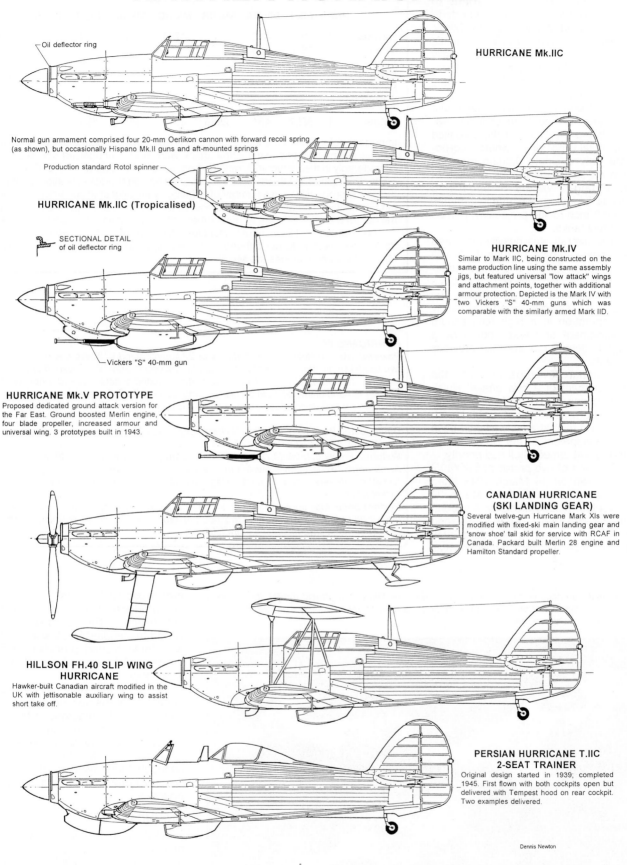

Oil deflector ring

HURRICANE Mk.IIC

Normal gun armament comprised four 20-mm Oerlikon cannon with forward recoil spring (as shown), but occasionally Hispano Mk.II guns and aft-mounted springs

Production standard Rotol spinner

HURRICANE Mk.IIC (Tropicalised)

SECTIONAL DETAIL
of oil deflector ring

HURRICANE Mk.IV
Similar to Mark IIC, being constructed on the same production line using the same assembly jigs, but featured universal "low attack" wings and attachment points, together with additional armour protection. Depicted is the Mark IV with two Vickers "S" 40-mm guns which was comparable with the similarly armed Mark IID.

Vickers "S" 40-mm gun

HURRICANE Mk.V PROTOTYPE
Proposed dedicated ground attack version for the Far East. Ground boosted Merlin engine, four blade propeller, increased armour and universal wing. 3 prototypes built in 1943.

CANADIAN HURRICANE (SKI LANDING GEAR)
Several twelve-gun Hurricane Mark XIs were modified with fixed-ski main landing gear and 'snow shoe' tail skid for service with RCAF in Canada. Packard built Merlin 28 engine and Hamilton Standard propeller.

HILLSON FH.40 SLIP WING HURRICANE
Hawker-built Canadian aircraft modified in the UK with jettisonable auxiliary wing to assist short take off.

PERSIAN HURRICANE T.IIC 2-SEAT TRAINER
Original design started in 1939; completed 1945. First flown with both cockpits open but delivered with Tempest hood on rear cockpit. Two examples delivered.

Dennis Newton

HURRICANE IV

The final Hurricane variant to achieve production was another dedicated ground attack model, the Mk.IV, of which 794 were built by Hawker. Of these, the first 270 were originally designated Mk.IIEs but this was subsequently changed. All were fully tropicalised.

The Hurricane IV was designated a 'low attack' model, its principal feature being the fitting of the so-called 'universal wing' which would incorporate only a single 0.303in machine gun on each side but be capable of accepting a variety of underwing stores including two 40mm cannon, eight 3-inch rocket projectiles, bombs and fuel tanks.

The aircraft was heavily armoured and powered by a 1,620hp (1,208kW) Merlin 24 or 27 with two speed supercharger, the ratios 'tailored' to produce maximum power at low altitudes. The Merlin 27 was developed specifically for operation in a high temperature environment and was cooled by a slightly deeper radiator than previous models.

Although investigations into the development of a 'low attack' Hurricane began in mid 1941, detailed design work didn't start until March 1942 and then at a fairly relaxed pace as development of the Hurricane IID and rocket armed Mk.II had priority.

The first of two prototypes (KX405) was flown on 14 March 1943 fitted with a 1,700hp (1,268kW) Merlin 32 and a four bladed propeller. A second aircraft with Merlin 27 and four bladed propeller followed a few days later. Both these aircraft also served as

	Proto	Mk.I	Mk.IIA	Mk.IIB	Mk.IIC	Mk.IID	IIE/IV	X–XII	Totals
HURRICANE PRODUCTION SUMMARY									
Hawker	1	1924	418	1781	4711	296	794	–	9925
Gloster	–	1850	33	867	–	–	–	–	2750
Austin	–	–	–	300	–	–	–	–	300
CCF	–	60	–	–	–	–	–	1391	1451
Fairey	–	3	–	–	–	–	–	–	3
Yugoslavia	–	20	–	–	–	–	–	–	20
Totals	1	3857	451	2948	4711	296	794	1391	14,449

Important note: One of the interesting things about the Hurricane's history is that no-one seems to know exactly how many were built! Recognised sources vary considerably in their estimates, ranging from about 14,230 up to 14,670. Canadian production figures are themselves subject to some considerable variation, perhaps due to the probability that a number of airframes were allocated serial numbers but not completed. The above table represents this author's attempt at establishing the number, and is different to most others although within the published range.

The Hurricane IIE/IV figure includes 270 aircraft which were originally designated the Mk.IIE but subsequently redesignated as Mk.IVs. The Canadian Mk.X-XII column includes the Mk.XI.

HURRICANE IV

Powerplant: One Rolls-Royce Merlin 24 or 27 liquid cooled V12 piston engine with two speed/single stage supercharger rated at 1,620hp (1,208kW) for takeoff and 1,640hp (1,223kW) at 2,000ft (610m); Rotol three bladed constant-speed propeller of 11ft 3in (3.43m) diameter. Fuel capacity 97imp gal (441 l) in wing and fuselage tanks; provision for two underwing 45imp gal (205 l) drop or 90imp gal (409 l) fixed ferry tanks.
Dimensions: Wing span 40ft 0in (12.19m); length 32ft 3in (9.83m); overall height 13ft 3in (4.04m); wing area 258sq ft (23.97m²).
Weights: Empty 6,150lb (2,790kg); normal loaded (with 40mm guns) 8,463lb (3,838kg).
Armament: Two 0.303in Browning machine guns in wings with 600 rounds per gun; two 40mm Vickers S cannon under wings with 15rpg; or eight 3in/60lb (7.62cm/27kg) rocket projectiles.
Performance: Max speed 273kt (505km/h) at 13,500ft (4,115m); range cruise 153kt (283km/h) at 2,000ft (610m); time to 2,000ft (610m) 0.75min; service ceiling 32,100ft (9,784m); range (internal fuel) 430nm (797km).

The final Hurricane version to enter production, the Mk.IV 'low attack' model. Its universal wing was capable of mounting a variety of underwing stores including eight 3-inch rocket projectiles, as shown here.

prototypes for the closely related but not produced Hurricane V, as described below. They subsequently reverted to standard Mk.IV specification with three bladed propellers and in the case of the second aircraft, a Merlin 27 engine.

The Hurricane IV remained in production until the second half of 1944 and equipped squadrons at home, in the Mediterranean theatre and in India-Burma. Several UK based squadrons also had Mk.IVs on strength, although these were mostly used in secondary roles such as gunnery co-operation.

HURRICANE V

Another dedicated ground attack model, intended for service in Burma and featuring a 1,700hp (1,268kW) low altitude rated Merlin 32 and four bladed Rotol propeller. Only three were produced, two of them also serving as prototypes for the closely related Hurricane IV. These were

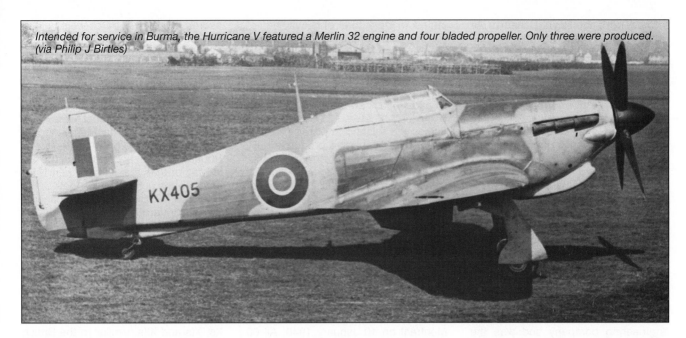

Intended for service in Burma, the Hurricane V featured a Merlin 32 engine and four bladed propeller. Only three were produced. (via Philip J Birtles)

KX405 and KZ193 (both flown in March 1943 and originally designated Mk.IVs) and NL255.

Engine overheating proved to be a problem with the Mk.V and as the RAF had sufficient stocks of Hurricane IICs, IIDs and IVs to meet its needs it was not put into production.

Performance figures achieved in testing included a maximum speed of 326mph (524km/h) at only 500 feet (152m) while the Mk.V's maximum weight of 9,300lb (4,218kg) was by far the heaviest of any Hurricane.

MISCELLANEOUS MARKS

Several other Hurricane marks were created by conversion for specific roles. Some of the designations listed below were applied retrospectively. Canadian built Hurricanes and Sea Hurricanes are covered elsewhere.

Tac R.I: About nine Hurricane Is serving in North Africa were converted in the field (by 103 Maintenance Unit at Aboukir) for tactical reconnaissance duties from October 1940. Several different camera installations were applied, with one, two or three cameras installed in the rear fuselage.

One aircraft had a forward facing camera in the wing root, while another (with three cameras) had its guns removed and the empty spaces fitted with fuel tanks containing an extra 194imp gal (882 l) of fuel, giving a range of over 1,100miles (1,770km).

Tac R.II: About 200 Hurricane IIAs, Bs and Cs were converted to either armed tactical reconnaissance or unarmed photo reconnaissance aircraft in North Africa, the former as Tac R Mk.IIs with a forward facing cine camera or F.24 stills camera in the starboard wing root.

Full gun armament was usually retained and the first conversion was performed in February 1942 for use by 6 Squadron. About 20 Hurricane Is were also converted to Tac R Mk.IIA standards by fitting a Merlin XX engine.

Tac R Mk.II conversions were also performed for use by Hurricane units in the India-Burma theatre from early 1943, in the case of the Mk.IIC usually with two of the four 20mm cannon removed to improve performance.

PR.I and II: Three North African based Hurricane Is were converted to dedicated photographic reconnaissance aircraft as PR Mk.Is in early 1940, two with a pair of oblique fuselage mounted F.24 cameras and the third with three F.24s, arranged with one vertically mounted and the others obliquely. These aircraft were unarmed, capable of operating above 30,000 feet (9,144m) and had their normal fuel capacity almost trebled by the fitting of tanks in the gun bays.

Photographic reconnaissance conversions of the Hurricane II began appearing in North Africa in 1942, about 20 of them entering service by the end of the year. Retrospectively dubbed PR Mk.IIs, these aircraft were based on Mk.IIB and IIC aircraft and also featured additional fuel capacity in the empty gun bays. After operating around the Mediterranean, most of the survivors were sent to serve in India-Burma.

Met.IIC: The collection of meteorological data was a twice daily routine for the RAF at home and abroad, and this was often performed by Hurricane IICs which received the official designation Met Mk.IIC when used in this role. One UK based met specialist unit was 521 Squadron which flew the Hurricane Met.IIC between August 1944 and February 1946. Meteorological Flights equipped with Hurricanes were also established elsewhere, notably in the Middle East.

CANADIAN HURRICANES

Like many other nations, Canada began a review of its armed forces in the second half of the 1930s in the light of the worsening international situation. The Hurricane was chosen

One of the more bizarre experimental Hurricanes was the Hillson slip wing which was briefly tested in 1943. The idea was to give the aircraft substantially more range by providing increased wing area which in turn would allow much heavier than standard takeoff weights to be achieved and therefore more fuel to be carried. After takeoff, the wing would be detached (or 'slipped') and the Hurricane would carry on as usual. The test aircraft was only ever flown as a fixed wing biplane and interest soon waned.

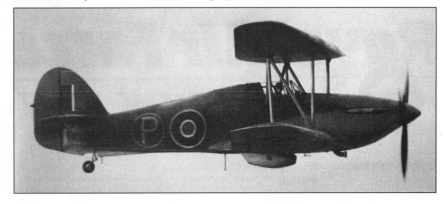

to modernise the Royal Canadian Air Force's fighter establishment and an order was placed for 20 Mk.I aircraft.

These were diverted from existing RAF contracts and delivered to Canada between February and August 1939. All were from the initial production batch and were therefore built to the early specification with fabric covered wings and two bladed Watts fixed-pitch propeller.

The seeming inevitability of war prompted Britain to approach the Canadian Government about establishing a production facility for the Hurricane in that country as a second source of aircraft as insurance against British production being interrupted. Plans for this venture were in place by the beginning of 1939, the Canadian Car & Foundry Co Ltd (CCF) at Montreal selected as prime contractor. CCF was a substantial Canadian engineering company and was the largest manufacturer of railway equipment in the country.

In March 1939 an initial contract for the production of 40 Hurricane Is for the RCAF was placed with CCF, simultaneous with the arrival in Canada of a pattern aircraft, L1848. Six months later, L2144 was sent across the Atlantic to provide sample material for Canadian production. By then, war had broken out and further orders had been placed with CCF covering an additional 20 Mk.Is for the RCAF and at that stage 600 more for the RAF.

Canadian Hurricane (and Sea Hurricane) production eventually reached 1,451 aircraft of all versions, excluding about 150 which it is believed were never assembled even though the basic airframes were built.

The first CCF built Hurricane I (P5170) recorded its maiden flight at Montreal on 10 January 1940. All 60 aircraft in the initial batch were built to the contemporary British standard with Merlin III engines, three bladed de Havilland propellers and metal skinned wings.

Although these early aircraft were originally intended to equip RCAF squadrons at home, most were shipped to Britain in the March-August 1940 period to equip No 1 (RCAF) Squadron which had arrived in the UK in May of that year. Others were allocated to the general RAF 'pool'.

About 50 CCF built Hurricane Is were converted to Sea Hurricane standards, as described later in this chapter, while a few others were fitted with ski undercarriages during 1942 for trials.

Hurricane X, XI and XII

The 60 CCF built Hurricane Is were followed by a further 1,391 Hurricane Xs, XIs and XIIs, similar to the British

Two views of the same Canadian built Hurricane, taken 25 years apart. Z7015 was built in Canada by CCF and completed as a Sea Hurricane IB. The top photograph shows the aircraft in 1971 before restoration to flying condition. The bottom shot shows the aircraft in 1996, shortly after being made airworthy again and operated jointly by the Shuttleworth Trust and Duxford. (Philip J Birtles/Vance Ingham)

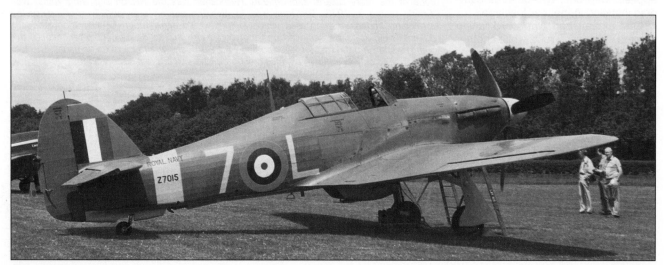

Canadian built Hurricane XIIA 'Z7381'/G-HURI, preserved at Duxford by The Fighter Collection. It is in the markings 71 Squadron RAF, the first 'Eagle' squadron manned by US personnel. (Philip J Birtles)

Hurricane II models but powered by Packard Merlin 28/29 engines, the American manufacturer's equivalents to the Rolls-Royce Merlin XX and similarly rated.

Britain placed contracts for a total of 1,140 CCF Hurricane Mks. X, XI and XII while a further 400 of the latter was ordered for use by the RCAF itself although most of these ended up in Britain or the Soviet Union. As noted above, not all were completed.

Deliveries of the Hurricane Mks.X-XII began in early 1941 and were completed in late 1942. A change in the financial structure of the Canadian Hurricane programme occurred earlier in the same year. Until then the venture had been underwritten entirely by Britain but the United States took over financial responsibility under the terms of Lend-Lease.

The CCF Hurricane X-XII variants were:

Hurricane X: Packard Merlin 28 of 1,300hp (969kW) for takeoff; Hamilton Standard Hydromatic propeller; first 100 (approximately) with eight or 12 0.303in Browning machine guns depending on batch; some converted to carry four 20mm Oerlikon cannon.

Hurricane XI: Similar to Mk.X but with Canadian rather than British equipment; eight gun wings, many subsequently modified to take four 20mm Oerlikon or Hispano cannon; some converted to Sea Hurricane XIBs with 12 gun wings.

Hurricane XII: Packard Merlin 29 engine of similar rating to 28 but with different reduction gear ratio; 12 gun wing, some subsequently fitted with four Hispano cannon.

Hurricane XIIA: As for Mk.XII but with eight gun wings although some later fitted with 12 machine guns or four cannon; a few converted to Sea Hurricane XIIAs.

SEA HURRICANE
Sea Hurricane IA

The suitability of the Hurricane for naval use was discovered almost by accident during the ill-fated Norwegian campaign of May 1940 when, after having been taken aboard in Britain, the Hurricanes of 46 Squadron RAF were flown off the carrier HMS *Glorious* to allow them to operate from land bases in Norway.

The failure of the campaign made it necessary for the Hurricanes to return to the *Glorious,* upon which they successfully landed into a strong headwind despite their pilots' inexperience of shipboard operations.

Glorious was unfortunately lost to the German battle cruisers *Scharnhorst* and *Gneisenau* on the return voyage with the loss of all the Hurricanes, but the fact that they were able to be successfully flown off and on to a carrier inspired Hawker to examine development of naval versions of the fighter.

Two lines of development were simultaneously explored: one with arrester hook and catapult spools for conventional operation from an aircraft carrier and the other involving launching the Hurricane from converted merchant vessels via a rocket powered catapult.

The latter resulted in the first Sea Hurricane variant and had some urgency attached to it as there was a need to defend the vital Atlantic convoys from German Focke-Wulf Fw 200 Condors and Heinkel He 111s which were operating from bases in western France. The long range Condors were a particular threat to shipping in the Western Approaches, assuming it had survived the U-boats encountered *en route*.

Thus was born the 'Hurricat', or Sea Hurricane Mk.IA, designed to operate from these converted merchantmen – CAM-Ships (Catapult Armed Merchant Ships) – each one of which would carry two Hurricanes, one

A 'Hurricat' (or more properly, Sea Hurricane IA) is launched by rocket catapult from a Catapult Armed Merchant Ship during training. The CAM-Ship Hurricanes scored several victories and equally as important, acted as a strong deterrent.

Sea Hurricane IB P2886 of 768 Squadron NAS displays its vee frame arrestor hook to good effect. About 260 Sea Hurricane IB conversions were performed from 1941. (via Neil Mackenzie)

mounted on the fo'c'sle catapult ready to go and the other stored in reserve.

The major problem was that which faced the Hurricat's pilot. It was obviously a one way trip for him once his aircraft was launched so he had to try to make his way back to land. If that was not possible, the only options were to ditch next to a friendly ship or bale out near the convoy and hope to be picked up.

Fifty ex RAF Fighter Command Hurricanes were initially allocated for conversion to Sea Hurricane IA standards, differing from its RAF equivalent only in that it had a catapult spool and naval radio fitted. The first conversion was handed over to the Royal Navy in January 1941. Thirty-five vessels were converted to CAM-Ships, the first of them sailing in May 1941.

The Hurricats scored several victories over the Fw 200 at a time when the convoys were being decimated and resources were severely stretched. The first of them was recorded by an Australian, Lt Cdr Robert Everett of 804 Squadron FAA on 2 August 1941, flying from HMS *Maplin*.

The CAM-Ships operated for a period of just over two years, during which time they undertook 175 voyages. Eight Hurricat launches were made during that time of which six resulted in a successful interception for the loss of one Hurricane pilot.

Although eight may not seem like a lot of sorties, the mere presence of the Hurricats served as a strong deterrent to the German aircraft which kept away, this itself offering a useful form of protection to the convoys and undoubtedly saving many ships and lives.

Sea Hurricane IB

The Sea Hurricane Mk.IB provided a more conventional naval airpower solution as it was intended to operate from both conventional aircraft carriers and a new class of small escort carrier known as MAC (Merchant Aircraft Carrier) ships, converted – as the name implies – from merchant vessels with a flight deck and arrestor cables incorporated. These ships could each accommodate about 12 Sea Hurricanes and provided invaluable protection for convoys in the Atlantic and Mediterranean.

The Sea Hurricane IB was also based on the RAF's Hurricane I and featured a V-frame arrestor hook under the rear fuselage as well as catapult launching spools. About 260 conversions were performed from early 1941, most of them by General Aircraft.

Sea Hurricane IC

The Sea Hurricane Mk.IC entered service in January 1942, this hybrid variant combining the Hurricane I's

Merlin III engine with the Mk.IIC's outer wing panels and four 20mm cannon armament. It lacked the Mk.II's more powerful engine, with the result that the extra weight of the cannon reduced maximum speed to 290mph (252kt/467km/h). All were conversions.

Sea Hurricane IIC

The performance penalties incurred by the Sea Hurricane IC were overcome with the introduction to service in late 1942 of the Mk.IIC with the more powerful Merlin XX of its land based equivalent in combination with the heavier four 20mm cannon armament. Featuring the usual catapult spools, V-frame arrestor hook and naval radio, the IIC equipped naval fighter squadrons aboard fleet and escort carriers in most theatres of operation.

Although originally planned to be a new production Sea Hurricane variant, the IIC was also produced as a result of conversions, most of them again performed by General Aircraft. Many of the conversions were performed on newly built aircraft, however.

Canadian production contributed to the Sea Hurricane tally with Mk.XIIs in particular ending up as naval aircraft. These differed from their British counterparts in having Packard Merlin engines and machine gun rather than cannon armament.

SEA HURRICANE IIC
Powerplant: *One Rolls-Royce Merlin XX liquid cooled V12 piston engine with two speed/single stage supercharger rated at 1,280hp (954kW) for takeoff and 1,460hp (1,089kW) at 6,250ft (1,905ft); Rotol or de Havilland constant-speed propeller of 11ft 3in (3.43m) diameter. Fuel capacity 97imp gal (441 l) in wing and fuselage tanks.*
Dimensions: *Wing span 40ft 0in (12.19m); length 32ft 3 in (9.85m); overall height 13ft 3in (4.04m); wing area 258sq ft (23.97m²).*
Weights: *Empty 5,800lb (2,631kg); normal loaded 7,300lb (3,311kg); max loaded 7,800lb (3,538kg).*
Armament: *Four 20mm Hispano Mk.I or II cannon with 100 rounds per gun.*
Performance: *Max speed 280kt (518km/h) at 13,500ft (4,115m); economical cruise 184kt (341km/h) at 20,000ft (6,096m); time to 22,000ft (6,705m) 9.1min; service ceiling 35,600ft (10,850m); range 400nm (740km).*

The total number of Sea Hurricane conversions is thought to be about 800, of which the Royal Navy had taken delivery of 600 by mid 1942. The aircraft was always regarded as an interim type intended to fill an urgent need until purpose built naval fighters became available. As such, its operational career was relatively short with most front line units changing to other types during 1943.

The last of 38 Fleet Air Arm squadrons to fly the Sea Hurricane relinquished its aircraft in April 1944.

HURRICANES FOR TWO

Although Hawker had studied a tandem two seat Hurricane with open cockpits in 1940, the project was shelved as the pressures of the war mounted. During the conflict, it is known that the Soviets converted some Hurricanes to two seaters with the second seat squeezed in behind the pilot, where the radio was normally mounted. Both cockpits featured a windscreen but no canopy.

Two 'official' two seat conversions were performed by Hawker for Persia (Iraq) postwar, based on the Hurricane IIB/C and initially fitted with four 20mm Oerlikon cannon. First flown in September 1947, these originally featured open cockpits with individual windscreens and a rollover pylon between them but testing revealed the rear cockpit was subject to severe turbulence and a modified Tempest canopy was fitted to help protect the occupant. The rear cockpit featured basic controls for an instructor and no radio was fitted as it occupied the space in which it was normally accommodated.

The two seaters were capable of a maximum speed of 320mph (515km/h) at 21,500ft (6,553m).

One of the two official Hurricane two seater conversions performed by Hawker for Persia in 1947. The original open rear cockpit was subject to severe buffeting and was subsequently covered. The front cockpit remained open.

HAWKER HURRICANE PRODUCTION and SERIALS

Mark	Qty	Serial Nos	Builder/Remarks	Mark	Qty	Serial Nos	Builder/Remarks
Proto	1	K5083	Hawker, F.36/34 prototype, ff 6/11/35	I	50	V7461-7510	Hawker
I	600	L1547-2146	Hawker, L1547 ff 12/10/37, del 12/37-10/39; L1702 first with Merlin III, L1980 first with v-p prop; exports to Belgium (20), Yugoslavia (24), Rumania (12), Iran (1), Sth Africa (6), Canada (22), Turkey (15)	I	40	V7533-7572	Hawker
				I	40	V7588-7627	Hawker
				I	47	V7644-7690	Hawker
				I	33	V7705-7737	Hawker
				I	40	V7741-7780	Hawker
				I	44	V7795-7838	Hawker
I	50	N2318-2367	Hawker, first delivered 29/09/39	I	12	V7851-7862	Hawker
I	30	N2380-2409	Hawker	I	4	W6667-6670	Hawker, delivered 07/40
I	20	N2422-2441	Hawker, N2423 first with metal covered wings	I	60	W9100-9159	Gloster
				I	40	W9170-9209	Gloster
I	50	N2453-2502	Hawker	I	30	W9215-9244	Gloster
I	40	N2520-2559	Hawker	I	20	W9260-9279	Gloster
I	50	N2582-2631	Hawker	I	30	W9290-9329	Gloster
I	30	N2645-2674	Hawker	I	20	W9340-9359	Gloster
I	30	N2700-2729	Hawker, last delivered 05/40	II	50	Z2308-2357	Hawker, first delivery 09/40
I	50	P2535-2584	Gloster, P2535 ff 20/10/39	II	45	Z2382-2426	Hawker
I	40	P2614-2653	Gloster	II	20	Z2446-2465	Hawker
I	30	P2672-2701	Gloster, P2682 first Gloster built with 3-blade prop	II	50	Z2479-2528	Hawker
				II	35	Z2560-2594	Hawker
I	20	P2713-2732	Gloster	II	20	Z2624-2643	Hawker
I	20	P2751-2770	Gloster	II	45	Z2661-2705	Hawker
I	45	P2792-2836	Gloster	II	35	Z2741-2775	Hawker
I	35	P2854-2888	Gloster	II	50	Z2791-2840	Hawker
I	25	P2900-2924	Gloster	II	50	Z2882-2931	Hawker
I	50	P2946-2995	Gloster	II	35	Z2959-2993	Hawker
I	50	P3020-3069	Gloster	II	20	Z3017-3036	Hawker
I	45	P3080-3124	Gloster	II	50	Z3050-3099	Hawker
I	40	P3140-3179	Gloster	II	45	Z3143-3187	Hawker
I	35	P3200-3234	Gloster	II	50	Z3221-3270	Hawker
I	15	P3250-3264	Gloster	II	50	Z3310-3359	Hawker
I	15	P3265-3279	Hawker, first delivery 02/40	II	20	Z3385-3404	Hawker
I	25	P3300-3324	Hawker	II	40	Z3431-3470	Hawker
I	20	P3345-3364	Hawker	II	35	Z3489-3523	Hawker
I	50	P3380-3429	Hawker	II	45	Z3554-3598	Hawker
I	45	P3448-3492	Hawker	II	50	Z3642-3691	Hawker
I	40	P3515-3554	Hawker	II	45	Z3740-3784	Hawker
I	50	P3574-3623	Hawker	II	20	Z3826-3845	Hawker
I	45	P3640-3684	Hawker	II	35	Z3885-3919	Hawker
I	40	P3700-3739	Hawker	II	50	Z3969-4018	Hawker, last delivery 07/41
I	35	P3755-3789	Hawker	I	50	Z4022-4071	Gloster
I	35	P3802-3836	Hawker	I	35	Z4085-4119	Gloster
I	50	P3854-3903	Hawker	I	45	Z4161-4205	Gloster
I	25	P3920-3944	Hawker	I	50	Z4223-4272	Gloster
I	25	P3960-3984	Hawker, last delivered 07/40	I	20	Z4308-4327	Gloster
I	40	P5170-5209	CCF, to Britain 03-08/40 redesignated Mk.X	I	45	Z4347-4391	Gloster
I	10	P8809-8818	Hawker, fabric covered wings	I	20	Z4415-4434	Gloster
I	10	R2680-2689	Hawker	I	35	Z4482-4516	Gloster
I	50	R4074-4123	Gloster	I	50	Z4532-4581	Gloster
I	30	R4171-4200	Gloster	I	50	Z4603-4652	Gloster
I	20	R4213-4232	Gloster	I	35	Z4686-4720	Gloster
I	20	T9519-9538	CCF	I	50	Z4760-4809	Gloster
I	50	V6533-6582	Gloster	I	45	Z4832-4876	Gloster
I	50	V6600-6649	Gloster	I	20	Z4920-4939	Gloster
I	40	V6665-6704	Gloster	IIA	30	Z4940-4969	Gloster
I	40	V6722-6761	Gloster	IIA	3	Z4987-4989	Gloster
I	50	V6776-6825	Gloster	IIB	17	Z4990-5006	Gloster
I	50	V6840-6889	Gloster	IIB	50	Z5038-5087	Gloster
I	50	V6913-6962	Gloster	IIB	45	Z5117-5161	Gloster
I	50	V6979-7028	Gloster	IIB	35	Z5202-5236	Gloster
I	40	V7042-7081	Gloster	IIB	20	Z5252-5271	Gloster
I	40	V7099-7138	Gloster	IIB	50	Z5302-5351	Gloster
I	40	V7156-7195	Gloster	IIB	20	Z5376-5395	Gloster
I	10	V7200-7209	Hawker, fabric covered wings, first delivery 07/40	IIB	50	Z5434-5483	Gloster
I	15	V7221-7235	Hawker, fabric covered wings	IIB	35	Z5529-5563	Gloster
I	25	V7236-7260	Hawker, metal covered wings	IIB	50	Z5580-5629	Gloster
I	43	V7276-7318	Hawker	IIB	45	Z5649-5693	Gloster
I	50	V7337-7386	Hawker	X	35	Z6983-7017	CCF
I	47	V7400-7446	Hawker	X	45	Z7049-7093	CCF
				X	20	Z7143-7162	CCF

HAWKER HURRICANE PRODUCTION and SERIALS (cont)

Mark	Qty	Serial Nos	Builder/Remarks	Mark	Qty	Serial Nos	Builder/Remarks
X	20	AE958-977	CCF	IIB/C	50	BP430-479	Hawker
X	155	AF945-999	CCF, 24 retained by RCAF	IIB/C	34	BP493-526	Hawker
X	145	AG100-344	CCF	IIB/C/D	29	BP538-566	Hawker
X	20	AG665-684	CCF	IIB/C	36	BP579-614	Hawker
X	100	AM270-369	CCF, most to USSR	IIB/C	48	BP628-675	Hawker
X	26	AP138-163	CCF	IIB/C	20	BP692-711	Hawker
IIB	35	AP516-550	Austin, all but AP516 to USSR	IIB/C	39	BP734-772	Hawker
IIB	50	AP564-613	Austin, all to USSR	IIA	20	BV155-174	converted from Mk.I
IIB	20	AP629-648	Austin, all to USSR	X	6	BW835-840	CCF
IIB	45	AP670-714	Austin, all to USSR	X	1	BW840	CCF
IIB	50	AP732-781	Austin, all to USSR	X	39	BW841-879	CCF
IIB	25	AP801-825	Austin, all to USSR	X	1	BW880	CCF
IIB	50	AP849-898	Austin, up to AP879 to USSR	X	4	BW881-884	CCF
IIB	25	AP912-936	Austin	XI	115	BW885-999	CCF
I	4	AS987-990	Hawker, delivered 02/41	XI	35	BX100-134	CCF
IIB/C	50	BD696-745	Hawker, first delivery 07/41	IIA	40	DG612-651	converted from Mk.I by Rolls-Royce
IIB/C	35	BD759-793	Hawker	IIA	36	DR339-374	converted from Mk.I, for USSR
IIB/C	20	BD818-837	Hawker	IIA	4	DR391-394	converted from Mk.I, for USSR
IIB/C	45	BD855-899	Hawker	IIB/C	48	HL544-591	Hawker
IIB/C	50	BD914-963	Hawker	IIB/C	32	HL603-634	Hawker
IIB/C	7	BD980-986	Hawker	IIB/C	30	HL654-683	Hawker
IIB/C	13	BE105-117	Hawker	IIB/C	50	HL698-747	Hawker
IIB/C	45	BE130-174	Hawker	IIB/C	43	HL767-809	Hawker
IIB/C	50	BE193-242	Hawker	IIB/C	40	HL828-867	Hawker
IIB/C	35	BE274-308	Hawker	IIB/C	35	HL879-913	Hawker
IIB/C	50	BE323-372	Hawker	IIB/C	17	HL925-941	Hawker
IIB/C	35	BE394-428	Hawker	IIB/C	45	HL953-997	Hawker
IIB/C	50	BE468-517	Hawker	IIB/C	48	HM110-157	Hawker
IIB/C	45	BE546-590	Hawker	IIB/C/D	43	HV275-317	Hawker
IIB/C	20	BE632-651	Hawker	IIB/C/D	38	HV333-370	Hawker
IIB/C	50	BE667-716	Hawker	IIB/C/D	50	HV396-445	Hawker
IIB	50	BG674-723	Gloster	IIB/C/D	49	HV468-516	Hawker
IIB	35	BG737-771	Gloster	IIB/C/D	27	HV534-560	Hawker
IIB	50	BG783-832	Gloster	IIB/C/D	36	HV577-612	Hawker
IIB	45	BG844-888	Gloster	IIB/C/D	41	HV634-674	Hawker
IIB	20	BG901-920	Gloster	IIB/C/D	50	HV696-745	Hawker
IIB	45	BG933-977	Gloster	IIB/C/D	32	HV768-799	Hawker
IIB	10	BG990-999	Gloster	IIB/C/D	44	HV815-858	Hawker
IIB	40	BH115-154	Gloster	IIB/C/D	49	HV873-921	Hawker, HV892-93 for SAAF
IIB	35	BH167-201	Gloster	IIB/C/D	47	HV943-989	Hawker
IIB	50	BH215-264	Gloster	IIB/C/D	32	HW115-146	Hawker
IIB	20	BH-277-296	Gloster	IIB/C/D	41	HW167-207	Hawker
IIB	50	BH312-361	Gloster	IIB/C/D	50	HW229-278	Hawker
IIB/C	39	BM898-936	Hawker, delivered from 10/41	IIB/C/D	33	HW291-323	Hawker
IIB/C	50	BM947-996	Hawker	IIB/C/D	29	HW345-373	Hawker
IIB/C	40	BN103-142	Hawker	IIB/C/D	46	HW399-444	Hawker
IIB/C	35	BN155-189	Hawker	IIB/C/D	35	HW467-501	Hawker
IIB/C	40	BN203-242	Hawker	IIB/C/D	40	HW533-572	Hawker
IIB/C	34	BN265-298	Hawker	IIB/C/D	29	HW596-624	Hawker
IIB/C	27	BN311-337	Hawker	IIB/C/D	36	HW651-686	Hawker
IIB/C	44	BN346-389	Hawker	IIB/C/D	45	HW713-757	Hawker
II/B/C	37	BN399-435	Hawker	IIB/C/D	30	HW779-808	Hawker
IIB/C	49	BN449-497	Hawker	IIB/C/D	48	HW834-881	Hawker, delivered 11/42
IIB/C	36	BN512-547	Hawker	XII	153	JS219-371	CCF built 1942
IIB/C	45	BN559-603	Hawker	XII	37	JS374-420	CCF, 12 gun wings
IIB/C	31	BN624-654	Hawker	XII	48	JS421-468	CCF, most with 4 cannon wings
IIB/C	39	BN667-705	Hawker	IIB/C/D	36	KW696-731	Hawker, first delivery 11/42
IIB/C	41	BN719-759	Hawker	IIB/C/D	33	KW745-777	Hawker
IIB/C/D	30	BN773-802	Hawker	II/IV	42	KW791-832	Hawker
IIB/C/D	29	BN818-846	Hawker	IIB/C/D	36	KW846-881	Hawker
IIB/C/D	24	BN859-882	Hawker	II/IV	44	KW893-936	Hawker
IIB/C	45	BN896-940	Hawker	IIC	34	KW949-982	Hawker
IIB/C/D	40	BN953-992	Hawker, delivered 03/42	IIC/D	46	KX101-146	Hawker
IIB/C/D	33	BP109-141	Hawker, delivered 03/42	IIC/D/IV	41	KX162-202	Hawker
IIB/C/D	47	BP154-200	Hawker	IIC/D	42	KX220-261	Hawker
IIB/C	29	BP217-245	Hawker	IIC/D	28	KX280-307	Hawker
IIB/C	44	BP259-302	Hawker	IIC	49	KX321-369	Hawker
IIB/C	47	BP316-362	Hawker	IIC	23	KX382-404	Hawker
IIB/C	39	BP378-416	Hawker	V	1	KX405	Hawker, later Mk.IV

Mark	Qty	Serial Nos	Builder/Remarks
IIC/IV	20	KX406-425	Hawker
IIC/D	40	KX452-491	Hawker
IIC/IV	47	KX521-567	Hawker
IIC/IV	43	KX579-621	Hawker
IIC/IV	46	KX691-736	Hawker
IIC	36	KX749-784	Hawker
IIC/IV	43	KX796-838	Hawker
IIC/D/IV	42	KX851-892	Hawker
IIC	46	KX922-967	Hawker
IIC	46	KZ111-156	Hawker
IIC/IV	24	KZ169-192	Hawker
V	1	KZ193	Hawker
IIC/IV	8	KZ194-201	Hawker
IIC/IV	35	KZ216-250	Hawker
IIC/IV	36	KZ266-301	Hawker
IIC/IV	38	KZ319-356	Hawker
IIC/IV	43	KZ370-412	Hawker
IIC	47	KZ424-470	Hawker
IIC	44	KZ483-526	Hawker
IIC/IV	43	KZ540-582	Hawker
IIC/IV	16	KZ597-612	Hawker, delivered 04/43
IIC/IV	20	KZ613-632	Hawker, first delivery 04/43
IIC/IV	44	KZ646-689	Hawker
IIC/IV	49	KZ702-750	Hawker
IIC	36	KZ766-801	Hawker
IIC	46	KZ817-862	Hawker
IIC/IV	44	KZ877-920	Hawker
IIC	17	KZ933-949	Hawker
IIC	44	LA101-144	Hawker
IIC	34	LB542-575	Hawker
IIC	37	LB588-624	Hawker
IIC/IV	49	LB639-687	Hawker
IIC/IV	38	LB707-744	Hawker
IIC/IV	33	LB769-801	Hawker
IIC/IV	36	LB827-862	Hawker
IIC	41	LB873-913	Hawker
IIC	47	LB927-973	Hawker
IIC/IV	14	LB986-999	Hawker
IIC/IV	32	LD100-131	Hawker
IIC/IV	29	LD157-185	Hawker
IIC/IV	21	LD199-219	Hawker
IIC/IV	35	LD232-266	Hawker
IIC/IV	29	LD287-315	Hawker
IIC	18	LD334-351	Hawker
IIC	48	LD369-416	Hawker
IIC/IV	36	LD435-470	Hawker
IIC/IV	22	LD487-508	Hawker
IIC	16	LD524-539	Hawker
IIC/IV	24	LD557-580	Hawker
IIC/IV	39	LD594-632	Hawker
IIC	45	LD651-695	Hawker
IIC	47	LD723-749	Hawker
IIC/IV	38	LD772-809	Hawker
IIC/IV	40	LD827-866	Hawker
IIC/IV	21	LD885-905	Hawker
IIC/IV	49	LD931-979	Hawker
IIC	7	LD993-999	Hawker, delivered 09/43
IIC/IV	26	LE121-146	Hawker, first delivery 09/43
IIC	21	LE163-183	Hawker
IIC	14	LE201-214	Hawker
IIC/IV	27	LE247-273	Hawker
IIC/IV	19	LE291-309	Hawker
IIC	35	LE334-368	Hawker
IIC/IV	19	LE387-405	Hawker
IIC	18	LE432-449	Hawker
IIC	29	LE456-484	Hawker
IIC/IV	37	LE499-535	Hawker
IIC/IV	42	LE552-593	Hawker
IIC/IV	49	LE617-665	Hawker
IIC	35	LE679-713	Hawker

Mark	Qty	Serial Nos	Builder/Remarks
IIB/C/IV	33	LE737-769	Hawker
IIB/C	33	LE784-816	Hawker
IIC/IV	39	LE829-867	Hawker, I only Mk.IIB (LE852)
IIC/IV	41	LE885-925	Hawker
IIC	29	LE938-966	Hawker
IIC	21	LE979-999	Hawker
IIC/IV	35	LF101-135	Hawker
IIC	32	LF153-184	Hawker
IIC	41	LF197-237	Hawker
IIC	43	LF256-298	Hawker
IIC	34	LF313-346	Hawker
IIC	47	LF359-405	Hawker
IIC/IV	18	LF418-435	Hawker
IIC/IV	32	LF451-482	Hawker
IIC/IV	23	LF494-516	Hawker
IIC	14	LF529-542	Hawker
IIC/IV	43	LF559-601	Hawker
IIC	41	LF620-660	Hawker
IIC	48	LF674-721	Hawker
IIC	38	LF737-774	Hawker
IIC	39	MW335-373	Hawker, 3 to Portugal
Sea IIC	36	NF668-703	Hawker
Sea IIC	24	NF716-739	Hawker
V	1	NL255	Hawker
IIB/C	32	PG425-456	Hawker
IIB/C	31	PG469-499	Hawker
IIB/C	43	PG512-554	Hawker
IIB/C	44	PG567-610	Hawker
XII	36	PJ660-695	CCF
XII	48	PJ711-758	CCF
XII	35	PJ779-813	CCF
XII	31	PJ842-872	CCF
IIC	49	PZ730-778	Hawker
IIC	45	PZ791-835	Hawker
IIC	18	PZ848-865	Hawker, last delivered 08/44

Conversions to Sea Hurricane (selection only)

N2351, 2352, 2367, 2399, 2409, 2429, 2433, 2467-69, 2488, 2489, 2590, 2591, 2618, 2630, 2631, 2648, 2660, 2671, 2706.

P2717, 2731, 2826, 2878, 2886, 2921, 2948, 2953, 2963, 2972, 2986, 2994, 3020, 3036, 3056, 3090, 3092, 3104, 3111, 3114, 3152, 3165, 3168, 3206, 3229, 3301, 3320, 3362, 3394, 3398, 3460, 3466, 3467, 3530, 3544, 3597, 3620, 3706, 3710, 3719, 3773, 3776, 3784, 3805, 3814, 3829, 3870, 3877, 3883, 3924-26, 3934, 3975, 3979, 5180, 5182, 5187, 5203, 5206, 5209.

R4077, 4078, 4089, 4095, 4105, 4177, 4178, 4214, 4226.

T9526.

V6536, 6537, 6541, 6545, 6555, 6556, 6564, 6577, 6610, 6649, 6697, 6700, 6723, 6727, 6731, 6751, 6756, 6759, 6760, 6779, 6794, 6799, 6801, 6802, 6815, 6817, 6843, 6954, 6858, 6867, 6881, 6886, 6923, 6924, 6933, 6944, 6952, 6957, 7001, 7005, 7027, 7043, 7046, 7049, 7050, 7063, 7070, 7071, 7077, 7100, 7113, 7125, 7129, 7130, 7133, 7135, 7157, 7161, 7162, 7172, 7182, 7189, 7191, 7194, 7195, 7207, 7208, 7229, 7241, 7244, 7246, 7252, 7253, 7301, 7311, 7339, 7349, 7465, 7498, 7501-06, 7588, 7600, 7623, 7646, 7647, 7650, 7665, 7675, 7681, 7685, 7745, 7824.

W9124, 9128, 9174, 9182, 9188, 9209, 9215, 9216, 9218, 9220-24, 9237, 9272, 9276, 9277, 9279, 9311-13, 9315, 9316, 9318, 9319.

Z4039, 4051, 4053, 4055-57, 4094, 4365, 4500, 4504, 4532, 4550, 4553, 4568, 4569, 4581, 4605, 4624, 4638, 4646, 4649, 4686, 4778, 4835, 4846, 4847, 4849, 4851-54, 4865-67, 4873, 4874, 4876, 4920-22, 4924-26, 4929, 4933-39, 6987, 6995, 6997, 7008, 7015, 7016, 7050, 7055, 7057, 7061, 7065, 7067, 7069, 7071, 7073, 7078-80, 7082-91, 7093, 7144, 7145, 7148, 7149, 7151-55, 7160-62.

HL673

AE958-976, 975, 977

AF945-47, 962, 963, 965-67, 969, 971, 973, 974, 976, 981, 982.

JS253, 328, 334, 336 etc.

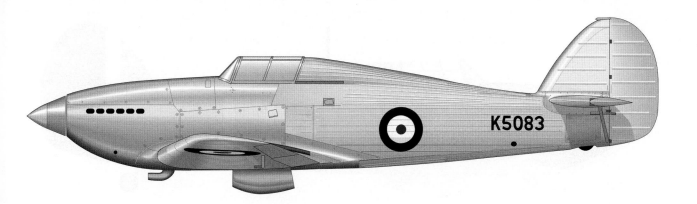

Hawker F.36/34 prototype at the time of its maiden flight on 6 November 1935. Note retractable tailwheel.

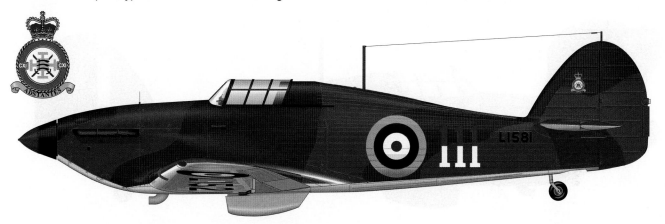

Hurricane I L1581 of 111 Sqdn RAF in July 1938 while taking part in the Bastille Day celebration flypast over Paris.

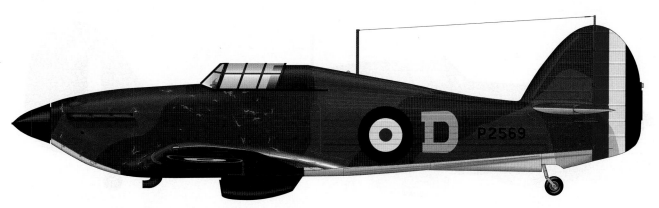

Hurricane I P2569/D of 73 Sqdn RAF in France 1939-40 during the 'Phoney War'.

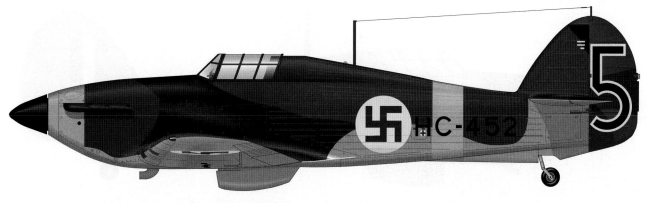

Hurricane I HC-452 (ex RAF N2394) in 1942 after repainting in Finnish colours and carrying Continuation War markings. Note the replacement rudder fitted after battle damage.

Hurricane I N2359/YB-J of 17 Sqdn RAF at Debden in September 1940. Aircraft originally built with fabric covered wings but shown after fitting of metal wings.

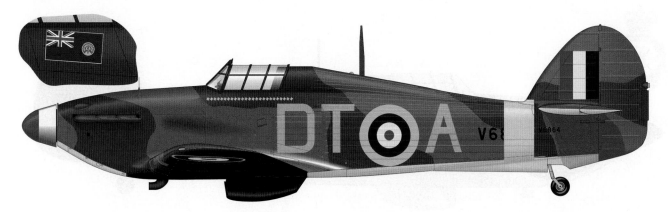

Hurricane I V6864/DT-A of 257 Sqdn RAF in late 1940. Aircraft of Sqdn Ldr Robert Stanford Tuck with 25 'kill' markings under canopy.

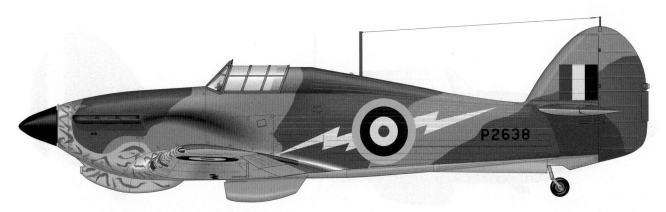

Hurricane I (Trop) P2638 of 208 Sqdn RAF, Western Desert 1941. Note Italian style mottled camouflage on nose and wing leading edges to confuse enemy anti aircraft gunners during low level attacks.

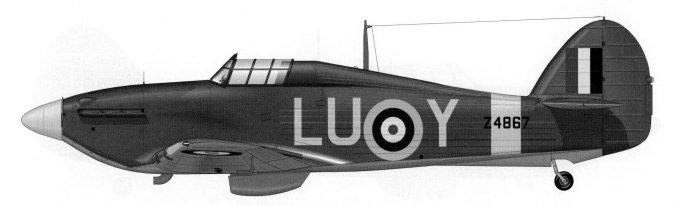

Sea Hurricane IA Z4867/LU-Y of the RN Merchant Ship Fighter Unit for operation from CAM-Ships 1941. Note lack of arrestor hook.

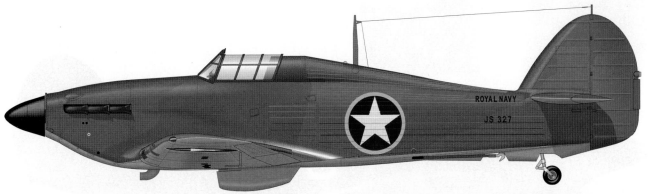

Sea Hurricane IIB (converted from Canadian Hurricane XII) JS327 of No 800 Sqdn RN Fleet Air Arm 1942. Operated from HMS Bitter during Operation Torch landings in North Africa and wore US insignia.

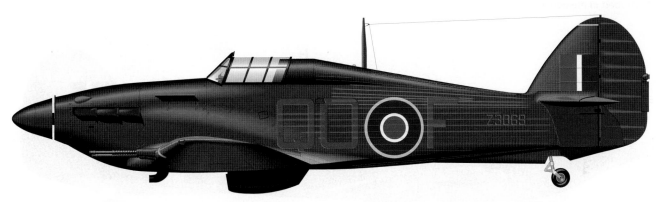

Hurricane IIC Z3069/QO-F of 3 Sqdn RAF 1942, night fighting duties.

Hurricane IIB BM959 '60' of Soviet Air Force late 1942. Pilot was nicknamed the 'Wolf of Vienna', thus logo on tail.

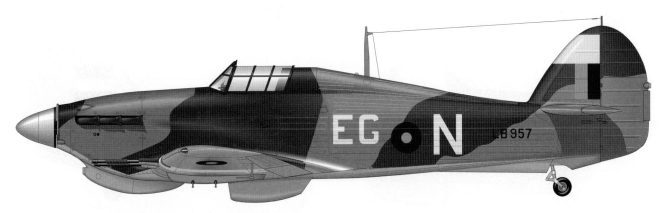

Hurricane IIC (Trop) LB957/EG-N of 34 Sqdn RAF, Burma 1943-44.

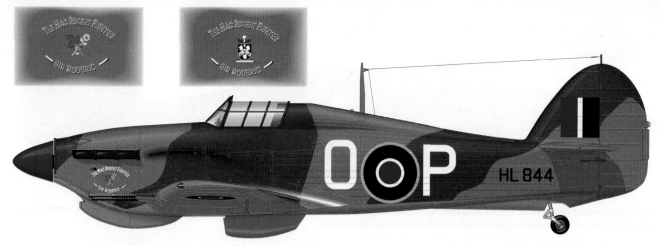

Hurricane IIC (Trop) HL844/O-P 'Sir Roderick' of 94 Sqdn RAF, Western Desert late 1942. One of three Hurricanes donated by Lady MacRobert in memory of her sons.

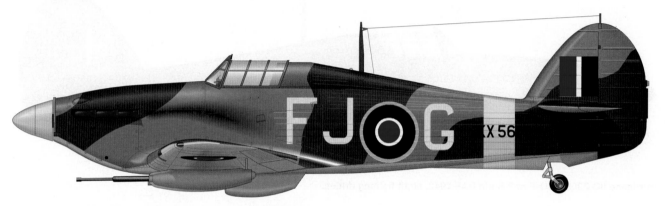

Hurricane IID KX561/FJ-G of 164 Sqdn RAF, Middle Wallop UK June 1943.

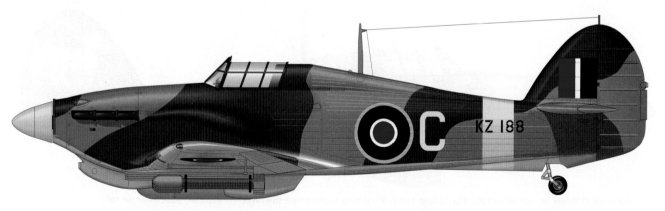

Hurricane IV KZ188 'C' of 6 Sqdn RAF, Italy May 1944. Note rocket projectiles under port wing and fuel tank under starboard.

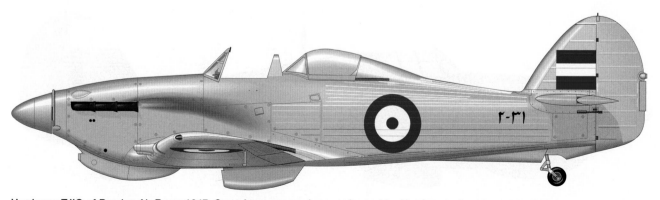

Hurricane T.IIC of Persian Air Force 1947. One of two conversions performed by Hawker post war.

HURRICANE AT WAR

The Hurricane was one of the most widely used RAF combat aircraft with no fewer than 146 RAF squadrons operating it at some stage. To this impressive tally should be added seven Commonwealth (Canadian, Australian and New Zealand) squadrons which flew under RAF control and 38 Royal Navy Fleet Air Arm squadrons which operated Sea Hurricanes.

By the outbreak of war in September 1939, just under 500 Hurricane Is had been delivered and 18 RAF and Auxiliary Air Force squadrons had the aircraft on strength. The first to re-equip had been 111 Squadron at Northolt at the beginning of 1938 followed by the end of that year by numbers 1, 3, 32, 43, 56, 73, 79, 85, 87 and 151. By September 1939 Nos 17, 46, 213, 501, 504 and 605 were also flying the RAF's first monoplane, eight gun fighter.

A new RAF organisation had come into effect from 1936 following implementation of the expansion plan promulgated the previous year. With the reorganisation came the creation of Fighter, Bomber, Coastal and Training Commands within the RAF.

Fighter Command's founding Commander-in-Chief and architect of the Battle of Britain victory, Air Marshal Sir Hugh Dowding.

Fighter Command's first Commander-in-Chief was Air Marshal Sir Hugh Dowding, a man of vision according to many and one whose strength of character and strength of leadership would be tested and passed with honour in 1940.

After an initial period of setting up and finding its feet, the Command was eventually divided into several Groups, each with its own geographical area of responsibility in Britain. No 11 Group was responsible for the heavily populated south-east and included London, No 10 the south-west, No 12 the midlands, and No 13 the north. Each was divided into sectors for controlling purposes, the ground controllers who would prove so vitally important during the Battle of Britain working in conjunction with one of the new wonders of the scientific age – Range and Direction Finding (RDF) equipment, or radar as it was subsequently known.

The first British 'Chain Home' radar station was established in March 1937 and proved so successful that orders were placed for stations to be built along the entire east coast of

A formation of No 1 Squadron Hurricane IICs based at Tangmere 1941-42. (via Neil Mackenzie)

England. These began to be commissioned in 1938, a truly significant year for Britain as it saw the elements which would soon save it from the *Luftwaffe* put into place – the radar system which could detect incoming enemy aircraft; the organisation of the system of controlling which would allow defending fighters to intercept the raiders; and the introduction to service of the eight gun fighters which would perform the interceptions, the Hawker Hurricane at the beginning of the year and the Supermarine Spitfire later on.

THE EARLY WAR

The Fight for France

The declaration of war on 3 September 1939 saw some of the RAF's Hurricane's almost immediately sent to France as part of the Advanced Air Striking Force (AASF) and an attachment to the Air Component of the British Expeditionary Force (BEF) . Four squadrons were initially involved – Nos 1, 73, 83 and 87 – and for many months during the period called the Phoney War their activities were minimal with the only combat opportunities coming from the occasional interception of *Luftwaffe* reconnaissance aircraft.

1 Squadron scored the first RAF victory in France on 30 October 1939 when one of its Hurricanes downed a Dornier Do 17.

The battle for France did not begin in earnest until May 1940, preceded by German attacks on the Low Countries which began on the same day Winston Churchill became British Prime Minister – May 10. Germany's invasion of France prompted more Hurricane squadrons to be attached to the BEF and by the middle of the month ten squadrons were either operating in France preparing to go there.

A vital link in Britain's defensive system, the Chain Home radar network which provided early warning of incoming raiders. The radar provided coverage around the south and east coasts of England but could not search inland.

Continuous and heavy fighting followed, the Hurricane squadrons finding themselves constantly on the move as the airfields from which they were operating were overrun by the advancing Germans. With this constant disruption came problems in maintaining the aircraft and properly planning operations. Losses mounted steadily as the position rapidly became untenable for France and the BEF.

By the last week of May 1940 the RAF had lost about 200 Hurricanes attached to the BEF in France, about 75 to enemy action and the remainder to other damage or unserviceability. As the Germans took over the airfields at which the Hurricanes were based, many had to be abandoned because they were unserviceable.

It was at this point that Dowding decided that Britain could no longer afford to lose its fighters at such a rate in the face of the fact that the French cause was obviously hopeless. He knew they would be needed very soon in order to protect Britain itself.

On 16 May, Dowding wrote a letter to the Chief of Air Staff, ACM Sir Cyril Newall, one which urgently called for his fighters to be no longer wasted in France. There were some attempts at diplomacy but typically, Dowding's words were very much to the point. The importance of this letter to Britain's future is such that it deserves to be reproduced in full:

Sir,

I have the honour to refer to the very serious calls which have recently been made upon the Home Defence Fighter Units in an attempt to stem the German invasion on the Continent.

I hope and believe that our Armies may yet be victorious in France and Belgium, but we may have to face the possibility that they may be defeated.

In this case I presume that there is no-one who will deny that England should fight on, even though the remainder of the Continent of Europe is dominated by the Germans.

For this purpose it is necessary to retain some minimum fighter strength in this country and I must request that the Air Council will inform me what they consider this minimum strength to be, in order that I may make my dispositions accordingly.

Early production Hurricane I L1592 after its 1961 restoration by Hawker for display in London's Science Museum. It carries the markings of 615 (County of Surrey) Squadron which flew in France in 1940. (Philip J Birtles)

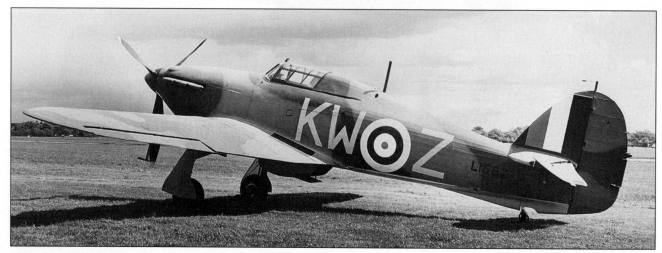

I would remind the Air Council that the last estimate which they made as to the force necessary to defend this country was 52 squadrons, and my strength has now been reduced to the equivalent of 36 squadrons.

Once a decision has been reached as to the limit on which the Air Council and the cabinet are prepared to stake the existence of the country, it should be made clear to the Allied Commanders on the Continent that not a single aeroplane from Fighter Command beyond the limit will be sent across the Channel, no matter how desperate the situation may become.

It will, of course, be remembered that the estimate of 52 squadrons was based on the assumption that the attack would come from the eastwards except so far as the defence might be outflanked in flight. We now have to face the possibility that attacks may come from Spain or even from the north coast of France. The result is that our line is very much extended at the same time as our resources are reduced.

I must point out that within the last few days the equivalent of 10 squadrons have been sent to France, that the Hurricane squadrons remaining in this country are seriously depleted, and that the more squadrons which are sent to France the higher will be the wastage and the more insistent the demands for reinforcements.

I must therefore request that as a matter of paramount urgency the Air Ministry will consider what level of strength is to be left to Fighter Command for the defences of this country, and will assure me that when this level is reached, not one fighter will be sent across the Channel however urgent and

Early Hurricane Is in formation. The battle for France was very expensive with some 300 Hurricanes lost before they were withdrawn to Britain. (via Neil Mackenzie)

insistent the appeals for help may be.

I believe that, if an adequate fighter force is kept in this country, if the fleet remains in being, and if the Home Forces are suitably organised to resist invasion, we should be able to carry on the war single handed for some time, if not indefinitely. But, if the Home Defence Force is drained away in desperate attempts to remedy the situation in France, defeat in France will involve the final, complete and irremediable defeat of this country.

This remarkable letter made its mark and no more Hurricanes were sent to France. The French naturally objected, saying they had been deserted by the British and considerable resentment followed.

The order to recall the BEF's Hurricanes was quickly issued and the survivors flown back to England from where they provided some of the air cover over the BEF's retreat from Dunkirk on 27-28 May. AASF Hurricanes remained in France for another three weeks before they were recalled

– two days after Paris fell – and were engaged in heavy fighting throughout. Losses for those squadrons amounted to 66 Hurricanes. These and the BEF's losses represented a substantial proportion of the RAF's Hurricane strength at the time and there was also the question of having lost many experienced pilots.

Norway

May 1940 was a particularly busy month for the RAF's Hurricanes as they were also involved in another ill-starred campaign, this time in Norway. Germany had attacked Norway and Denmark in early April and at the beginning of May the Norwegians surrendered.

Britain had ground forces in the country which were very heavily engaged and needed support. It was therefore decided that No 46 Squadron and its Hurricanes would be sent to the area but because of the distances involved they would be transported on the aircraft carrier HMS *Glorious* and flown off. Eighteen Hurricanes were involved.

The flying off operation on 26 May was successful but by then the British forces were being withdrawn in the face of a German naval and land onslaught and the situation was worsening. Ten surviving Hurricanes were landed back on the *Glorious* in early June (without the benefit of arrestor equipment – for non naval pilots a remarkable feat) and *Glorious* began steaming for the relative safety of home. Unfortunately, she was sunk by the battlecruisers *Scharnhorst* and *Gneisenau* shortly after departure with the loss of all but two of 46 Squadron's pilots and all of its Hurricanes.

The Norwegian adventure had one positive outcome and that was providing inspiration for Hawker to look at the possibility of developing naval versions of the Hurricane which were capable of conventional operation from aircraft carriers. These investigations were successful and the Sea Hurricane was the result.

A 46 Squadron Hurricane I being loaded aboard HMS *Glorious* before departing for Norway in May 1940. This ill-starred adventure gave birth to the Sea Hurricane concept. (via Neil Mackenzie)

A symbol of the Battle of Britain – a Luftwaffe Dornier Do 17 bomber lies burning in an English field after being brought down by RAF fighters.

THE BATTLE OF BRITAIN

The Hurricane's next test would be the most important of its operational career – the Battle of Britain – on which the very survival of Britain depended.

Even though the battle for France had been expensive in terms of aircraft losses, Britain at least had the situation by mid 1940 that production of the arms it would need to defend itself against Germany was building up. Fighter aircraft production was especially important and under the control of Minister for Aircraft Produc-tion, Lord Beaverbrook, had signifi-cantly increased.

Hurricane production had aver-aged only 64 aircraft per month over the last three months of 1939 but had jumped to an average 236 per month in the first quarter of 1940, largely thanks to the second production source at Gloster having come on line. Spitfire production was also growing, although it was still at a lower rate than the Hurricane.

The quality of the aircraft had also improved during 1940 with few if any Hurricanes and Spitfires retaining the original fixed-pitch propellers by the early months. There were also fewer Hurricanes with the early fabric cov-ered wings.

The Hurricane's Battle

Much has been written about the Battle of Britain elsewhere and in great detail so there is little point here to attempt to repeat that in the limited space available. The intention here is therefore to merely summarise the Hurricane's part in the battle and to hopefully emphasise its importance.

Generally speaking, the battle comprised several distinct stages. The preliminaries took place over the two month period starting in the first week of June 1940 when *Luftwaffe* activities were directed mainly against the ports on England's south coast.

The battle proper is considered to have started on 13 August, the day *Reichsmarschall* Hermann Goering declared as *Adlertag* – the 'Day of Ea-gles'. On that day, the *Luftwaffe* be-gan a series of large, sustained and well escorted attacks on RAF airfields and other military targets.

After a period of about three weeks during which the RAF suffered heavy losses and appeared to be in trouble, Goering suddenly switched the main thrust of his attacks away from mili-tary targets and on to major cities, particularly London. This move gave the RAF some breathing space and ultimately helped it in its quest to re-pel the *Luftwaffe,* although it did not mean any slackening in the intensity of the fighting.

The climax of the battle was reached on 15 September 1940 – now commemorated as Battle of Britain Day – when the *Luftwaffe's* last major offensive was launched and repelled by the RAF fighters. After that, Ger-many had to concede it had not achieved the air superiority over Britain that Goering had promised and inva-sion plans were indefinitely postponed.

Two Hurricane Is of 17 Squadron 1940 with N2359 in the lower shot. 17 Squadron converted to Hurricanes in mid 1939 and relinquished them five years later after serving in France, Britain and Burma. (via Neil Mackenzie)

The raids continued into October, the officially recognised last day of the Battle of Britain being 31 October. After that, the *Luftwaffe* switched to a new phase of raids on England, the night *Blitz*.

In early July 1940, RAF Fighter Command had 50 squadrons at its disposal of which half were equipped with Hurricanes. A month later, at the time of the official start to the Battle of Britain, the total number of squadrons had increased to 55, including 29 equipped with Hurricanes.

Broken down, RAF Fighter Command's Order of Battle in early August looked like this:

No 10 Group: three Hurricane squadrons (87, 213 and 238) with 59 aircraft plus four Spitfire squadrons (71 aircraft).

No 11 Group: 13 Hurricane squadrons (1, 17, 32, 43, 56, 85, 111, 145, 151, 257, 501, 601, 615) with 238 aircraft plus six Spitfire squadrons (100 aircraft).

No 12 Group: five Hurricane squadrons (46, 63, 229, 242, 249) with 87 aircraft plus six Spitfire squadrons (103 aircraft).

No 13 Group: the equivalent of eight Hurricane squadrons (3, 79, 232, 245, 253, 263, 504, 605, 607) two of which were regarded as half a squadron only; 143 Hurricanes on strength plus three Spitfire squadrons with 47 aircraft.

Overall, there were 527 Hurricanes and 321 Spitfires available on this date with 160 and 132, respectively, in reserve. A few Boulton Paul Defiants and Bristol Blenheims were also on strength and facing them was four German *Luftflotten* comprising a total of 1,610 bombers (He 111s, Ju 87s, Ju 88s and Do 17/215s) plus 760 Messerschmitt Bf 109s and 250 Bf 110s.

Despite its numerous qualities, it was recognised at an early stage that the Hurricane's performance was inferior to that of the Bf 109. It was therefore allocated the primary role of

(right) 242 Squadron pilots at Duxford in 1940. In the centre is the legendary Douglas Bader, one of the main proponents of the controversial 'Big Wing' theory in conjunction with 12 Group's C-in-C, AVM Trafford Leigh-Mallory. This caused considerable friction between Leigh-Mallory on the one hand and Dowding and 11 Group's Keith Park on the other. The idea of the Big Wing was to send up several squadrons of fighters as one group to intercept the Germans, the theory being that numbers would meet numbers and therefore be more effective. In practice, it was unwieldy compared to a single squadron, taking time to assemble and therefore slower to reach its targets. Considerable ill feeling was generated by Leigh-Mallory on this and other matters and even today prompts sometimes heated discussion.

The 11 Group Headquarters operations room, the nerve centre for controlling the Group's Hurricane and Spitfire fighters as the German raiders attacked.

Typical of the many foreign units and pilots which fought in the Battle of Britain is 310 (Czech) Squadron which formed on Hurricanes at Duxford in July 1940.

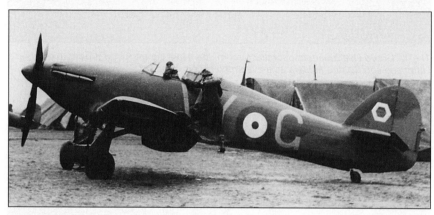

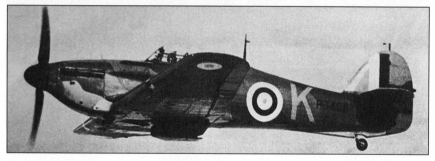

Battle of Britain Hurricanes (top to bottom): L2124/SD-H of 501 Squadron, VY-G of 85 Squadron and P3408, also of 85 Squadron. (via Neil Mackenzie)

Fighter ace Sqdn Ldr Robert Stanford Tuck of 92 (Spitfire) and 257 (Hurricane) Squadrons during the Battle of Britain. He scored 14 kills during the Battle.

taking on the *Luftwaffe* bomber formations which tended to operate at medium altitudes and leave the escorting fighters to the Spitfires. This was a fine theory but in the confusion of a raging air battle it was rarely possible for such a neat and tidy arrangement to be put into practice.

Because of their greater number, the Hurricanes took on a larger share of the responsibilities than the Spitfires and claimed more kills as a result. The same applied to Fighter Command's No 11 Group which due to the geographic area it covered, took the lion's share of the interceptions and had the greatest number of squadrons within it.

That victory was achieved is very much down to the superb leadership displayed by 11 Group's commander, Air Vice-Marshal Keith Park, working closely with the inspirational Dowding.

By the end of September 1940, 448 Hurricanes had been lost in combat over the previous two months and a further 144 had suffered repairable damage. Another 240 were destroyed or damaged in October.

A vital part of the effort was provided by the United Kingdom Hurricane Repair Organisation, established in 1940 by Lord Beaverbrook and comprising some 20 companies and RAF Salvage, Repair and Maintenance units throughout Britain. Companies such as de Havilland, Airwork, Gloster, Rollasons, Rolls-Royce, Scottish Aviation, Short Bros, Austin, Taylorcraft and of course Hawker were involved in this massive programme which saw nearly 1,000 damaged Hurricanes repaired and returned to service in 1940 alone. The organisation remained in place until 1945 (in diminishing numbers after 1943) and overall, some 4,500 Hurricanes passed through it.

Nicolson VC

There were countless examples of heroism during the Battle of Britain but one was rewarded with Britain's highest award for valour, the Victoria Cross. Of the 22 VCs awarded to RAF personnel during the war, only one went to a fighter pilot, Flt Lt James Nicolson of 249 Squadron based at Boscombe Down.

On 16 August, 249's Hurricanes were scrambled to intercept a large formation of enemy aircraft which had been reported crossing the coast. Nicolson was leading the squadron's red section which was attacked from behind by a number of Messerschmitt Bf 110s. Nicolson's Hurricane was hit by four 20mm cannon shells, two of which wounded the pilot while another ignited the fuel tank in front of the cockpit.

A fierce blaze ensued and as

Nicolson was preparing to bail out a 110 appeared in front of him. Ignoring his injuries and the fire which was causing him burns, Nicolson decided to attack the 110. He remained in the Hurricane long enough to deliver a long burst of machine gun fire which hit the Messerschmitt and caused it to fall out of control.

Nicolson then abandoned his aircraft and parachuted to safety. He recovered from his injuries and was later promoted to the rank of Wing Commander but died in 1944 when the aircraft in which he was flying disappeared over the Indian Ocean.

AT HOME 1941-45
Night Fighters

The Luftwaffe's switch from day to night bombing attacks in late 1940 caught the RAF ill prepared to deal with this new problem as it had few aircraft suitable for the role. Fighter Command's night fighter element comprised just 12 squadrons in November 1940, six of which had Blenheims and Beaufighters equipped with very early forms of Airborne Interception (AI) radar.

The number of night fighter squadrons had grown to 15 within six months but half of these still had unsuitable equipment including Hurricanes which were guided to the general vicinity of targets plotted on ground radar and after that relied on the good old 'Mark 1 Eyeball' to achieve a successful interception.

The more powerful Hurricane II began to appear in the latter stages of the Battle of Britain but didn't become available in numbers until early 1941.

Flt Lt James Nicolson VC, the only RAF fighter pilot of the war so honoured.

The most important of these new models was the cannon armed Mk.IIC with substantially increased firepower.

Despite its shortcomings as a night fighter, the Hurricane was fairly widely used in this role for a year or so until more specialist radar equipped aircraft such as the night fighter Mosquito and Beaufighter models became more readily available. Throughout 1941 many of the home based Hurricane squadrons were employed in night activities either as interceptors or for use on night intruder missions.

A night fighter Hurricane had very little equipment installed to distinguish

it from its daytime counterparts. Apart from a coat of black paint, the only other difference was the installation of anti glare strips between the exhaust stubs and the pilot's field of vision.

As mentioned in the previous chapter, Hurricanes were extensively involved in the 'Turbinlite' trials where the Hawker fighter operated in concert with a Douglas Havoc fitted with AI radar and a large searchlight in the nose. The theory was that the Havoc's radar would lead the two aircraft to the target which would then be illuminated by the light, allowing the Hurricane to shoot it down.

This was generally unsuccessful (the heavily laden Havoc's lack of manoeuvrability a contributing factor) as was the Hurricane's use as a solo night fighter, but despite its basic unsuitability for the role a few exceptional pilots recorded kills, all of which helped in the fight against the *Luftwaffe's* Winter *Blitz* of 1940-41 and afterwards. The main squadrons flying Hurricane IICs as night fighters during this period were Nos 1, 3, 43, 87 and 247 while 253 flew IIBs. Nos 1 and 43 were involved in Turbinlite combat operations.

Onto the Offensive

The Hurricane was much happier being used in daylight offensive sweeps into Europe. These began in earnest from early 1941 when the RAF's mood changed from defence to offence following the Battle of Britain. Early excursions were little more than cheeky displays of defiance but they soon became organised and effective incursions over enemy occupied terri-

Hurricane I N2479/US-B of 56 Squadron, complete with starting trolley. This squadron flew its Hurricane Is in France and the Battle of Britain and kept them until early 1941. (via Neil Mackenzie)

The aptly named 'Night Duty', an 87 Squadron Hurricane IIC night fighter. The squadron operated over England's south-west mainly in that role from July 1940 (with Mk.Is) until late 1942, by which time it had been flying IICs for several months. (via Neil Mackenzie)

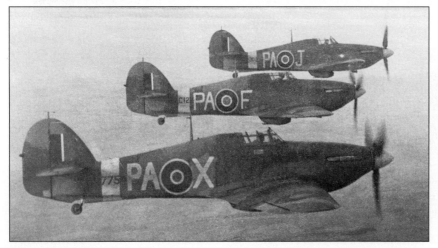

Gloster built Hurricane I W9200 of 245 Squadron at Aldergrove in Northern Ireland during 1941 while flying air defence and convoy patrols. (via Neil Mackenzie)

tory. At first, the Hurricanes were armed only with guns but from late 1941 underwing bombs began to be carried, creating genuine fighter-bomber versions of the Hurricane.

There were several variations of these offensive operations, each with a specific purpose:

Circus: a bomber or fighter-bomber operation heavily escorted by fighters and intended mainly to entice enemy fighters into the air.

Sweep: general term covering fighters flying offensive missions over enemy territory or the sea, with or without accompanying bombers.

Rodeo: fighter sweep over enemy territory without accompanying bombers.

Ramrod: similar to a Circus but with the aim of destroying a specific target.

Rhubarb: freelance fighter operations on a small scale attacking targets of

opportunity. These were often conducted in bad weather so as to introduce an element of surprise.

The first of these missions were flown in late 1940 and involved anti shipping patrols in the Channel along the French coast. From there, the first ventures over enemy held territory were made. Circus No 1 was flown on 10 January 1941 and involved three Hurricane squadrons (Nos 46, 242 and 249), three Spitfire squadrons and six Blenheims. The mission was flown over north-west France and was regarded as successful with enemy fighters drawn into combat.

Some 30 UK based Hurricane squadrons operated in these roles from 1941 as the aircraft became less frequently used in the interceptor fighter role for which it had originally been designed. The Hurricane's usefulness increased with its ability to carry more external ordnance and as such often became the 'bomber' element of the sweeps, usually escorted by Spitfires. Enemy airfields, transports, supply depots and other targets of opportunity were all attacked, causing disruption and creating considerable 'nuisance' value.

Anti shipping patrols were added to the Hurricane's repertoire as were night intruder missions usually attacking *Luftwaffe* airfields in occupied Europe, taking advantage of the long range drop tanks which had become available. The Hurricanes used on these sorties would often intercept German bombers returning to their bases.

The only UK based Hurricane squadron to operate the Hurricane IID with 40mm cannon was No 184, which received its first aircraft in December 1942. No 137 Squadron was the first to receive rocket armed Mk.IVs in June 1943 and between them these units helped develop the ground attack techniques which would shortly be so successfully employed by squadrons equipped with Hawker Typhoons.

As the Hurricane came to be replaced in the UK based squadrons over the last year or so of the war it was more often used in support duties such as target towing, army co-operation and anti aircraft co-operation. A large number of squadrons performed these roles, as can be seen from the accompanying 'RAF Hurricane Squadrons' table.

Most had been disbanded by the middle of 1945 and only two home based regular squadrons continued operating Hurricanes into 1946 – Nos 518 and 521, both of them Meteorological Units.

The training never stopped. These Hurricanes (including Mk.I V7754 nearest camera and Canadian built Mk.X AG122, centre) are pictured while serving with No 55 Operational Training Unit in 1942. (via Neil Mackenzie)

RAF HURRICANE SQUADRONS

Sqn	Marks Flown	Dates	Areas of Operation
1	I, IIA, IIB, IIC	10/38-09/42	UK, France
3	I, IIA, IIB, IIC	03/38-05/43	UK
5	IIC, IID	06/43-09/44	India
6	I, IIC, IID, IV	03/41-12/46	Egypt, Tunisia, Palestine, Italy
11	IIC	09/43-06/45	Burma
17	I, IIA, IIB, IIC	06/39-06/44	UK, France, Channel Islands, Burma, India
20	IIB, IID, IV	02/43-09/45	India, Burma
28	IIB, IIC	12/42-10/45	India, Burma
29	I	08/40-12/40	UK
30	I, IIA, IIB, IIC	05/41-07/44	Egypt, Ceylon, Burma
32	I, IIB, IIC	10/38-08/43	UK, Algeria
33	I, IIB. IIC	09/40-12/43	Palestine, Greece, Crete, Egypt
34	IIC	08/43-03/45	India, Burma
42	IIC, IV	10/43-06/45	Ceylon
43	I, IIA, IIB, IIC	11/38-03/43	UK, Gibraltar, Algeria
46	I, IIA, IIC	02/39-06/41	UK, Norway
56	I, IIB	05/38-01/42	UK
60	IIC	08/43-07/45	India, Burma
63	IIC, IV	03/44-05/44	Scotland
67	IIB, IIC	02/42-02/44	India, Burma
69	IIA	01/41-02/42	Malta
71	I, II	11/40-08/41	UK
73	I, IIA, IIB, IIC	07/38-07/43	UK, France, Egypt, Tunisia
74	IIB	12/42-09/43	Palestine, Iran, Egypt
79	I, IIB, IIC	11/38-07/44	UK, France, India, Burma
80	I, IIB, IIC	02/41-04/43	Greece, Syria, Palestine, Western Desert, Cyprus
81	IIB	09/41-11/41	Russia
85	I	09/38-07/41	UK, France
87	I, IIC	07/38-01/44	UK, France, Gibraltar, Sicily
94	I, IIB, IIC	05/41-04/44	Egypt, Western Desert
95	I	07/41-10/41	Sierra Leone
96	I, IIC	12/40-03/42	UK
98	I	06/41-07/41	UK
111	I, IIA	01/38-05/41	UK, France (first Hurricane squadron)
113	IIC	09/43-04/45	India, Burma
116	IIA	06/42-05/45	UK
121	I, IIB	05/41-11/41	UK
123	I, IIC	11/42-08/44	Western Desert, India, Burma
126	I, IIB	06/41-03/42	Malta
127	I, IIB, IIC	06/41-03/44	Iraq, Egypt, Libya, Cyprus, UK
128	I, IIB	10/41-03/43	Sierra Leone
133	IIB	08/41-12/41	UK
134	IIA, IIB, IIC	09/41-08/44	Russia, UK, Egypt, India, Burma
135	IIA, IIB, IIC	08/41-09/44	India, Burma
136	IIB, IIC	08/41-10/43	UK, India, Burma
137	IV	06/43-01/44	UK
145	I	03/40-02/41	UK
146	IIB, IIC	05/42-06/44	India, Burma
151	I, IIB	12/38-02/42	UK, France
153	IIC	08/44-09/44	Algeria, Sardinia
164	IID, IV	02/43-03/44	UK
174	IIB	03/42-04/43	UK
175	IIB	03/42-04/43	UK
176	IIC	05/43-01/44	India, Burma, Ceylon
182	I, X	09/42-10/42	UK (training only pending Typhoons)
184	IID, IV	12/42-03/44	UK
185	I, IIA, IIB	04/41-03/42	Malta
186	IV	08/43-11/43	UK
193	I, IIC	01/43-02/43	UK (training only pending Typhoons)
195	I	12/42-02/43	UK
208	I, IIA, IIB	11/40-12/43	Egypt, Palestine, Iraq
213	I, IIA, IIC	01/39-03/44	UK, Egypt, Cyprus, Libya
225	I, IIC	01/42-04/43	UK, North Africa
229	I, IIC	03/40-04/42	UK, Egypt, Malta
232	I, IIB	07/40-02/42	Scotland, Singapore, Java
237	I, IIC	09/41-12/43	Western Desert, Iraq, Iran, Egypt, Libya
238	I, IIB, IIC	06/40-09/43	UK, Western Desert, Egypt
239	I, IIC	01/42-05/42	UK (army co-operation)
241	IIC	11/42-12/43	Tunisia
242	I, IIB	01/40-02/42	UK, France, Singapore, Sumatra, Java
245	I, IIB	03/40-01/43	UK
247	I, IIA, IIB, IIC	12/40-02/43	UK
249	I, IIA, IIB	06/40-03/42	UK, Malta
250	I, IIB	02/42-04/42	Palestine
253	I, IIA, IIB, IIC	02/40-09/43	UK, France, Algeria, Tunisia
255	I	03/41-07/41	UK (night fighter)
257	I, IIA, IIB, IIC	06/40-09/42	UK
258	I, IIA, IIB, IIC	12/40-08/44	UK, Singapore, Sumatra, Java, Ceylon, India, Burma
260	I	11/40-02/42	UK, Egypt, Western Desert, Palestine, Lebanon
261	I, IIB, IIC	08/40-06/44	Malta, Iran, Palestine, Cyprus, Ceylon, India, Burma
263	I	06/40-11/40	UK
273	I, IIB, IIC	08/42-03/44	Ceylon
274	I, IIB, IIC	08/40-10/43	Western Desert, Egypt, Libya, Tunisia, Cyprus
279	IIC, IV	04/45-06/45	UK (air-sea rescue)
284	IIC	09/44-03/45	Italy, Corsica
285	IIC	01/44-06/45	UK (target towing etc)
286	I, IIC, IV	11/41-05/45	UK (target towing etc)
287	IIB, IV	11/41-02/44	UK (target towing etc)
288	I, IIC	11/41-10/44	UK (target towing etc)
289	I, IIC, IV	12/41-06/45	UK (anti aircraft co-operation)
290	IIC	12/43-01/45	UK, Belgium (anti aircraft co-operation)
291	IIC	03/44-06/45	UK (target towing etc)
302	I, IIA, IIB	07/40-10/41	UK (Polish)
303	I, IIA	08/40-01/41	UK (Polish)
306	I, IIA	08/40-07/41	UK (Polish)
308	I	10/40-04/41	UK (Polish)
309	IIC, IV	02/44-04/44	UK (Polish)
310	I, IIA	07/40-12/41	UK (Czech)
312	I, IIB	08/40-12/41	UK (Czech)
315	I	02/41-07/41	UK (Polish)
316	I, IIA, IIB	02/41-10/41	UK (Polish)
317	I, IIA, IIB	02/41-10/41	UK (Polish)
318	I, IIB	04/43-02/44	UK, Egypt (Polish)
331	I, IIB	07/41-11/41	UK (Norwegian)
335	I, IIB, IIC	10/41-01/44	Greece, Western Desert, Egypt, Libya (Greek)
336	IIC	02/43-05/44	Western Desert (Greek)
351	IIC, IV	07/44-06/45	Libya, Italy, Yugoslavia (Yugoslav)
352	IIC	04/44-07/44	Mediterranean (Yugoslav)
501	I	03/39-05/41	UK
504	I, IIB	03/39-11/41	UK, France
516	IIB, IIC	12/43-12/44	Scotland (combined operations training)
518	II	09/45-10/46	Northern Ireland (met unit)
520	IIC	06/44-12/45	Gibraltar (met unit)
521	II	08/44-02/46	UK (met unit)
527	I, IIB	06/43-04/45	UK (radar calibration)
530	IIC	09/42-01/43	UK (Turbinlite trials)
531	IIC	09/42-01/43	UK (Turbinlite trials)
532	IIB, IIC	09/42-01/43	UK (Turbinlite trials)
533	IIC	09/42-01/43	UK (Turbinlite trials)
534	IIB/C, X, XI, XII	09/42-01/43	UK (Turbinlite trials)
535	IIC	09/42-01/43	UK (Turbinlite trials)
536	IIC	09/42-01/43	UK (Turbinlite trials)
537	IIC	09/42-01/43	UK (Turbinlite trials)
538	IIC	09/42-01/43	UK (Turbinlite trials)
539	IIC, X	09/42-01/43	UK (Turbinlite trials)
567	IV	12/43-06/45	UK (anti-aircraft co-operation)

RAF HURRICANE SQUADRONS (cont)

Sqn	Marks Flown	Dates	Areas of Operation	Sqn	Marks Flown	Dates	Areas of Operation
577	IIC, IV	12/43-07/45	UK (anti-aircraft co-operation)	680	I, IIB	02/43-12/44	North Africa, Tunisia, Sardinia, Sicily, Libya, Cyprus, Italy (photo recce)
587	IIC, IV	12/43-07/45	UK (anti-aircraft co-operation)				
595	IIC, IV	12/43-12/44	UK (anti-aircraft co-operation)				
598	IIC, IV	02/44-04/45	UK (anti-aircraft co-operation)	681	IIB	01/43-09/43	Burma, Siam (photo recce)
601	I, IIB	03/40-01/42	UK, France	691	I, IIC	12/43-05/45	UK (anti-aircraft co-operation)
605	I, IIA, IIB	08/39-03/42	UK, Singapore, Sumatra, Java, Malta detachment	695	IIC	12/43-09/45	UK (anti-aircraft co-operation)
607	I, IIA, IIB, IIC	06/41-09/43	France, UK, India				
610	I	09/39 only	UK				
615	I, IIA, IIB, IIC	04/40-10/43	France, UK, India, Burma				
631	IIC	03/44-07/45	UK (target towing etc)				
639	IV	08/44-04/45	UK (anti-aircraft co-operation)				
650	IV	04/44-06/45	UK (gunnery co-operation)				
667	IIC	04/44-08/45	UK (gunnery co-operation)				
679	IIC, IV	12/43-06/45	UK (anti-aircraft co-operation)				

Notes: table excludes Commonwealth squadrons which operated Hurricanes under RAF control. These were Nos 401, 402 and 439 (Canadian); 3, 450 and 451 (Australian); 488 (New Zealand).

Royal Navy Fleet Air Arm Sea Hurricane Squadrons were Nos 700, 702, 731, 748, 759, 760, 761, 762, 766, 768, 769, 774, 776, 778, 779, 781, 787, 788, 789, 791, 792, 794, 795, 800, 801, 802, 803, 804, 813, 824, 825, 880, 882, 883, 885, 891, 895 and 897.

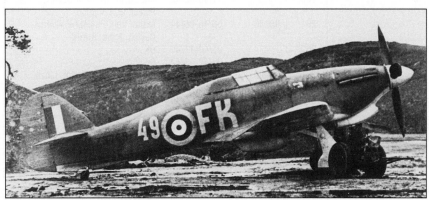

One of 39 RAF Hurricanes of Nos 81 and 134 Squadrons which went to Russia in August 1941. This is Mk.IIB Z3768 of 81 Squadron, photographed at Vaenga in late 1941. (via Neil Mackenzie)

RUSSIAN INTERLUDE

The Soviet Union was a major recipient of Hurricanes, taking delivery of nearly 3,000 aircraft from late 1941. To help the Soviets get their Hurricanes into service and also to provide some air protection for the ports from which they would be unloaded, two RAF squadrons (Nos 81 and 134) were formed in August 1941 and sent to Russia.

The two squadrons had 39 Hurricane IIA and IIBs between them, 24 of which were in flying trim and the remainder dismantled and crated. The aircraft were put on board the carrier HMS *Argus* and upon arrival the 24 airworthy Hurricanes were flown off to an airfield near Murmansk. The others were subsequently assembled.

The two squadrons began operations in mid September and almost immediately ran into the *Luftwaffe*, the first encounter by 81 Squadron resulting in the destruction of three Bf 109s for the loss of one Hurricane.

Another 12 German aircraft were downed by the Hurricanes between then and late November when they were handed over to the Soviet Union Northern Fleet Air Force's 72nd Regiment.

NORTH AFRICA and the MED

Malta

The Hurricane saw extensive service in these theatres of operation, starting in June 1940 when a quartet of Mk.Is arrived in Malta to help in the defence of that strategically vital island. On Malta, they joined the famous Gloster Gladiators which had been providing heroic defence in the absence of anything else.

The arrival of the Hurricanes meant a quantum leap in the island's defensive capability but it was still not enough against the onslaught it would have to endure. Ammunition was so scarce the Hurricanes used only six of their eight guns in order to

Partners on Malta. This Sea Hurricane and Gloster Gladiator belong to the Shuttleworth Collection at Duxford and were photographed in 1996 but side by side they represent the early air defence of Malta when the old biplane struggled on alone until the first Hurricanes arrived in June 1940. (Vance Ingham)

conserve it. Another 12 Hurricane Is arrived in early August 1940 – flown off the carrier HMS *Argus* from 200 miles (320km) away – and an additional four arrived in November. These later 16 Hurricanes were operated by 261 Squadron.

Malta's defences received a substantial boost in April 1941 when 50 Hurricane IIAs and IIBs arrived to replace 261 Squadron's Mk.Is and to equip a new squadron, No 185. A third squadron – No 126 with Hurricane IICs – arrived on Malta in May 1941 but later in the year the *Luftwaffe* began the series of heavy and constant raids on Malta from which the legend of the island's resilience grew.

It was quickly discovered that the Hurricanes were no match for the Messerschmitt Bf 109F in combat and losses were constant. By April 1942 only 18 serviceable Hurricanes remained but by then the situation was being relieved with the arrival of Spitfires in adequate numbers.

Middle East Ubiquity

The Hurricane carried a substantial burden of responsibility during the North African campaign – especially in the early stages when it was the only British monoplane fighter in the area – and later on when it was put to use in specialised ground attack and anti armour roles.

By the end of 1940 there were three Hurricane squadrons in the Western Desert equipped with Mk.Is fitted with the standard desert/tropical kit of the Vokes filter under the nose. Delivery of Hurricanes to the area was a serious problem at the time due to the influence of the enemy near the most direct delivery routes, so most aircraft arrived at their mainly Egyptian bases via a long

Hurricane I Z4172 of 260 RAF/450 RAAF Squadrons. The two units operated in combination against the Vichy French in Syria. (via Neil Mackenzie)

'Bombing up' in the desert. As the war progressed, so did the Hurricane's employment as a ground attack aircraft. (via Neil Mackenzie)

RAF 'erks' inspect the damage done to a Hurricane after a wheels up landing in the desert. (via Neil Mackenzie)

Propeller change for a Hurricane in North Africa. Maintenance was almost always an outdoors activity. (via Neil Mackenzie)

The 'MacRobert Fighters' lined up for inspection in North Africa. The Hurricane IICs were named 'Sir Alasdair', 'Sir Ian' and 'Sir Roderic' after three brothers all killed in the war. Flt Lt Sir Roderic MacRobert was the last to die, shot down while flying with 94 Squadron in the Middle East. To commemorate her sons, Lady MacRobert donated three Hurricane IICs to the Middle East Air Command, each one carrying the family crest and the brothers' names. The photograph shows Air Marshal McClaughry inspecting the aircraft. (via Neil Mackenzie)

trans-Africa route which involved shipping them to the Gold Coast and then flying them overland.

The Hurricanes were soon flying far and wide throughout the North Africa/Mediterranean area and saw action in Greece, Crete, Iraq, Syria, the Suez Canal zone and elsewhere.

Hurricane IIs began arriving in the area from in the first half of 1941, initially to replace the Mk.Is already in service and then to equip new squadrons. By November 1941 (when the British 8th Army launched its second Western Desert campaign) there were 25 Hurricane squadrons in the Middle East including Australian and South African units operating under RAF control.

The see-sawing nature of the North African campaign saw little chance for the Hurricane squadrons to relax, activities reaching a peak in mid 1942 when Rommel's *Afrika Korps* once again went on the offensive.

The Hurricanes were in constant use to attack German supply lines, while the pivotal Battle of El Alamein in October and November 1942 had no fewer than 22 Hurricane squadrons in the desert flying close support missions. One group of six squadrons flew 842 sorties in the first 17 days of this battle and was responsible for the destruction of 39 tanks, 212 trucks and armoured troop carriers, 26 fuel bowsers, 42 guns and over 200 other vehicles.

Hurricane IIC BP586 of 80 Squadron on approach to El Bassa, Palestine during September 1942. (Via Mike Kerr)

Rare shot of a 33 Squadron Hurricane I (V7419) in Greece in early 1942. The squadron flew bomber escort missions over Albania but had to evacuate to Crete in April 1942 and then to Egypt. (via Neil Mackenzie)

One of the first aircraft on Italian soil, a Hurricane IIC. This aircraft is photographed at Reggio de Callabria being refuelled. (via Philip J Birtles)

Desert Hurricane with makeshift stores building. In some areas and at certain times of the year, rain could turn the dry dust into impassable mud within minutes. (via Neil Mackenzie)

The Hurricane IID with two 40mm cannon served with No 6 Squadron during the Alamein campaign and proved to be highly effective against armour. The squadron quickly picked up the nickname 'The Tin Openers'. This concept was quickly extended with the Mk.IIE/IV which could carry rocket projectiles and bombs as alternative loads.

Heading North

German and Italian forces began retreating from El Alamein in early November 1942 beginning a series of victories which would eventually see the Allies gain control of North Africa.

Also in November, the Allies began Operation Torch, starting with assaults on French Morocco and Algeria and in effect opening up a second front in the area. These were the first actions in a series of operations which would see the Allies take Benghazi in November 1942, Tunisia in May 1943, Sicily the following July and in September, the surrender of Italy.

Hurricane squadrons were involved in all of this as well as in Yugoslavia and Greece but in diminishing numbers from mid 1943 when most of the 20 Squadrons based in the Mediterranean area were relegated to second line duties such as training, communi-

cations, convoy patrol and second line patrols.

There were some exceptions, notably 6 Squadron, which fought in the north-west Africa campaigns, converted to rocket firing Hurricane IVs in July 1943. These were flown in Italy and from there on operations with the Balkan Air Force operating in Greece and Yugoslavia. Ground attack and anti shipping missions were flown until the end of the war whereupon the squadron returned to Palestine. No 6 was the last front line RAF operational squadron to keep the Hurricane on strength, not relinquishing the aircraft until December 1946 in favour of Spitfires.

Means of transport centuries apart. Hurricane IIC LE336 of 34 Squadron (and bullock cart) in Burma during 1944. The squadron re-equipped with P-47 Thunderbolts in March 1945. (via Neil Mackenzie)

THE FAR EAST

A total of 51 Hurricanes arrived in Singapore in early January 1942 to bolster the defences of the area against the rapidly advancing Japanese. Comprising MK.Is and early production Mk.IIAs, they were operated by Nos 258 and 605 Squadrons but the strength of the Japanese invasion force quickly saw their numbers reduced and with the fall of Singapore in February the seven survivors were withdrawn to Sumatra.

Twenty-four other Hurricane Is which were intended for Singapore but diverted to Java were flown by pilots of the Netherlands East Indies Air Force against the Japanese. The Dutch East Indies and its defenders were also quickly overwhelmed by March 1942, but not before the Hurricanes were able to inflict some useful damage on the invaders.

Burma

Another batch of 30 Hurricanes also intended for Singapore went instead to Burma in late January 1942 for operation by Nos 17 and 67 Squadrons. The area's defences were further strengthened with the arrival in Ceylon of 30 Squadron's Hurricane Is aboard the carrier HMS *Indomitable*, direct from some hard work in North Africa. Another squadron which had seen considerable action in the Middle East – No 261 – arrived at about the same time equipped with Hurricane IIs. It was the beginning of a lengthy campaign in the India-Burma theatre, a campaign in which the Hurricane would play a prominent part.

The two Burma based Hurricane squadrons also suffered at the hands of Japan at first and had to withdraw to India as the Japanese advanced. 17 Squadron subsequently moved further south to Ceylon.

A counter offensive in Burma was considered to be a vital part of the overall plan to defeat Japan and considerable efforts were made during 1942 by the Allies to build up their forces in the area. During the course of the year 11 squadrons were formed (or reformed) with Hurricane IIAs or IIB fighter-bombers. Another four squadrons arrived in mid 1943 including some with Hurricane IIDs and within a year seven more were based in India.

Overall, 20 Hurricane squadrons served in the India-Burma-Ceylon area, including No 681 equipped with Mk.IIBs for photo-reconnaissance duties. As time went on these squadrons were equipped with more effective Hurricane IIC fighter-bombers plus the dedicated ground attack Mk.IID and IV, indicative of the Hurricane's primary role in the campaign. They were used for continuous and effective attacks on Japanese lines of

In Burma, the Hurricane was used very effectively as flying artillery.

A 607 Squadron Hurricane IIC at Chittagong (India) in 1943 during the Burma campaign. Note the underwing drop tanks. The squadron converted to Spitfire Vs later in the year. (W Goold via Mike Kerr)

Open air briefing for Hurricane pilots of 42 Squadron during the Burma campaign. The squadron operated in that theatre from October 1942, converting from Blenheims to Hurricanes a year later. (via Neil Mackenzie)

A Sea Hurricane IB of 768 NAS is manhandled into position on the deck of HMS Argus in 1943. (via Neil Mackenzie)

communication and supply lines as well as providing fighter escort for transport aircraft supplying Allied troops in remote jungle areas.

The Hurricane began to be replaced by other types from mid 1944 but some squadrons retained the type after that, two of them – Nos 20, and 28 – keeping their Hurricanes until the end of hostilities.

HURRICANES AT SEA

The origins and development of the Sea Hurricane (plus the use of the Catapult Armed Merchant Ships variant) are described in the previous chapter. The Sea Hurricane IB with catapult spool and arrestor hook for operation from conventional aircraft carriers first equipped the RN FAA's No 880 Squadron aboard HMS Furious in July 1941 and were used in the Petsamo and Kirkenes raids in that month.

The same month saw Nos 803 and 806 Squadron Sea Hurricanes flying from land bases in the Mediterranean area, operating in support of the British Army in the defence of Egypt. It was the Mediterranean which saw the bulk of Sea Hurricane operations aboard the carriers *Avenger, Eagle, Indomitable* and *Victorious* including in the case of the former, participation in the Operation Torch landings in north-west Africa.

The Sea Hurricane was intimately involved in efforts to supply the besieged island of Malta. In June 1942 HMS *Eagle's* aircraft provided the primary air cover for the Operation Harpoon convoy to Malta, while in August, Operation Pedestal saw that vitally important convoy – which was subsequently immortalised in book and film – protected by five squadrons of Sea Hurricanes from the carriers *Eagle, Indomitable* and *Victorious.* This convoy included the tanker *Ohio* which although badly damaged made it to Malta, bringing with it desperately needed fuel.

The Allies expended considerable effort in their attempts to keep Malta supplied and defended, fully realising – as did the enemy – its strategic importance. The cost was high, Operation Pedestal witnessing the loss of HMS *Eagle* to four torpedoes from a German U-Boat. Sixteen Hurricanes went down with the ship.

The Sea Hurricane began to be replaced by the Supermarine Seafire from 1943 despite the more effective cannon armed Mk.IIC becoming available from late in the previous year. The last FAA squadron to relinquish the Hawker fighter was No 842 in April 1944. The squadron's final operation with the Sea Hurricane was aboard the escort carrier HMS *Striker*, providing cover for the carrier's Swordfish torpedo bombers as they attacked shipping along the Norwegian coast.

It will be remembered that it was during the ill fated Norwegian campaign of 1940 that the idea of a naval version of the Hurricane first developed – albeit almost by accident – so perhaps it's appropriate that the aircraft's final combat sorties in its brief career should have been in those same waters.

FOREIGN HURRICANES

Several nations other than Britain flew Hurricanes before, during and after World War II. These are summarised below:

Australia: The RAAF made limited use of the Hurricane, three squadrons (Nos 3, 450 and 451) operating the type in the Middle East under RAF control. No 3 Squadron was the first to arrive in Egypt in August 1940 initially equipped with Gladiators and then Hurricanes from January 1941. It kept them

A Sea Hurricane departs HMS Striker *with two recently airborne Fairey Swordfish just visible in the distance. A total of 38 RN Fleet Air Arm squadrons had Sea Hurricanes on strength at some stage.*

only until the following May when Curtiss P-40s were received but several 'kills' were recorded in the meantime.

Nos 450 and 451 Squadrons arrived in the Middle East during 1941, the former initially operating in conjunction with 260 (RAF) Squadron against the Vichy French in Syria. For the remainder of 1941 it flew tactical reconnaissance missions before re-equipping with P-40s.

No 451 Squadron kept its Hurricanes rather longer and among its duties was providing a Flight for the air defence of Cyprus. After a period of relative inactivity through most of 1942 the squadron was re-established in Egypt in early 1943 equipped with Hurricane IIs and made responsible for providing part of the defence for the Nile Delta area. The level of activity was low and the squadron moved to Corsica in March 1944 where it re-equipped with Spitfire IXs.

Only one Hurricane was taken on RAAF strength 'at home'. Tropicalised Mk.I V7476 was delivered in 1941 and used for trials, pilot evaluation and even as means of fund raising. The aircraft was allocated the RAAF serial A60-1 but it wore the British identity during its time in Australia.

Belgium: Belgium concluded a licence production deal for the Hurricane in April 1939 at the same time ordering 20 Mk.Is from British production. Fifteen of these had been delivered by the time war broke out in September 1939 and the remainder were retained by the RAF. Only 11 remained on strength by the time Germany began its assault on the Low Countries in May 1940 and all but two were destroyed on the first day when they were bombed and strafed by the *Luftwaffe* at their base. The other two managed to get airborne but were quickly shot down.

Three RAAF squadrons flew Hurricanes in the Middle East. This is 451 Squadron's Mk.I W9346 starting up at Rayak in early 1942. (via G Morley-Mower/Mike Kerr)

The licence production contract had been placed with Avions Fairey and covered 80 aircraft. These differed from British Hurricane Is in having four 12.65mm (0.50in) instead of the standard eight 0.303s but only three had been built by the time of Belgium's capitulation.

Canada: Canada was the major source of Hurricane production outside Britain, some 1,450 leaving the Montreal production line of the Canadian Car & Foundry Co from January 1940. Most of these were delivered to Britain or the Soviet Union and many were converted to Sea Hurricanes.

The Royal Canadian Air Force had selected the Hurricane in 1938 and placed an order for an initial batch of 20 Mk.I aircraft. These were diverted from RAF contracts and deliveries began in February 1939 equipping No 1 Squadron at Calgary. With the outbreak of war it was decided to send the squadron to Britain to serve under RAF control flying British built Hurricanes. The squadron arrived in time to participate in the Battle of Britain and was heavily involved in the fighting.

Commonwealth squadrons serving with the RAF were numbered in the 400 series from late 1940 with the result that 1 Squadron became No 401 (RCAF) Squadron. It remained in the UK throughout the war operating Hurricane Is and IIs until converting to Spitfires in 1942. Before that, it had been involved in the Channel sweeps and as such had helped pioneer the use of the Hurricane IIB fighter-bomber. Four other Canadian squadrons (Nos 438, 439, 440 and 417) also flew in Britain, all of them equipped with Hurricanes at some stage.

Egypt: Although technically neutral during the war, Egypt received some Hurricane Is and IIs from RAF stocks from 1941, these equipping Nos 1 and 2 Squadrons until 1945.

Finland: In an attempt to strengthen Finland's air force in its battle with the Soviet Union, 12 Hurricane Is were transferred from the RAF in January 1940. They fought in the Winter and Continuation Wars with some success. A captured Russian Hurricane IIB was added to the fleet in 1942.

France: Following France's surrender to Germany in June 1940, numerous Free French pilots and groundcrew

The only Hurricane delivered to the Royal Australian Air Force 'at home', Mk.I V7476.

joined the Allies and eventually formed several units which flew alongside the RAF and USAAF in the Middle East. Of these, *Escadrille de chasse* No 1 (EC1) and EC2 were equipped with Hurricanes, operating them at Tobruk, in Syria and the Western Desert until September 1942 when they went to Britain to re-equip with Spitfires. The two units together formed *Groupe de Chase* No 1 (GCI).

Two more Free French squadrons also received Hurricanes, GCII/3 operating Mk.IICs briefly in 1943, while GCIII/3 also received Mk.IICs in 1943 and operated them in Syria and Algeria before re-equipping with P-39 Airacobras later in the same year.

India: Several Indian Air Force squadrons received Hurricanes from RAF stocks, starting in June 1942 with the handover of some Mk.IIBs. These initially equipped No 1 Squadron, followed by Nos 2 and 6 which served alongside RAF units in Burma. Included in their fleets were some of the

Tac R (tactical reconnaissance) sub-variant.

Altogether, about 300 Hurricane IIBs, IICs, IVS and Canadian built XIIs were handed over, equipping eight squadrons in all, some of which took part in Burma operations while others remained at home providing air defence.

Ireland: The Irish Air Corps' first Hurricane was a Canadian built Mk.I which had force landed in Eire during 1942. Two others were obtained by the same means but in 1943 four ex RAF Mk.Is were supplied direct followed by another seven Mk.Is and six Mk.IICs. They remained in service until after the war.

Persia: A long time Hawker customer, Persia ordered 18 Hurricane Is from the company in 1939 but only two were delivered. During the war, 10 more were taken on strength from aircraft operated by the RAF's No 74 Squadron in the country during 1942, while the original contract was hon-

oured postwar when 16 ex RAF Mk.IICs were delivered. With these went a pair of two seat trainer Hurricane IICs with conversions performed by Hawker. These were the only 'official' two seat Hurricanes produced.

Poland: In March 1939 the Polish Air Force ordered a single Hurricane I which was delivered the following July. Nine others were subsequently ordered and were ready for shipping when Poland was overrun by Germany.

Portugal: A 1943 agreement for the use of facilities in the Azores by the RAF and Royal Navy included the supply of 15 Hurricane IICs to the *Arma da Aeronautica* in August of that year. A further 125 Hurricane IIBs and IICs were supplied before the end of the war, equipping several squadrons including the Lisbon Defence Squadron.

Romania: Britain agreed to supply 12 Hurricane Is to Romania following a visit by King Carol of Romania in late 1938. Deliveries began in late August 1939.

South Africa: The South African Air Force was an early Hurricane operator, receiving six Mk.Is from RAF stocks at the beginning of 1939. Twenty-four others were supplied after the outbreak of war, these and the originals equipping No 1 Squadron which went to Kenya and Sudan to counter the threat posed by Italy in Abyssinia.

Five other SAAF squadrons (Nos 2, 3, 7, 40 and 43) were also equipped with Hurricanes during the war including Mk.IIBs and IICs. The South African Hurricanes saw action against Italy in 1940 and in North Africa after that, remaining there until 1944.

Soviet Union: As discussed earlier, 39 Hurricanes were transferred from the RAF to the Soviet Naval Air Fleet's 72nd Regiment in November 1941 as part of the arrangement which would eventually see the Russians receive 2,952 Hurricanes from British and Canadian production under Lend-Lease between then and 1944.

Of the total there were 210 Mk.IIAs, 1,557 Mk.IIB/XI/XIIs, 1,009 Mk.IICs, 60 Mk.IIDs and about 100 Mk.IVs.

Little is known of Soviet Hurricane operations except they were often used as bomber escorts. Several were converted to two seat trainers while some were modified to carry 0.50in (12.7mm) machine guns instead of the normal 0.303s.

The Russians apparently liked the Hurricane, an October 1942 issue of the *Soviet War News* describing a mission in which the aircraft successfully escorted Il-2 bombers on a mission, fighting off eight attacking Bf 109s. According to the newspaper: "The fight ended in the complete defeat of the German airmen, who, after

Among the several countries to receive Hurricanes pre war and shortly after hostilities began was Yugoslavia. Twenty-four were delivered from Hawker but planned licence production was interrupted by the war and only 20 locally built examples were completed.

losing three of their aircraft, were forced to give up the attack ... the quality of the Hurricane has made it possible to solve the important problem of ensuring the safety of the Il-2 ... the British machines have proved equally successful on reconnaissance duty and in guarding troops and military objectives. In two months past, Major Panov's unit has been flying Hurricanes. With some 20 machines at his disposal, his unit has brought down 83 Germans aircraft in aerial combat, including 31 bombers, and this for the price of only four pilots and ten aircraft".

Turkey: Turkey ordered 15 new production Hurricane Is which were delivered from mid September 1939, two weeks after hostilities began. Further small quantities of Mks.IIB and IICs were supplied as part of an aid programme in 1942, some of which remained in service three years later.

Yugoslavia: Yugoslavia and Britain concluded a deal in 1938 which would see the Royal Yugoslav Air Force take delivery of 24 Hurricane Is from British production and then undertake licence production at the Zmaj and Rogozarski factories. The first British built aircraft was handed over in December 1938 and the remainder of the first batch of 12 followed during 1939. The second batch of 12 aircraft followed in February 1940.

A total of 100 Hurricanes were ordered from the two local factories but by the time of the German attack on Yugoslavia in April 1941 only 20 had been built, all from the Zmaj plant. Including those, 38 Hurricanes were on strength at the time, equipping three squadrons. They were used extensively as interceptors and for strafing German troops while the invasion was in progress but within a week of the attack's beginning it was over. As the Germans overran the airfields, the Yugoslavs managed to destroy most of the Hurricanes.

The Soviet Union received nearly 3,000 Hurricanes from 1941 under the terms of Lend-Lease, many of them from Canadian production. This is Gloster built Mk.IIB Z5252.

LOCKHEED
P-38 LIGHTNING

The classic profile of the Lightning, in this case an F-4 photographic reconnaissance version of the Royal Australian Air Force. (DoD)

THE FORK TAILED DEVIL

The Germans called it *"der Gabelschwanz Teuful"* – the fork tailed devil – the Americans relied on it for extensive service during World War II in both the European and Pacific theatres and the pundits wondered at its radical (and unique in its day) twin boom configuration and the technical innovations it introduced.

It was the Lockheed P-38 Lightning, one of the more significant combat aircraft of the 1939-45 war and along with the Republic P-47 Thunderbolt and North American P-51 Mustang, one of the trio of fighters upon which the United States Army Air Force relied most heavily for much of the conflict.

The P-38 was manufactured in *relatively* modest numbers compared with some of its contemporaries, just over 10,000 leaving the production line. By comparison, the P-47 and P-51 both reached production totals of well over 15,000. They, of course, were single engined fighters while the P-38 was a twin, and although this meant the Lockheed aircraft suffered slightly in its manoeuvrability, it also provided long range and twin engined security on the far reaching penetrations into enemy airspace at which it excelled.

Not that the Lightning was in any way a failure as a dogfighter as the two highest scoring American aces of

the war, Major Richard Bong (40 victories) and Major Thomas McGuire (38) both flew Lightnings in the Pacific, usually against more nimble Japanese opposition.

Apart from its configuration, the Lightning introduced several 'firsts'. It was the first twin engined fighter put into service by the USAAF, it was the first fighter with turbosupercharged engines to enter regular service, the first with power boosted controls, the first with metal skinned control surfaces from the outset and the first with tricycle undercarriage. These innovative and technically risky features guaranteed that considerable attention would be directed towards the P-38 when it first appeared in late 1938 but its career got off to an unfortunate start.

The first flight was recorded on 27 January 1939 but the prototype was damaged beyond repair in a landing accident just two weeks later at the end of a new trans America record flight, flown at an average speed of 350mph (563km/h), then an almost unbelievable achievement. Not surprisingly, the record and the crash attracted enormous publicity!

The Lightning survived that interesting start to its career and grew from there. There were problems to overcome on the way but at the end

of it all the aircraft was quickly recognised as having made an outstanding contribution to the allied cause in World War II.

Constant Innovation

By the mid 1930s, the company founded two decades earlier by brothers Allen and Malcolm Loughead was a well established operation based at Burbank, California. Originally established as the Loughead Aircraft Manufacturing Company in 1916, the firm was liquidated in 1921 but re-established another five years later as the Lockheed Aircraft Company of Hollywood. Its best known product over the next few years was the Vega, a single engined high wing monoplane of wooden construction powered by the 450hp (337kW) Pratt & Whitney R-1340 Wasp engine.

Designed by Jack Northrop, the seven seat Vega was noted for its aerodynamic cleanliness (despite fixed undercarriage) and cantilever wing which removed the need for bracing struts. Vegas were used in many record breaking flights in the late 1920s and early 1930s, the best known being Wiley Post's *Winnie Mae* which set two around the world records. In 1931 Post flew with Harold Gatty; in 1933 he completed the trip solo, the first to do so.

Portrait of the devil. A P-38J (foreground) and F-5B photo-reconnaissance version formate for the camera. (Lockheed)

The successful line of Lockheed twins began in 1934 with the L.10 Electra. This is a version for the US Navy, the XR2O-1 used as a personal transport by the Secretary of the Navy. (Lockheed)

In 1937 the Vega Aircraft Corporation was formed as a Lockheed affiliate and in 1941 the company became a wholly owned subsidiary of what was now called simply the Lockheed Aircraft Corporation. The Vega name officially disappeared completely two years after that, although it remained in general use.

Lockheed had quickly established a reputation as a manufacturer offering innovative, high performance designs to the market. The name became linked to record breaking flights by not only Wiley Post but also the likes of Howard Hughes and Amelia Erhart.

The company's road to more permanent commercial success began with the first of a series of high performance twin engined aircraft which were developed to meet the needs of commercial air travel in the 1930s. These would eventually evolve into the company's first maritime patrol (or

reconnaissance bomber) aircraft, the Hudson. This type of aircraft would soon become an area of particular expertise for Lockheed.

The L.10 Electra was the first of the new commercial twins, first flying in 1934 and capable of carrying 10 passengers or freight at a speed of close to 200mph (320km/h). Of all metal construction and featuring retractable undercarriage, the L.10 was powered by Pratt & Whitney or Wright radial engines of between 400 and 450 horsepower (300 and 335kW) and could be considered advanced for its day and a total of 148 was built, almost all of them for the airlines. Like subsequent Lockheed twins, a distinctive feature of the Electra was its twin endplate fin and rudder assemblies.

Next came the similar in configuration but smaller and faster L.12 Electra, designed to carry six passengers. This first appeared in 1936 and was followed in 1937 by the much larger

L.14 Super Electra. Powered by Pratt & Whitney or Wright radials of 750-820hp (562-615kW), the 14 was capable of carrying 12 passengers and from it came the military Hudson.

The Hudson was Lockheed's first maritime patrol/reconnaissance bomber and was originally developed to meet the needs of the Royal Air Force. Armed with bombs, depth charges and machine guns (including two in a mid-upper gun turret), the Hudson was built in large numbers mainly for the RAF and supplied through Lend-Lease.

The prototype first flew in December 1938 (one month before the P-38) and the type remained in production until 1943, in the meantime serving with the armed forces of Great Britain, Australia (which operated 257 from early 1940), New Zealand, Canada, the Netherlands, China and of course the United States. The Hudson was more powerful than the L.14 upon

The one-off Lockheed XC-35 of 1937 was an experimental version of the Electra built for conducting cabin pressurisation and engine supercharging trials for high altitude flight. It had a circular fuselage and very small windows for the pressure cabin and contributed a great deal to the knowledge of these areas. (Lockheed)

which it was based, featuring Pratt & Whitney R-1830 Twin Wasp or Wright R-1820 Cyclone engines of between 1,000 and 1,200hp (750 and 900kW), depending on the variant.

From there the idea developed. From the L.14 came the 14 passenger L.18 Lodestar transport of 1939 with two 1,000hp (750kW) R-1820s and its patrol bomber development, the PV and PV-1 Ventura with 1,850 or 2,000hp (1,385 or 1,500kW) Pratt & Whitney R-2800 Double Wasp engines. The final expression of the line was the PV-2 Harpoon which was similarly powered and capable of carrying a larger payload of bombs, mines and torpedoes.

The performance of this series of aircraft grew along with their weight, weapons load, range and electronic detection (radar) capability. The Hudson was capable of a top speed of 253mph (407km/h) at optimum altitude while the PV-1 Ventura was some 60mph (96km/h) faster.

These aircraft, along with the P-38 Lightning, enabled Lockheed to enter the postwar military and commercial aircraft markets as a major player with a wide range of usually long lasting products including the P2V Neptune and P-3 Orion maritime patrol aircraft, the C-130 Hercules, C-5 Galaxy and C-141 Starlifter military transports, the Constellation, Electra and L-1011 TriStar commercial transports and some remarkable combat aircraft such as the pioneering P-80 Shooting Star jet fighter, U-2 and Mach 3 SR-71 spyplanes, F-104 Starfighter and F-117 Nighthawk stealth fighter-bomber.

Lockheed has long been one of the major US defence contractors and achieved the number one spot in 1995 following its acquisition of Martin. In that year, Lockheed Martin won US military contracts worth $US10.5bn, or just under nine per cent of the total market.

The Hudson maritime patrol bomber was developed from the L.14 Super Electra transport for the Royal Air Force. It was the first Lockheed aircraft subject to large orders and required rapid company expansion to cope with them.

Specification X-608

Despite the USA's isolationist posture during the 1930s and the generally minor part the armed forces played in the politicians' overall scheme of things, there was always some within the military who could see that it would not be peaceful forever and that much of the equipment used by the services would be inadequate if the shooting ever started.

Such people existed within the US Army Air Corps, those who by the mid 1930s could see that all was not well on the international front with the rise of Nazi Germany, the rearmament which accompanied that and the generally warlike rumblings which were starting to come from the other side of the Atlantic. There was also the general direction Japan seemed to be heading.

One of the inadequacies facing the USAAC was the fact that its fighters' armament was severely weight limited by the available power, bearing in mind that at the time, the service's 'pursuit' types were all single engined. In most cases, this meant that

the aircraft's gun armament was restricted to just two machine guns and their ammunition. Clearly, heavier armament was going to be needed for the next generation of fighters and at the time, the solution seemed to lie in building a twin engined fighter. Twice the power, therefore twice the armament.

In late 1935 the Air Corps drew up two Circular Proposals and in early 1936 issued them to selected manufacturers. These were for 'interceptor' rather than 'pursuit' aircraft, a deliberate move to avoid the former term which was unfashionable among those who handed out funding at the time. The first proposal was for a single engined fighter and the other for a twin, both with heavy armament for the time and the then radical configuration of a tricycle undercarriage and turbosupercharged engine/s. A high rate of climb was a requirement as was long range on internal fuel, bearing in mind that at the time, the concept of fitting long range drop tanks was not considered viable by the USAAC.

The 14 passenger L.18 Lodestar spawned its own patrol bomber development, the PV-1 Ventura.

Two views of P-38s show some of the aircraft's salient features. The under view (top) shows the arrangement of the undercarriage and flaps while the lower view shows the placement of the turbochargers in the tail booms and the radiators behind them.

Lockheed was one of the companies to receive the circular but it was to be another year before a more detailed Specification (X-608) was issued in February 1937. This called for a twin engined aircraft which could reach a top speed of 360mph (579km/h) at optimum altitude and climb to 20,000 feet (6,096m) in six minutes.

To put this high performance request into the perspective of the times, the production Supermarine Spitfire I which first flew in May 1938 had a similar maximum speed but took 9.4 minutes to reach 20,000 feet, the Messerschmitt Bf 109B of 1937 took 10 minutes to climb to the same height and the Hawker Hurricane I a few seconds less than that. The single engined interceptor requirement was covered by Specification X-609.

First Concepts

By the time Specification X-608 arrived at Lockheed, the company's

preliminary design group – comprising chief engineer Hal Hibbard and Clarence L 'Kelly' Johnson – had been working on designs to meet the requirements of the original Circular Proposal for a twin engined, single seat fighter. Under the company designation Model 22, six different configurations had been penned by Johnson and all of them very different to anything which had gone before.

Three had a conventional, albeit very streamlined fuselage with a forward located and extensively glazed cockpit. Of these, one had its engines mounted in normal nacelles and two had the engines buried in the fuselage with geared shafts driving the wing mounted propellers which in one case were tractor and in the other pusher, the latter also featuring a twin fin tail assembly.

The other three concepts featured twin tailbooms joined aft by the horizontal tail surfaces. One had the pi-

lot's station in the port boom above the wing in a layout similar to the later North American P-82 Twin Mustang but without the second crew member; another had an extended central fuselage pod which accommodated the pilot with the engines in front of and behind him driving tractor and pusher propellers (years later Cessna called this 'centreline thrust' in its Skymaster light twin); and the third featured a shortened pod for the pilot and armament with the two engines mounted as forward extensions of the twin tailbooms.

The last of these was considered to offer the most promise and design of the Lockheed Model 22 was based on it. All were designed around the Allison V-1710 liquid cooled vee-12 engine.

Development and Acceptance

Lockheed submitted its proposals to the Air Corps in April 1937, Kelly's design based on the twin boom configuration and featuring the innovative design features mentioned earlier. The Allison V-1720-C engines drove Curtiss Electric three bladed propellers and were rated at 1,150hp (857kW) maximum power with the exhaust driven General Electric Type F turbosuperchargers mounted flush in the top surface of the tail booms behind the wing. The engines were cooled by ethylene glycol with the radiators located on each side of the tail booms behind the turbochargers.

The result of all this was some fairly complex plumbing which resulted in persistent engine cooling problems with power limitations being applied to the P-38 through its earlier variants. Engine oil coolers were mounted beneath the engines, fed by small intakes behind the propeller spinners.

Performance estimates were impressive – maximum speeds of 417mph (671km/h) at 20,000 feet (6,096m) and 350mph (563km/h) at sea level; initial climb rate a staggering 4,670ft (1,423m)/min; time to 35,000 feet (10,668m) an equally impressive 10.6 minutes and to 20,000 feet 4.5 minutes, and service ceiling 39,100 feet (11,917m). The planned large internal fuel capacity of 400 US gallons (1,514 litres) gave an estimated range of 1,386 miles (2,230km), although by the time the first aircraft appeared this had been reduced.

The Model 22 was a large aeroplane for an interceptor, spanning 52 feet (15.84m) and also heavy, the maximum takeoff weight initially estimated at 10,500lb (4,762kg) but quickly increasing to 14,500lb (6,577kg) by the time the prototype was flown. By comparison, Lockheed's own L.10 Electra 10 passenger transport had a maximum weight of 10,500lb (4,762kg).

A central feature of the new fighter was its armament, which as the whole point of the exercise was considerably heavier than anything the USAAC had seen before. The five guns – one 23mm Madsen cannon and four 0.50in Browning M-2 heavy machine guns – were to be all mounted in the nose so as to provide a highly concentrated and very powerful cone of fire.

Complementing the aircraft's numerous 'firsts' in its configuration and design features were construction methods using the latest all metal technology. The fuselage pod and tailbooms were both of semi monocoque design with Alclad skinning, the wing was of single main spar design with a shear web plus ribs and spanwise stiffeners under the metal skinning; all control surfaces were metal covered (extremely rare in 1937) and for the moment manually operated (power boosted controls came later – another first); and the area increasing Fowler-type flaps were presented in four separate sections, two under the centre section and one on each of the outer wing panels.

The flaps were hydraulically operated as was the retractable tricycle undercarriage, the main and nose units each featuring a single wheel and rearwards retraction into the tail booms and fuselage pod, respectively.

On 23 June 1937 it was announced that Lockheed had won the X-608 contract against substantial competition from Bell, Vultee, Curtiss and Douglas. The contract (Air Corps number 9974) called for the construction of a single prototype under the designation XP-38 and the USAAC serial number 37-457 was allocated to the aircraft.

The parallel X-609 contract for a single engined fighter was won by Bell with its P-39 Airacobra, itself a radical design with tricycle undercarriage, heavy cannon armament and mid mounted Allison engine driving the propeller via a long extension shaft.

There were major changes made to the Model 22/XP-38 design after the contract was awarded: reducing the fuel capacity by 25 per cent to 300 US gallons (1,135 litres) and fitting 'handed' (opposite rotating) versions of the Allison V-1710-C engines to eliminate the torque effect normally associated with propeller driven aircraft.

A Short Life

Construction of the XP-38 was completed at Lockheed's Burbank facility in December 1938, at which time the aircraft was transported by road to March Field, California, for reassembly and preparation for first flight. The pilot who would perform the initial flights was Lt B S (Ben) Kelsey, one of the Procurement Board officers responsible for the X-608 specification being issued in the first place. He was now XP-38 Project Officer.

The XP-38's life was short and spectacular and not without its problems, even before the first flight was recorded. Despite this, its potential was partially demonstrated and enough was done to convince the powers-that-be that its continued development was worthwhile.

Taxying tests revealed the first problem – brake failure – which resulted in Ben Kelsey having no choice but to park the aircraft in a ditch. The necessary repairs resulted in the first flight being delayed until 27 January 1939, and that very nearly ended in disaster.

As the XP-38 climbed away on this most momentous of occasions in any aircraft's history, a severe vibration set in. This was caused by poor gap sealing and under strength flap supporting brackets, three out of four of which broke in the early stages of the flight. This left the flaps loose and dangling in the airstream, a situation which very nearly forced Kelsey to abandon the aircraft.

After taking stock of the situation, Kelsey found that if he maintained a very high angle of attack (about 18 degrees) the vibration reduced to just about manageable levels. After what must have been an extremely harrowing 34 minutes, Kelsey dragged the XP-38 back onto the ground intact, maintaining the necessary angle of attack throughout and scraping the aircraft's fins on the runway as he landed. The flap support brackets were immediately strengthened!

By 10 February 1939 the XP-38 had recorded a total of six flights which amounted to 4hr 49min in the air. These flights had revealed more problems including longitudinal instability (cured by increasing the size of the horizontal tail surfaces), elevator buffeting, poor engine cooling (a redesign of the cooling system was performed) and ongoing problems with the brakes. Regardless of all this, the aircraft's performance was proving to be not too far off estimates and it was judged to be ready for evaluation by the USAAC at Wright Field at Dayton, Ohio.

It was then decided that the delivery flight to Wright should include a record attempt to the base and if conditions were right, a flight from there to Mitchell Field, New York to break the US transcontinental mark.

Kelsey departed March Field early on the morning of 11 February, headed for Wright via a refuelling stop at Amarillo, Texas. The refuellers at Amarillo were unaware of the record attempt and performed their work at a leisurely pace, but despite this the XP-38 reached Wright in good time. Kelsey was greeted there by the Chief of the Army Air Corps, Maj Gen 'Hap' Arnold and after some discussion of the situation, was told to carry on to

The prototype XP-38 at the time of its rollout in December 1938. (Lockheed)

New York. This was duly done, the XP-38 arriving at Mitchell in a flying time of 7hr 02min since leaving California, an average speed of 350mph (563km/h). Ground speeds of up to 420mph (676km/h) were achieved, all of which served to fire up the publics' (and politicians') imaginations when the details were released.

The only problem with the whole adventure was the XP-38's arrival at Mitchell Field. It should be noted that there were flutter problems with the flaps which meant that the engines had to be throttled well back before the flaps could be lowered, and the very poor brakes were used up after the landings at Amarillo and Wright. This meant that Kelsey had to drag the aircraft in for landing with a flat approach using lots of power, and at the end of it was the prospect of stopping it with next to no braking.

When the time came for Kelsey to open the XP-38's throttles and bring the aircraft in, nothing happened. The engines remained at idle speed but would not respond to the request for more power, thought to be the result of picking up some carburettor ice when they were throttled back. Try as he might, the pilot could not coax the engines into the required amount of life, leaving him next to no chance of getting the aircraft onto the ground in one piece.

The XP-38 came down well short of the runway, on a golf course. The aircraft was damaged beyond repair but thankfully, Ben Kelsey was uninjured.

Despite its disastrous ending, that transcontinental flight assured the P-38's future as the speeds it recorded created much official interest. Things would have been very different if the aircraft had been lost on the first flight, just 15 days earlier!

In April 1939 Lockheed received a contract to build 13 YP-38 service test aircraft and the 'Fork Tailed Devil's' career was underway.

The XP-38's life was short but spectacular. It barely survived its first flight and crashed just two weeks later at the end of a record breaking transcontinental flight.

A rare colour shot (top) of YP-38s lined up at Lockheed's Burbank plant with Hudsons destined for the RAF in the background; and much further down the line, a P-38J-15 (bottom).

Two views of P-38H-5 42-67079, a Lightning much photographed by Lockheed's PR people.

Photo-reconnaissance F-5B Lightning in the foreground and a P-38J-10 formate for the camera (top). P-38J-10 42-67543 (bottom) was operated by The Fighter Collection at Duxford until 1996 when it was destroyed in an airshow accident at its home airfield. This shot was taken in May 1996, shortly before the crash. (Philip J Birtles)

P-38J-20 44-23296 'Yippee' was temporarily painted in this overall red colour scheme to celebrate the fact it was the 5,000th Lightning built. It subsequently reverted to more normal combat colours and was put into service.

DEVELOPING THE DEVIL – P-38 VARIANTS

YP-38

The short but spectacular life of the prototype XP-38 (refer previous chapter) had generated sufficient enthusiasm for Lockheed's new fighter to ensure the US Army Air Corps' continued interest, the speed and range performance it had so briefly demonstrated forming the basis of what many considered to be a potentially great combat aircraft.

One of those who put his considerable influence behind the project was Maj Gen Henry H ('Hap') Arnold, chief of the Air Corps from 1937. Arnold's lobbying of the government was a major factor in the rapid decision to order a batch of 13 YP-38 (Lockheed Model 122-62-02) service test aircraft. The order was placed on 27 April 1939, less than nine weeks after the XP-38's crash.

As is often the case with such things, there was a fair bit of conning involved with Arnold's arguments, ably assisted by Ben Kelsey, who extolled the virtues of the aeroplane without having much hard data to back it up thanks to the prototype's short life. The irony is that this lack of information undoubtedly helped Arnold as there was no way his 'facts and figures' could be disproved!

There was a considerable gap between the issue of the YP-38 contract and the maiden flight of the first example (39-689) on 17 September 1940 by test pilot Milo Burcham due to the substantial amount of redesign which had to be incorporated to meet Army (and Lockheed) requirements. The delivery rate of the YP-38 was also slow, with the 13th and last not handed over until May 1940. It must be remembered that for its time the P-38 was a highly advanced combat aircraft incorporating many new and untried features and as a result was never going to be an 'overnight' aircraft, especially in view of the substantial detail redesign which took place.

In addition, the US aircraft industry was itself run down after two decades of neglect and time was needed to build it up again. The massive production figures being achieved just two years later emphasise the remarkable achievement of all involved.

Substantial Redesign

The most notable difference between the YP-38 and the prototype was the installation of 'F' series Allison V-1710 engines which although still 'handed' (opposite rotating) did so in the opposite direction to before. Viewed from the cockpit, the propellers now rotated outwards so as to reduce airflow disturbance over the tailplane. The engines were V-1710-27 (port) and -29 (starboard) rated at 1,150hp (858kW) and fitted with General Electric B2 turbosuperchargers.

Some internal redesign incorporated in these engines resulted in completely new shape nacelles being fitted. The engines' reduction gear cases were now installed on the front of the crankshaft (an extension of which became the propeller mounting shaft), resulting in a higher thrust line.

There was also some reorganisation of the various air scoops on and around the nacelles largely to do with the need to almost completely redesign the oil and engine cooling systems, a major problem in the prototype. The retractable oil cooler intake on the underside of the XP-38's nacelles was replaced with two intakes directly under the propeller spinners and a retractable oil cooler exhaust door was fitted further aft.

In addition, the retractable exhaust port on the top of the tailboom behind the turbocharger was deleted and incorporated into the rear of enlarged radiator scoops on either side of the booms. Despite these modifications, engine cooling would remain a problem until the P-38J came along in 1943.

The internals of the YP-38's nose also required modification due to the revised specified armament of one Colt-Browning M9 37mm cannon with 15 rounds plus two 0.50in (12.7mm) and two 0.30in (7.62mm) machine guns with 200 and 500 rounds per gun, respectively. The original intention was to fit one 23mm Madsen or 25mm Hotchkiss cannon plus four 'fifties, but both failed to materialise resulting in the need to adopt the M9 cannon instead and to adjust the machine gun armament.

Other changes incorporated in the YP-38 included the addition of external mass balances to the elevator in an attempt to control the buffet problem described below and replacement of the original single piece wraparound windscreen with a three panel (unarmoured) unit on all but the first few aircraft.

Design maximum weight was 14,348lb (6,508kg) and performance estimates included a maximum speed of 405mph (652km/h) at 20,000ft (6,069m), an initial climb rate of 3,333ft (1,016m)/min, service ceiling 38,000ft (11,582m) and maximum range 1,050 miles (1,690km).

The first YP-38 (39-689) over Los Angeles shortly after its first flight in September 1940. Lockheed test pilot Milo Burcham is at the controls. This aircraft crashed in November 1941 when the tail failed during a high speed dive. (Lockheed)

Lockheed built 13 YP-38 service evaluation aircraft and it was in these aircraft that the compressibility problem was first discovered.

Testing The 'Yippee'

After extensive testing by Lockheed, evaluation of the YP-38 (quickly nicknamed the 'Yippee') by the Army began in the northern spring of 1941, performed by service test pilots of the 1st Pursuit Group at Selfridge Field in Michigan.

A very large proportion of these tests was taken up with attempts to solve ongoing problems with tail buffet and compressibility in high speed dives. The phenomenon appeared at Mach numbers above about 0.67 and its first serious occurrence was recorded in May 1941 when the fifth YP-38 (39-693), flown by Major Signa Gilkie, entered a power dive from above 30,000 feet (9,144m). As the aircraft's true airspeed built up to about 500mph (805km/h) its tail began to buffet severely, and it became increasingly nose heavy until the point was reached where the control column was 'solid' and Gilkie could not pull it back.

Gilkie began using the elevator trim in his attempts to raise the aircraft's

nose. These were unsuccessful at first but as the YP-38 entered more dense air at lower altitudes the nose gradually came up and the speed reduced. Gilkie eventually regained straight and level flight at just 7,000 feet (2,133m).

Opinions differed as to the cause of this. The popular Army opinion was that the elevator was incorrectly balanced, which resulted in the installation of the external mass balances which would adorn all future P-38s. Only a few thought that compressibility was the problem with the result that research carried on down the tail flutter/imbalance path, a false one and one which ate up a lot of effort.

There was some result from the research including the development of small fairings for the wing/fuselage leading edge junction (a number of different designs were tried) which helped reduce elevator buffet – as opposed to flutter – by redirecting the disturbed air flow which came from the wing/fuselage junction. This was discovered when the second YP-38

(69-690) was installed complete minus propellers in the full scale NACA wind tunnel at Langley Field, Virginia.

The *real* problem – compressibility and the 'tuck' caused by high speed stalling of the wing centre section and the loss of elevator control which accompanied it – took rather longer to solve and it wasn't until mid 1944 and the introduction of dive flaps and other control modifications on late model P-38Js that it was finally beaten. Until then, P-38 pilots were told to fly the aircraft within limits that ensured the problem didn't arise.

The flight test programme continued with Lockheed test pilots James Mattern, Ralph Virden and Milo Burcham constantly exploring the compressibility and other aerodynamic problems which existed. Between them, for example, the pilots flew with some 15 different wing/fuselage junction fillets fitted before the correct combination was found and adopted as standard.

The Lockheed fighter claimed its first fatality on 4 November 1941 when the first YP-38 crashed with Ralph Virden on board. The aircraft was fitted with newly installed spring loaded servo tabs on the elevator trailing edge, the intention being to give the pilot some artificial help when he needed to pull back on the stick during a high speed dive.

Unfortunately for Virden, the tab proved to be a fatal hindrance rather than a help. Reaching a true airspeed of 535mph (860km/h) in the dive, Virden began pulling back on the stick to recover, but the servo tabs were so effective they simply overstressed the tail assembly and pulled it off the aircraft.

Despite these problems, the potential offered by the aircraft was clear. The YP-38s had achieved a maximum speed of 413mph (665km/h) at optimum altitude, a substantial figure in 1940/41 and about 40-50mph (64-80km/h) faster than most other fighters of the time including the Supermarine Spitfire and Messerschmitt Bf 109.

It was also clear that by the end of 1941 the P-38 was not yet fully combat worthy. Neither was Lockheed yet ready to build the vast numbers of aircraft of several types which would be needed in the very near future. The company was used to producing aircraft at a modest rate and the P-38s which had been ordered by then was already stretching resources.

The orderbook stood at 490 including the XP-38 and YP-38s for what since 20 June 1941 was called the United States Army Air Force (USAAF) and another 667 for the Royal Air Force and France's *Armee de l'Air,* the latter having been ordered as early as

A lineup of YP-38s at Lockheed's Burbank facility with Hudsons destined for Britain in the background.

Early production P-38s in formation. The first of 30 was flown in June 1941.

May 1940, five months before the first YP-38 was flown.

Lockheed had already been 'caught short' in its production capacity in 1938 when Britain ordered an initial 200 Hudson maritime reconnaissance bombers for the RAF. One of the terms of the purchase contract was that the company should deliver 200 aircraft "and as many more up to a total of 250" by December 1939, just 18 months after the contract was signed.

This presented large problems to the manufacturer as it had until then been producing relatively small quantities of aircraft and had been short of work, capital and working space. Rapid expansion became necessary, and to meet its obligations Lockheed borrowed $US1.25m, raised another $US3m through a stock issue, nearly trebled its workforce to some 7,000 during the course of 1939 and subcontracted a healthy amount of parts assembly work.

At least all this was largely in place by the time significant orders for the P-38 began coming in, but in order to meet the demand considerably more had to be done before what could be called mass production (by US standards) could begin.

P-38 'ATLANTA'

In July 1940, the USAAC ordered 66 production examples of Lockheed's new fighter, designating them as simply the P-38 or Lockheed Model 222-62-02. Of these, 29 were completed to this standard, one as the XP-38A with experimental pressure cabin and the remainder as the P-38D as discussed below.

The name 'Atlanta' was originally given to the aircraft but this was subsequently dropped in favour of the British appellation 'Lightning', the changeover occurring in October 1941, four months after the first P-38 had been flown. Obviously someone had decided the Brits came up with better aircraft names than the Yanks, especially when it came to fighters where an aggressive style of name became desirable – Spitfire, Hurricane, Thunderbolt, Mustang, Typhoon, Tempest, Lightning and so on.

The production P-38 differed from the service evaluation YP-38 only in detail, the major differences restricted to the incorporation of a three piece windscreen with armoured glass protecting the front panel, some armour protection for the pilot and a further revision of the armament, now one 37mm cannon and four 0.50in (12.7mm) machine guns.

The first P-38 (40-744) was flown in June 1941 and the aircraft spent relatively uneventful service lives with the 1st Pursuit Group (which had flown the 'Yippees') and taking part in various tests and trials. They were flown in various exercises but during the course of 1942 were relegated to non combat duties and subsequently redesignated as RP-38s, the 'R' for restricted flight. The XP-38A with pressure cabin was the 19th production airframe, serial number 40-762.

A P-38 on the approach with everything down. The four segment flaps (two on each side) are apparent, as is the lack of guns.

The P-38D was considered by the USAAF to be the first combat worthy Lightning version. Production was just 36 aircraft in 1941.

P-38D LIGHTNING

The last 36 of the original order for 66 P-38s were designated P-36D (Lockheed Model 222-62-08), the first of which (40-774) has handed over to the USAAF in July 1941. Going straight to the 'D' designation suffix (missing A, B and C) is explained by the fact that at the time there was a briefly enforced policy to standardise on D as the suffix for the first variant of a new aircraft which was considered 'combat worthy'. Other exam-

ples were the P-39D Airacobra and B-24D Liberator.

Similar to the initial production P-38 apart from the addition of self sealing fuel tanks, extra armour protection and a high pressure oxygen system which was subsequently replaced with a safer low pressure system, on late aircraft the P-38D also featured the fuselage/wing junction fillets which had previously been tested on the YP-38s. These reduced the amount of disturbed air flowing

over the tailplane and helped contain the buffeting problem.

The P-38Ds initially served with the 1st Pursuit Group at Selfridge Field and the 14th at Hamilton Field, California. With the renaming of the Army Air Corps to the Army Air Force, these units were retitled the 1st and 14th Fighter Groups (FG).

RAF LIGHTNINGS

As far back as May 1940, the British and French Purchasing Commissions had ordered P-38s and other aircraft during a visit to the USA. By then, of course, both countries were at war with Germany but the USA was neutral and would remain so for another 19 months.

Among the aircraft ordered was the substantial quantity of 667 P-38s, comprising 417 for the *Armee de l'Air* and 250 for the RAF. With the fall of France in June 1940, Britain took over the entire order. These aircraft were given the Lockheed model number 322 and were the first of the P-38 series to be allocated the name 'Lightning', a title quickly taken up by the Americans. The order was split into two with the first 143 aircraft designated Lightning Is and the remainder Lightning IIs. The RAF serial numbers AE978-AF220 and AF221-744 were allocated to the aircraft.

The British experience with the Lightning was brief and largely unhappy, mostly due to the unique specification to which the aircraft were built. The fundamental difference between these and American P-38s was the installation of C-series V-1710-33 engines producing a maximum 1,090hp (813kW) at 14,000ft (4,267m). These lacked the General

---

P-38D LIGHTNING
Powerplants: Two Allison V-1710-27/29 vee-12 liquid cooled turborcharged piston engines each rated at 1,150hp (857kW); Hamilton Standard three bladed constant-speed and feathering propellers. Internal fuel capacity 300 USgal (1,135 l) in four wing tanks.
Dimensions: Wing span 52ft 0in (15.85m); length 37ft 10in (11.53m); height 9ft 10in (3.00m); wing area 327.5sq ft (30.42m²).
Weights: Empty 11,780lb (5,343kg); max loaded 15,500lb (7,031kg).
Armament: One 37mm Browning M9 cannon and four 0.50in (12.7mm) Browning machine guns in nose.
Performance: Max speed 339kt (627km/h) at 20,000ft (6,096m); max cruise 260kt (482km/h); time to 20,000ft (6,096m) 8.0min; service ceiling 39,000ft (11,887m); max range 847nm (1,569km).

AF105 was one of only three Lightnings to fly with the RAF out of an order for 667. It arrived in Britain in March 1942 for evaluation. (via Neil Mackenzie)

Lightning I AE979, intended for the RAF but delivered to the USAAF instead on cancellation of the British order. Note the lack of turbochargers, normally recessed into the top of the tail booms. (Lockheed)

Electric turbosupercharger and had a conventional mechanical supercharger instead, and also were not 'handed' – that is they both rotated in the same direction. These features combined to rob the Lightning I of two of the P-38's main attributes – its superb performance at altitude and its docile handling at low speeds. The lack of handed engines also introduced a rudder trim problem to the aircraft.

The RAF had little choice when it came to the lack of turbosuperchargers on the aircraft as General Electric was having difficulty in building sufficient to meet US needs. Britain's aircraft could have been so equipped, but only if delivery delays were accepted. After due consideration it was decided that the complex nature of the turbos and the maintenance problems they would most likely introduce were not worth a delay.

The non handed engines were entirely the RAF's choice, the reasoning

behind selection of the V-1710-33 being that of spares and maintenance commonality with the RAF's fleet of Curtiss Tomahawks, the propeller also being common to both aircraft. Use of this engine changed the nacelle shape back to that of the YP-38 along with the original lower thrust line.

Other distinctive features of the Lightning I included installation of the wing/fuselage junction fillet, a revised nosewheel leg retraction mechanism which allowed more space in the nose for ammunition, and removal of the 37mm cannon and the fitting of two 0.50in and two 0.303in machine guns only.

The first Lightning I for the RAF was flown at Burbank in August 1941 but in the event, only three were delivered to Britain – AF105, AF106 and AF108, arriving in late March 1942. Testing by the Aircraft & Armament Experimental Establishment (A&AEE) at Boscombe Down was generally

favourable although the aircraft was noted as being "not particularly manoeuvrable for a fighter but comparable with other twin engined fighter types". The Lightnings were restricted to a maximum true airspeed of just 300mph (483km/h) due to the ongoing problems with tail buffet and compressibility, meaning that a full evaluation could not be performed.

This speed limitation in combination with poor altitude performance and changing requirements meant the RAF quickly lost interest in the Lightning and cancelled its orders. By then, the Lightning I was in full production at Burbank but luckily for Lockheed the USAAF decided to take over the order, the remaining 140 aircraft from the initial order receiving the designation P-332 (after the Lockheed model number) and given employment as fighter trainers and to provide air defence for the US west coast. Later aircraft off the line were fitted with handed and turbocharged F-series Allison V-1710 engines of 1,150hp (857kW) with most others retrofitted. All retained RAF serial numbers while in USAAF service.

The 524 Lightning IIs were to have turbocharged engines from the start, Lockheed promising a maximum speed of 415mph (668km/h) at 27,000ft (8,230m). The first aircraft came off the production line in October 1942, by which time the entire order had been taken over by the USAAF. These Lightnings were therefore built as 150 P-38Fs and 374 P-38Gs and were added to the orders already placed for these variants by the USAAF. US serial numbers were applied to these aircraft.

The USAAF took over 143 RAF Lightning Is and redesignated them the P-322 after their Lockheed model number. They retained RAF serial numbers in US service. (via Neil Mackenzie)

P-38E LIGHTNING

Although the P-38D was officially regarded as being the first combat worthy version of the Lightning to enter service, the first true combat variant was the P-38E (Model 222-62-09) which was also the first to be built for the USAAF in other than very small quantities with a total of 210 delivered between October 1941 and March 1942.

Retaining the V-1710-27/29 engines of its predecessor, the P-38E differed mainly in its armament, the 37mm cannon replaced with a 20mm Hispano weapon built under licence in the USA by Bendix as the M1. This had 150 rounds of ammunition and the quartet of 50-calibre machine guns had their ammunition supply increased from 200 to 500 rounds each thanks to the extra space in the nose provided by the smaller 20mm cannon and the revised nosewheel retracting mechanism which had first been incorporated in the Lightning Is intended for the RAF. This armament fit remained standard throughout the Lightning's production life.

The P-38E also had upgraded radio equipment, revised electrical and hydraulic systems and later aircraft had the original Hamilton Standard propellers with dural blades replaced by Curtiss Electric Hydromatics with hollow steel blades. Photo-reconnaissance derivatives of the P-38E were also developed and are described later.

P-38Es were rushed to the Aleutian Islands in mid 1942 to counter the Japanese threat to Alaska. Operated mainly by the 343rd Fighter Group's 54th Fighter Squadron, it was one of these aircraft which recorded the Lightning's first 'kill' of the war in August 1942 when Lt Stan Long shot down a Kawanishi H6K *Mavis* flying boat over Dutch Harbour in the Aleutians.

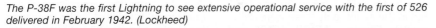

The P-38E was the first Lightning variant to be built in other than very small numbers, with 210 delivered from October 1941. It was also the first with the definitive fixed armament of one 20mm cannon and four 0.50in machine guns.

The P-38F was the first Lightning to see extensive operational service with the first of 526 delivered in February 1942. (Lockheed)

P-38F LIGHTNING

The first Lightning variant to see extensive operational service, the P-38F (Model 222-60-09) differed from its immediate predecessor mainly in having more powerful engines and the ability to carry ordnance or external fuel tanks on two underwing pylons mounted on a strengthened wing centre section.

This was also the first Lightning to be manufactured in substantial numbers with 526 delivered between February and September 1942 including 150 originally intended for the RAF as the Lightning I and upgraded. Other P-38F airframes were completed as F-4A photo-reconnaissance aircraft. The P-38F also introduced production block suffixes to the aircraft's designation.

The first 128 were simply P-38Fs followed by 148 P-38F-1s, 100 P-38F-5s,

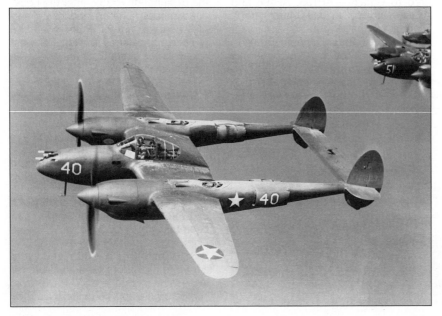

29 P-38F-13s (ex RAF order) and 121 P-38F-25s (also ex RAF). The latter was significant in that it introduced the 'combat flap' setting which allowed the Fowler flaps to be extended to a maximum of eight degrees at combat speeds, increasing lift and enhancing manoeuvrability.

Power was provided by two Allison V-1710-49/53 engines uprated to produce 1,325hp (988kW) each, operational weights increased and on all but the earliest aircraft, a rear hinged and upwards opening canopy replaced the original side hinged unit. The P-38F's underwing hardpoints were each capable of carrying either a bomb or a fuel tank, weapons of up to 1,000lb (454kg) being the maximum.

Two drop tanks of up to 150 USgal (568 l) capacity were the alternative external load, doubling the aircraft's total fuel capacity. The first drop tanks fitted to Lightnings were 75 USgal (284 l) units as was used on the Bell P-39 and Curtiss P-40, while 300 USgal (1,135 l) tanks were subsequently developed for the P-38F and later models.

The long range capability of the Lightning fitted with these large tanks was ably demonstrated in August 1942 when a P-38F undertook a non stop endurance test which lasted more than 13 hours and covered just over 2,900 miles (4,670km). The aircraft carried no armament but its takeoff weight of 19,128lb (8,676kg) was more than 3,000lb (1,360kg) greater than the F's normal maximum of the time.

The first two seat Lightning was converted from a P-38F, the two crewmembers sitting 'piggy back' in very cramped circumstances under a standard canopy with the rear seater occupying the space normally filled with radio equipment. Dual controls were not fitted and several P-38Fs

A P-38F demonstrates the substantial firepower provided by the guns in the nose. (Lockheed)

The idea of using the Lightning as a torpedo bomber was tested using a P-38F. Two torpedoes are under the wing centre section and although trials were successful, the concept faded as there was no operational requirement. (Lockheed)

were thus converted for use as familiarisation trainers and utility aircraft.

The P-38F was used extensively for testing various operational ideas. One explored the idea of using the Lightning as a torpedo bomber carrying one or two 1,927lb (874kg) torpedoes on the centre section hardpoints. If only one torpedo was carried it was balanced by a 300 USgal drop tank. Although the late 1942 trials were successful no operational requirement was developed for the Lightning torpedo bomber. The same P-38F was also used to trial the carriage of a single 2,000lb (907kg) bomb on one of the pylons, this idea being put into service in Europe from late 1944.

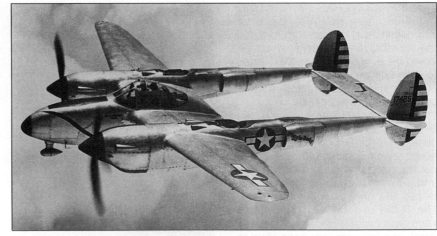

One of the piggyback P-38Fs converted for familiarisation training and utility duties. The back seater was crammed into the space normally filled by radio equipment and covered by the standard canopy. (Lockheed)

P-38F LIGHTNING
Powerplants: Two Allison V-1710-49/53 vee-12 liquid cooled piston engines with General Electric turbochargers, each rated at 1,325hp (988kW) maximum and 1,000hp (745kW) continuous; Curtiss Electric three bladed constant-speed and feathering propellers of 11ft 6in (3.50m) diameter. Internal fuel capacity 300 USgal (1,136 l) in four wing tanks; provision for two 150 or 300 USgal (568 or 1,136 l) drop tanks.
Dimensions: Wing span 52ft 0in (15.85m); length 37ft 10in (11.53m); height 9ft 10in (3.00m); wing area 327.5sq ft (30.42m²).
Weights: Empty 12,265lb (5,563kg); combat weight 15,300lb (6,940kg); normal loaded 15,800lb (7,167kg); max loaded 18,000lb (8,165kg).
Armament: One 20mm Type M1 cannon with 150 rounds and four 0.50in (12.7mm) machine guns with 500rpg in nose; provision for two underwing bombs of up to 1,000lb (454kg) each.
Performance: Max speed 301kt (558km/h) at 5,000ft (1,524m), 326kt (605km/h) at 15,000ft (4,572m), 343kt (635km/h) at 25,000ft (7,620ft); max cruising speed 265kt (491km/h); max rate of climb 2,900ft (884m)/min; time to 20,000ft (6,096m) 8.8min; service ceiling 39,000ft (11,887m); range (internal fuel) 608nm (1,126km); range (with drop tanks) 1,238nm (2,293km); max ferry range 1,520nm (2,816km).

Lockheed's outdoor assembly lines were unusual, but the Californian climate meant that rarely was production interrupted by rain. As the song says: "... it never rains in southern California".

P-38G LIGHTNING

By the time the P-38G (Model 222-68-12) appeared in September 1942, the production rate of the Lightning was starting to increase at Lockheed's Burbank plant. Only 207 aircraft were built in 1941 compared with 1,478 the following year. The P-38G accounted for 1,082 of the overall tally with the last example handed over to the USAAF in March 1943. Of these, 374 were originally intended as Lightning IIs for the RAF.

The P-38G differed from its predecessor in relatively minor ways, the major innovation being the incorporation of V-1710-51/55 engines which produced the same maximum power as before but had an increased continuous rating of 1,100hp (820kW). The engines also featured improved controls. The P-38G was slightly faster than the F, recording a maximum speed of 400mph (644km/h) at 25,000ft (7,620m). Maximum cruising speed increased considerably, from 305 to 340mph (491-547km/h). Rate of climb and ceiling were similar. Other minor changes included the incorporation of improved radio and oxygen systems.

The P-38G was modified as production went on to carry increasingly heavy loads on the centre section pylons. Early aircraft had basically the same carrying capability as the P-38F, but from the P-38G-10 block (aircraft number 161) two 1,600lb (726kg) bombs could be carried while the last 200 aircraft in the same production block could carry a total of 4,000lb (1,814kg) under its wings, comprising either two 2,000lb (907kg) bombs or a pair of the 300 USgal (1,135 l) drop tanks developed during 1942. These increased the P-38G's maximum fuel capacity to 900 USgal (3,407 l) and its maximum ferry range to 2,300 miles (3,700km).

P-38H LIGHTNING

Continued development of the V-1710 engine by Allison resulted in

The P-38H featured a useful increase in power from its Allison V-1710-89/91 engines but ongoing cooling problems meant it couldn't be used at altitude.

P-38H LIGHTNING

Powerplants: Two Allison V-1710-89/91 vee-12 liquid cooled engines with General Electric B33 turbochargers, each rated at 1,425hp (1,063kW) for takeoff and at 25,000ft (7,620m) the latter restricted to 1,240hp (925kW), max continuous 1,100hp (820kW); Curtiss Electric three bladed constant-speed and feathering propellers of 11ft 6in (3.50m) diameter. Internal fuel capacity 300 USgal (1,135 l) in four wing tanks; provision for two 150 or 300 USgal (568/1,135 l) drop tanks.
Dimensions: Wing span 52ft 0in (15.85m); length 37ft 10in (11.53m); height 9ft 10in (3.00m); wing area 327.5sq ft (30.42m²).
Weights: Empty 12,380lb (5,616kg); combat weight 16,300lb (7,394kg); max loaded 20,300lb (9,208kg).
Armament: One 20mm AN/M2C cannon with 150 rounds and four 0.50in (12.7mm) machine guns with 500rpg in nose; provision for two underwing bombs of up to 2,000lb (907kg) each.
Performance: Max speed 300kt (555km/h) at 5,000ft (1,524m), 323kt (598km/h) at 15,000ft (4,572m), 349kt (647km/h) at 25,000ft (7,620m); cruising speed 260kt (483km/h); max climb 2,800ft (853m)/min; time to 25,000ft (7,620m) 9.7min; range (large drop tanks) 1,695nm (3,138km); max ferry range 1,912nm (3,540km).

---

the F15 series offering more power, upgraded General Electric B33 turbochargers and fully automatic turbocharger and oil radiator flaps with the latter enlarged. Under the military designation V-1710-89/91, this engine was installed in the P-38H (Model 422-81-20), 600 of which were delivered between March and August 1943 following a single preproduction example (42-13559) which

had been flown in September 1942.

The new Allisons promised a useful increase in power and they were rated at a maximum 1,425hp (1,063kW) for takeoff and at 25,000ft (7,620m). Despite this, the actual power available was restricted to just 1,240hp (924kW) at altitude, the result of ongoing engine cooling problems which weren't properly solved until the introduction of the P-38J with its redesigned cooling system.

Other modifications incorporated in the P-38H included replacing the 20mm M1 cannon with an improved AN/M2C weapon of the same calibre and carrying the same 150 rounds of ammunition. Like later P-38Gs, the H was capable of carrying a 300 USgal (1,135 l) drop tank under each centre section pylon, or two 1,600lb (726kg) or 2,000lb (907kg) bombs.

P-38J LIGHTNING

The introduction of the P-38J (Model 422-81-14) finally saw the true potential of the Lightning realised with the ongoing engine cooling difficulties tackled and the compressi-

A P-38H demonstrates its engine out capabilities. Lockheed built 601 Hs in 1942-43.

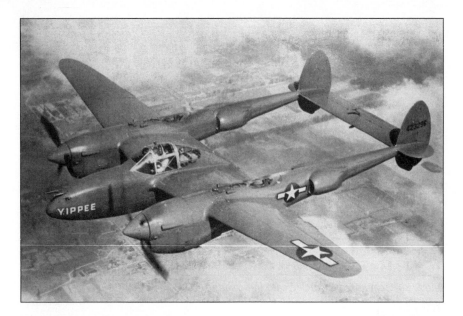

'Yippee' – the 5,000th Lightning, a P-38J-20 (44-23296) and painted overall red to celebrate the occasion. It subsequently reverted to more standard military colours.

tion by using Dallas to perform non standard tasks such as converting newly built aircraft to photo-reconnaissance standards.

In addition, 22 major sub contractors supplied components to Burbank and the result was that the P-38 production rate peaked at 432 per month in January 1945.

The major innovation introduced on the P-38J was a complete reorganisation of the engines' cooling systems, resulting in a new nacelle shape and the ability of the V-1710-89/91 engines – as used in the P-38H – to develop their full power at altitude. On the P-38H the engines' potential 1,425hp (1,063kW) was limited to just 1,240hp (924kW) at 25,000 feet (7,620m) due to the cooling problems. The P-38J suffered no such limitations and additional benefits included the availability of max continuous power (1,100hp/

bility problem also dealt with, at least in the final production batch.

The P-38J was also the first Lightning subject to mass production with 2,970 built from August 1943. In order to cope with this increased production rate, Lockheed installed a mechanised moving production line at Burbank and established a major modification centre at Dallas, Texas. The intention was to minimise interruptions to the main flow of produc-

The Lightning's potential was finally realised with the P-38J, introduced to production in the second half of 1943. This interesting shot shows Lockheed's indoor production line at Burbank with P-38J-10s on the line. In the background an early Constellation (C-69) transport can be seen nearing completion. (Lockheed)

820kW) to a higher altitude and war emergency power of 1,600hp (1,193kW) at 26,500ft (8,077m).

The result was the fastest of all the Lightning production variants, performance figures including a maximum speed of 414mph (666km/h) at 30,000 feet (9,144m).

The modified cooling system involved moving the turbocharger intercoolers from the inner wing leading edges and housing them (and the oil radiators) in the cowlings under the engine with air fed from a 'chin' type intake below the propeller spinner. This gave the P-38J's engine nacelles a completely different appearance which was similar to that of the Curtiss P-40 fighter. The Prestone coolant radiators on either side of the tailbooms were also modified, being made wider than the originals while at the same time creating less drag.

Ongoing Improvements

Further improvements were incorporated in the P-38J as production progressed. From Block 5 (P-38J-5) some aircraft had an extra 110 USgal (416 l) fuel in the wing leading edge space formerly occupied by the intercoolers, bringing total internal capacity to 410 USgal (1,552 l). This extra capacity became standard from Block 15 aircraft onwards.

The P-38J-10 introduced a new optically flat windscreen panel with the bullet proof armoured glass section mounted externally rather than inside and affording the pilot increased protection; the J-15 had an updated electrical system in which fuses were replaced by circuit breakers; and the J-20 had new turbocharger regulators.

Cockpit changes were also introduced on the P-38J including a revised instrument layout; improved heating incorporating a foot warmer for the pilot; a hot air defrosting tube which could be directed onto any part of the canopy; and a modified control wheel which was cut back to a 'half wheel' shape to give the pilot a bit more space.

Apart from the engine cooling system modifications, the most significant changes introduced to the P-38J were those to its flight control system. The compressibility problem was finally dealt with in the P-38J-25, the final batch of 210 aircraft, with the incorporation of 'dive flaps' under the wing, or 'compressibility flaps' as Kelly Johnson preferred to call them.

(right) Designer Kelly Johnson and test pilot Milo Burcham stand under the wing of a P-38J-25, the first batch of Lightnings fitted with the dive recovery flaps which finally solved the compressibility problem. The flap can be seen above the pair's heads. (Lockheed)

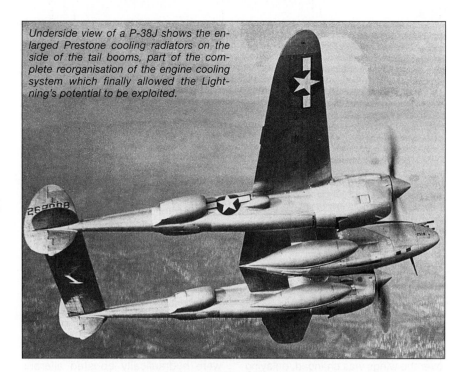

Underside view of a P-38J shows the enlarged Prestone cooling radiators on the side of the tail booms, part of the complete reorganisation of the engine cooling system which finally allowed the Lightning's potential to be exploited.

A P-38J-10 at Burbank. The 2551 on the nose is the aircraft's construction number, although the system employed by Lockheed does not mean this was the 2,551st Lightning built – it was actually the 3,501st. (Lockheed)

These flaps were mounted outboard of the tailbooms and were 4ft 10in (1.47m) wide.

Electrically operated by a button on the control wheel, the flaps could flip to the fully open position of 35 degrees in just one second and were a vital addition as they meant recovery from an extremely steep dive was possible as the airflow characteristics over the wings was changed, delaying buffeting and Mach 'tuck'. This considerably opened up the tactical possibilities for a Lightning's pilot as well as for the first time ensuring safety in a terminal velocity dive.

Interestingly, the flaps had been tested as early as February 1943, but it took more than a year for them to be incorporated into the production line. Many earlier P-38Js had the flaps installed as a field modification.

Supplementary to the dive flaps were hydraulically boosted ailerons which in combination with the 'combat flap' setting introduced earlier considerably enhanced the Lightning's manoeuvrability and meant it could hold its own with most single engined fighters. The P-38 was the first fighter to have powered flight controls.

Many field modifications were applied to the P-38J, particularly in the area of external ordnance. Among them were the addition of third and fourth pylons under the wing centre section allowing the carriage of both bombs and drop tanks, the fitting of three 4.5in (11.4cm) bazooka rocket tube launchers on each side of the lower forward fuselage, and the installation of 'tree' rocket launchers under the wings, each of them capable of carrying five 5-inch (12.7cm) HVARs (high velocity aircraft rockets).

P-38J-25 LIGHTNING

Powerplants: Two Allison V-1710-89/91 vee-12 liquid cooled piston engines with General Electric turbochargers, each rated at 1,600hp (1,193kW) war emergency power at 26,500ft (8,077m), 1,425hp (1,063kW) for takeoff and at 26,500ft (8,077m) and 1,100hp (820kW) max continuous to 32,500ft (9,906m); Curtiss Electric three bladed constant-speed and feathering propellers of 11ft 6in (3.50m) diameter. Internal fuel capacity 410 USgal (1,552 l) in four wing and two leading edge tanks, provision for two 75, 150, 165 or 300 USgal (284, 568, 624 or 1,135 l) underwing drop tanks.

Dimensions: Wing span 52ft 0in (15.85m); length 37ft 10in (11.53m); height 9ft 10in (3.00m); wing area 327.5sq ft (30.42m²).

Weights: Empty 12,780lb (5,797kg); combat (clean) 17,500lb (7,938kg); normal loaded 19,800lb (8,981kg); max loaded 21,600lb (9,798kg).

Armament: One 20mm AN-M2 cannon with 150 rounds and four 0.50in (12.7mm) machine guns with 500rpg in nose; provision for two underwing bombs of up to 2,000lb (907kg) each.

Performance: Max speed 313kt (579km/h) at 5,000ft (1,524m), 339kt (627km/h) at 15,000ft (4,572m), 360kt (666km/h) at 25,000ft (7,620m); max cruise speed 252kt (467km/h); range cruise speed 162kt (299km/h); maximum climb rate 3,670ft (1,118m)/min; time to 20,000ft (6,096m) 7.0min; service ceiling 43,800ft (13,350m); range (max external fuel) 1,634nm (3,025km) at normal cruise; max ferry range 1,964nm (3,637km); range with two 1,600lb (726kg) bombs 630nm (1,167km).

(left) A QEC (quick engine change unit) or self contained 'power egg' for a P-38J. The unit contained the V-1710 engine and its ancillaries. (Lockheed)

LOCKHEED P-38 LIGHTNING

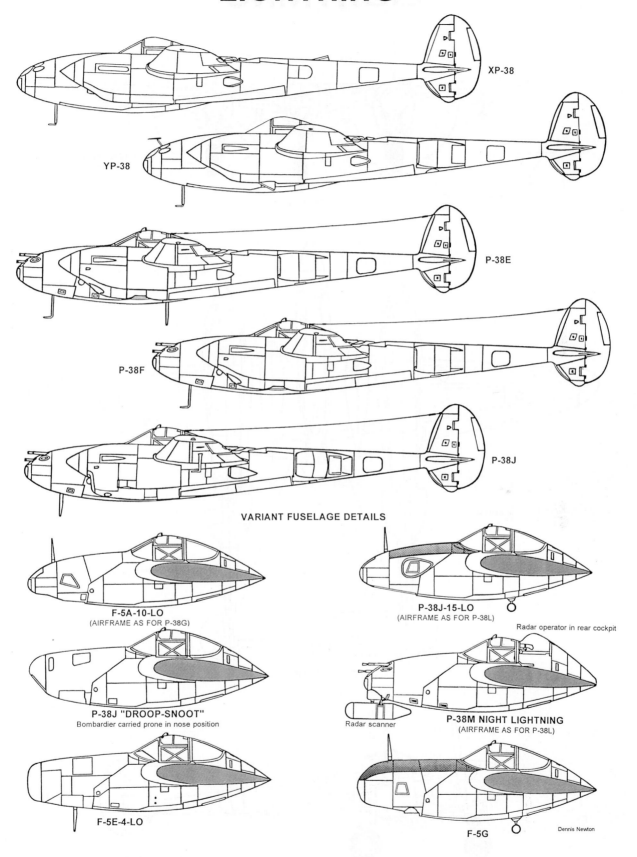

XP-38

YP-38

P-38E

P-38F

P-38J

VARIANT FUSELAGE DETAILS

F-5A-10-LO
(AIRFRAME AS FOR P-38G)

P-38J-15-LO
(AIRFRAME AS FOR P-38L)

P-38J "DROOP-SNOOT"
Bombardier carried prone in nose position

Radar operator in rear cockpit

P-38M NIGHT LIGHTNING
(AIRFRAME AS FOR P-38L)

Radar scanner

F-5E-4-LO

F-5G

Dennis Newton

LOCKHEED P-38L LIGHTNING

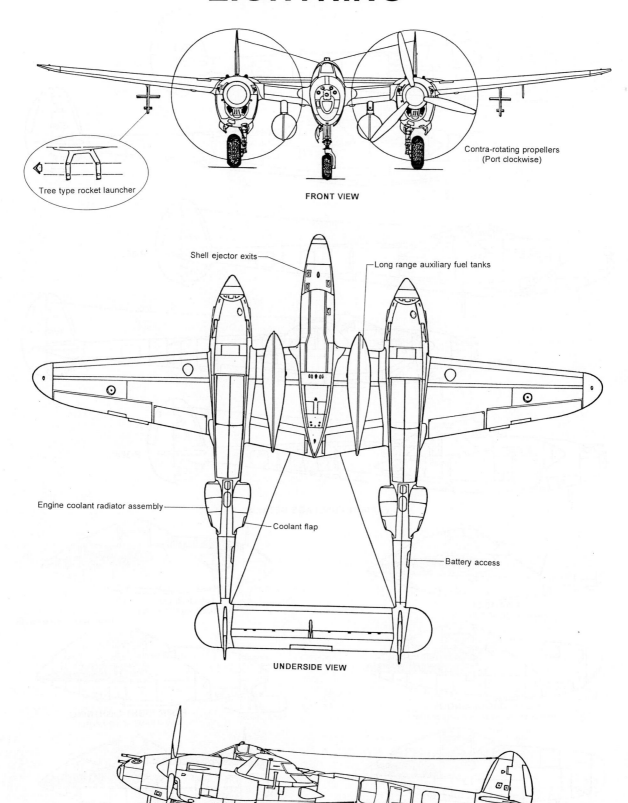

Tree type rocket launcher

Contra-rotating propellers
(Port clockwise)

FRONT VIEW

Shell ejector exits

Long range auxiliary fuel tanks

Engine coolant radiator assembly

Coolant flap

Battery access

UNDERSIDE VIEW

Tail bumper skid shoe

SIDE VIEW (PORT)

Dennis Newton

LOCKHEED P-38L LIGHTNING

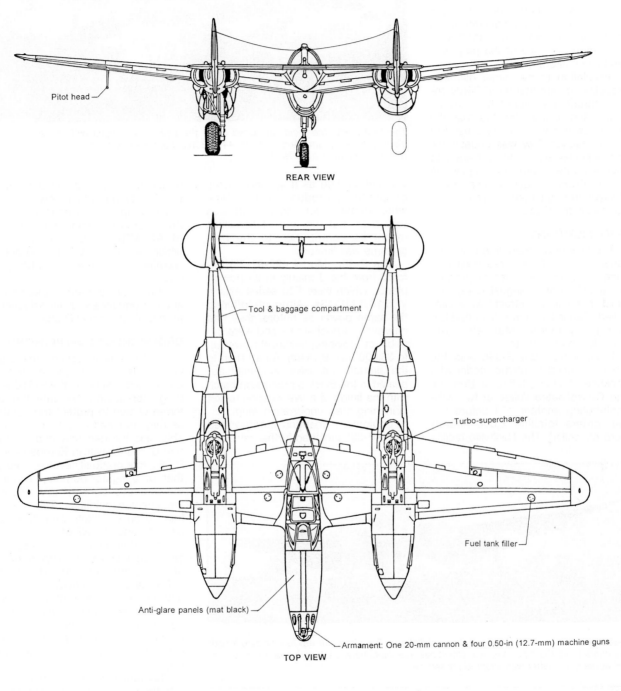

Pitot head

REAR VIEW

Tool & baggage compartment

Turbo-supercharger

Fuel tank filler

Anti-glare panels (mat black)

Armament: One 20-mm cannon & four 0.50-in (12.7-mm) machine guns

TOP VIEW

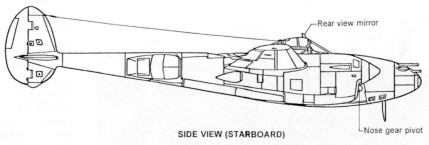

Rear view mirror

Nose gear pivot

SIDE VIEW (STARBOARD)

Dennis Newton

P-38K LIGHTNING:

The P-38K designation was applied to an experimental version of the Lightning powered by uprated V-1710-75/77 engines driving increased diameter and more efficient high activity Hamilton Standard propellers. The prototype (designated XP-38K) was converted from the first P-38E (41-1983) and a second aircraft based on P-38G airframe 42-13558 was more representative of the proposed production aircraft.

Installation of the larger diameter propellers meant that the P-38K's engine thrust line would have to be raised and it was decided that the disruption this would have caused to the production flow was undesirable and unnecessary, so the project was shelved. Other improvements planned for the P-38K – such as even more efficient turbochargers – were incorporated in the P-38L.

P-38L LIGHTNING

The final new production Lightning variant, the P-38L entered service in June 1944 and remained in production until VJ Day in August 1945, after which remaining contracts were cancelled. Cancellation of orders had begun the previous May after the capitulation of Germany.

Despite this, the P-38L was the most produced Lightning model with Lockheed building 3,810 at Burbank and Consolidated-Vultee at Nashville contributing another 113 before further orders totalling 2,000 aircraft were cancelled. The Nashville facility

The P-38L was the most produced of all the Lightning variants with more than 3,900 manufactured up until August 1945. 44-23856 is from the first production block, deliveries of which began in June 1944.

was established as a second source of Lightning production at a time when demand for the aircraft was very high, but the end of hostilities meant its contribution to the programme was limited.

The P-38L (Model 422-87-23) differed from the J mainly in its powerplants, which were F30 series Allison V-1710-111/113s. Although offering the same power as before, they had improved turbochargers and were capable of providing sea level power up to 30,000 feet (9,144m). An addition to the aircraft's offensive armament appeared in the Block 5 production batch with the fitting of a five weapon rocket launching 'tree' under each wing.

Equipment changes incorporated in the P-38L included further revisions

P-38Ls with different underwing rocket installations. The aircraft at top has 14 zero length launchers while the other has two 'Christmas tree' launchers, each with five 5-inch weapons aboard. The latter was adopted for service.

to the instrument panel and an expanded radio fit which now featured a radio compass and beacon receiver. An important addition was the fitting of AN/APS-13 tail warning radar which provided a visible and audible warning of another aircraft's presence.

The P-38L's basic specification and performance was almost identical to that of late model P-38Js.

DROOP SNOOTS and PATHFINDERS

As 1944 progressed, the Lightning's role as a an escort fighter in Europe diminished as the P-51D Mustang increasingly became the preferred choice to protect the bombers as they attacked targets in Germany. This plus the generally changing nature of the air war in Europe saw the P-38's role gradually evolve more into that of a fighter-bomber, exploiting the aircraft's considerable offensive armament capabilities. This was enhanced once rockets were able to be carried under the wings.

Low altitude fighter sweeps became an increasingly important part of the Lightning's repertoire after D-Day and this activity was further developed when the 8th Air Force in Britain realised that the aircraft could be used in conventional bombing missions using a modified P-38 as a navigation and bomb aiming lead ship.

This required a two seat Lightning with the second seat accommodating a bombardier/navigator who would operate a Norden bombsight. The project was given the name Droop Snoot and involved removing the gun armament from the Lightning's nose and installing a new and enlarged nose section capable of carrying the bombardier, the Norden, a navigation table and the various instruments and controls associated with this new role. A plexiglass section was attached to the front of the nose.

A Droop Snoot P-38J showing the enlarged nose capable of carrying a bombardier/navigator and Norden bombsight.

A Pathfinder conversion based on a P-38L. This time the enlarged nose accommodated a bombardier/radar operator and AN/APS-15 bombing through overcast (BTO) radar.

the 55th Fighter Group – led by a Droop Snoot – bombed targets in the St Dizier area from 20,000 feet (6,096m). A third squadron provided an escort and the raid was regarded as successful, leading to wider use of the concept. This meant that the P-38 – a fighter – was in effect now being used as a strategic bomber!

The Droop Snoot concept was also used by P-38s based in China during the last two years of the war, India's Hindustan Aircraft performing conversions on P-38Ls flown in this theatre. One of them lacked the bombing equipment but had a VIP front seat instead and was used as a personal transport by General George Stratemeyer.

A further development of the theme resulted in the Pathfinder conversion during 1944. This involved the installation of ground mapping AN/APS-15 BTO (Bombing Through Overcast), or 'Mickey' radar in a more bulbous enlarged nose section. A radar operator/bombardier was accommodated and the radar replaced the Norden bombsight installed in the Droop Snoots.

The prototype conversion was based on the P-38J but most of the 'production' conversions used the P-38L as their basis. The work was performed by Lockheed's modification centre at Dallas and the Pathfinder served in both the European and China-Burma-India theatres.

Design work was carried out at Lockheed's modification centre at Langford Lodge near Belfast in Northern Ireland. A wooden mockup of the new nose was installed on P-38H 42-67086 to test its aerodynamic properties and the aircraft was flown in its new configuration in late 1943.

The tests proved successful and the first true conversion – a new P-38J – was flown in February 1944.

Between 25 and 100 P-38J Droop Snoot conversions were subsequently performed at Langford Lodge and operations began in April 1944 when two Lightning squadrons from

A pleasing portrait of a P-38M Night Lightning showing its main distinguishing features – the undernose radar pod and second, raised cockpit. All P-38Ms were converted from P-38Ls. (Lockheed)

P-38M NIGHT LIGHTNING

Early model Lightnings had often been used in the night fighting role during their operational careers, mainly P-38Gs and Hs in the New Guinea/Pacific area albeit usually in unmodified form and at the behest of the individual units involved. Some field modifications were also developed to increase the aircraft's efficiency in this role, notable examples being the conversion of two New Guinea based P-38Gs to two seaters with SCR-540 radar installed in a drop tank Two single seat P-38Js were fitted with AN/APS-4 radar mounted in an underwing pod and used successfully by the 547th Night Fighter Squadron in the Philippines from late 1944.

Official interest in a night fighter Lightning grew during the course of 1944 as the need for a stop gap dedicated aircraft grew due to delays in the development of the Northrop P-61 Black Widow. Initial trials revolved around a P-38J which had AN/APS-4 airborne intercept radar installed in an underfuselage pod behind the nosewheel, although this was quickly moved to an underwing position

A closeup of the P-38M's rear cockpit shows the radar operator's cramped conditions with the radar scope hood prominent. (Lockheed)

when it was discovered that firing the guns resulted in the ejected spent cartridges hitting and damaging the pod.

Several other radar conversions of P-38Js were also made, some of which were 'piggy back' two seaters which were subsequently (and unofficially) designated TP-38Js. These aircraft were used for trials in the second half of 1944 and to train night fighter crews after that.

In October 1944 Lockheed was contracted to convert a P-38L to a two seat night fighter with the AN/APS-4 radar mounted in a pod under the nose. The second cockpit was mounted immediately behind and above the pilot's, the radar operator sharing his somewhat cramped space with a console and other equipment associated with the radar. The standard fixed armament of one 20mm cannon and four 0.50in (12.7mm) machine guns in the nose was retained.

Designated P-38M and dubbed Night Lightning, the converted aircraft (44-25237) flew for the first time on 5 February 1945 but it was destroyed in a crash after completing just six flights. Despite this, the USAAF ordered a further 75 P-38Ms, all of them converted from late production P-38Ls by Lockheed's Dallas modification centre.

Testing began in July 1945 and the aircraft proved to be superior to the purpose built Northrop P-61 Black Widow in some areas but the war ended before any of the Night Lightnings saw combat. Their service career was therefore short, the aircraft spending a few months in Japan from late 1945 as part of the Occupation Forces there.

Compared to the P-38L on which it was based, the P-38M suffered little in performance, the main penalty being in a reduction in maximum speed from 414mph (666km/h) to 391mph (629km/h) at optimum altitude due to

P-38M nose showing the radar pod installation for the AN/APS-4 airborne intercept radar. (Lockheed)

An F-4 photo-reconnaissance Lightning of the Royal Australian Air Force. The camera window can be clearly seen. (via Mike Kerr)

the increased drag provided by the radar pod and raised rear cockpit.

PHOTO-RECCE LIGHTNINGS

The Lightning's good performance at high altitudes made it a natural for the photo-reconnaissance role and it was widely used for such duties with more than 1,400 aircraft modified either from new or from existing fighter variants. Most of the conversions were performed at Lockheed's Dallas modification centre.

The basis of the photo-reconnaissance conversion was removal of the guns in the aircraft's nose and replacing them with cameras and the appropriate transparencies through which they could shoot. When modified, the aircraft were designated either F-4 or F-5 depending on the P-38 variant on which they were based. These are detailed below:

F-4: The first PR Lightning conversions, based on the P-38E and first flown in December 1941. Fitted with two K-17 vertical cameras, autopilot and drift sight, most of the 99 F-4s built were unarmed but several retained two fifty-calibre machine guns. These early aircraft were rushed to serve in the Pacific in early 1942, their importance illustrated by the fact that in January 1942 production of the F-4 outstripped that of the P-38E by 84 to 32. Three were delivered to the Royal Australian Air Force in 1942-43.

F-4A: Based on the P-38F, the F-4A differed from the original F-4 in having a trimetrogon K-17 setup involving vertical and oblique cameras and extra windows. Twenty were built.

F-5A: Based on the P-38G and therefore offering improved performance over the F-4 models, the first F-5A was flown in September 1942 and 181 were completed. The camera installation was similar to the F-4A but with improved mounts and equipment.

F-5B: Based on the P-38J and therefore sharing that variant's greatly enhanced performance, 200 F-5Bs were built. Several camera configurations were installed, with two K-17 obliques, one K-17 vertical and one K-18 vertical common.

F-5C: Designation covering 128 P-38J-5s converted to photo-reconnaissance configuration.

XF-5D: A single F-5A (42-12975) converted to carry a second (prone) crewman (observer/photographer) in a redesigned nose section which also had a single vertical K-17 camera and two machine guns within its confines. A second (oblique) camera was mounted in one of the tail booms. The intention was to develop a specialised low altitude reconnaissance version but was not proceeded with.

F-5E-2/3: Conversions from P-38Js, with a total of 205 completed. Normal camera installation was three vertical K-17s and two K-22 obliques.

F-5E-4: The major Lightning photo-reconnaissance variant with 508 converted from P-38Ls and equipped with four K-17 trimetrogon cameras.

F-5F: Also based on the P-38L and featuring an extended camera bay containing three vertical and two ob-

The F-5B was based on the P-38J and was capable of carrying several different camera combinations. 200 were built. (Lockheed)

The F-5G was a conversion of the P-38L, the reshaped nose capable of housing a forward facing oblique camera as well as the usual verticals and obliques.

lique cameras. The number of conversions performed is unknown.

F-5G: Another P-38L conversion with a restyled nose section capable of accommodating a forward facing oblique camera in the extreme nose in addition to the normal verticals and obliques. Sixty-three conversions were performed.

ASSORTED LIGHTNINGS

There were several planned developments of the P-38 or at least its basic concept which failed to make production, although a couple of these flew as prototypes. These and some other Lightnings which were modified for use in tests and trials are described below.

XP-49: Developed to meet a 1939 requirement for an advanced interceptor, Lockheed proposed its Model 522 with pressure cabin and two 24 cylin-

der Pratt & Whitney X-1800 four bank engines. The aircraft was basically a P-38 airframe with the above modifications and retained about two-thirds commonality. The military designation XP-49 was applied.

The sole prototype (40-3055) was flown on 11 November 1942, by which time the Pratt & Whitney engines had been replaced by a pair of 1,540hp (1,148kW) Continental XIV-1430-9/11 inverted vee-12 powerplants. After initial testing it was decided not to proceed with the XP-49 as it offered an insufficient performance advantage over the P-38 and there were doubts about the future of the Continental engine. The XP-49 spent the remainder of its days as a high altitude research and pressure cabin development aircraft.

Specification highlights included: max speed 353kt (653km/h) at 15,000ft (4,572m); initial climb 3,300ft

(1,006m)/min; range 591nm (1,094km); loaded weight 18,750lb (8,505kg); planned armament two 20mm cannon and four 0.50in (12.7mm) machine guns.

XP-58 Chain Lightning: Intended as a heavy, long range bomber escort fighter, the XP-58 retained the overall configuration of the P-38 but was considerably larger and heavier with a wing span of 70ft 0in (21.34m) and a length of 49ft 5in (15.07m).

Although given the go ahead in July 1940, the one and only prototype (41-2670) didn't appear until four years later due to changes to the official requirement and the non availability of the selected powerplants. The aircraft finally recorded its maiden flight on 6 June 1944 (D-Day) without the planned pressurisation system and powered by two 3,000hp (2,237kW) Allison V-3420-11/13 engines, basically two of the P-38's

The sole XP-49, basically a P-38 airframe with a pressure cabin and Continental XIV-1430 engines. The revised canopy shape can be seen in this shot.

The XP-58 Chain Lightning was designed as a heavily armed, long range bomber escort. It was considerably larger and heavier than the P-38, despite sharing a similar configuration. Only one prototype was built in 1944.

V-1710s joined together. The intended heavy armament (which included a 75mm cannon in the nose and remotely controlled barbettes) was not fitted.

The Chain Lightning flew about 25 times before it was cancelled, the Allison engines' turbochargers tending to ignite regularly and the requirement to which the aircraft was built having lapsed anyway.

Specification highlights: max speed 379kt (702km/h) at 25,000ft (7,620m); initial climb 2,660ft (811m)/min; service ceiling 38,400ft (11,704m); range 1,086nm (2,011km); normal loaded weight 39,192lb (17,777kg).

XFO-1: Designation applied to five F-5Bs assigned to the US Navy in North Africa. They carried the BuAer serial numbers 01209-01213.

TP-38L: Two P-38Ls converted to two seaters for training in 1945.

Swordfish: P-38E 41-2048 was modified in 1943 to test various aerodynamic means to improve the Lightning's overall flying characteristics, some of which had been developed in the wind tunnel and required confirming in real flight.

The aircraft acquired a much longer fuselage pod with 2ft 6in (0.76m) added to its forward part and 4ft 0in (1.22m) to its rear, a second cockpit was added behind the pilot, and the canopy narrowed. It first flew in June 1943 and although the modifications incorporated were not adapted for production, the aircraft went on to a long career as a Lockheed test aircraft for many concepts including trying out different aerofoil sections.

Floatplanes: The use of floatplanes in the Pacific was well exploited by the Japanese and the idea was also explored in 1941/42 by the Americans using the P-38 as a basis. The plan was to fit expendable floats to the aircraft in addition to the standard undercarriage but the concept was never developed as the operational need did not arise.

One P-38E (41-1986) was used in these trials. A note is required here. This aircraft featured lengthened and upswept tail booms which raised the elevator by 16 inches (41cm) as part of the trials. Conventional wisdom says that this was done as part of the investigations into the tail buffet problems but some evidence suggests otherwise, at least initially. Certainly, the aircraft was subsequently used for this purpose (with the tail upswept even more) and it crashed when it failed to pull out of a high speed dive as part of those tests.

Skiplanes: Testing of Lightnings on skis was conducted in Alaska during 1943-44, beginning with a P-38G and followed by a modified P-38J. The Federal skis were retractable but once again the operational requirement did not materialise and the project was abandoned.

Others: There were a couple of other 'oddball' Lightnings apart from the many aircraft used to test new armament installations. One was P-38 40-744 (the first production aircraft) which was used to study the effects on the human body of flying in a position other than the conventional one in the centre of the aircraft. 40-744

was accordingly modified to have a second cockpit installed in the port tailboom where the turbocharger would normally sit.

Glider tug trials were also carried out using the Lightning as the tow aircraft. Special tips were developed for the tailplane to which a towing harness was attached. Tests using a Waco CG-4A light assault glider were carried out in 1942 and plans were made to adapt the Lightning to tow three of these simultaneously. The decision to allocate transport aircraft to glider tug duties meant the Lightning's services were not required for this role.

P-38 LIGHTNING PRODUCTION SUMMARY	
XP-38	1
YP-38	13
P-38	29
XP-38A	1
P-332	143
P-38D	36
P-38E	210
P-38F	526
P-38G	1082
P-38H	601
P-38J	2970
P-38K	1
P-38L	3923
F-4	99
F-4A	20
F-5A	181
F-5B	200
Total	**10,036**
All others were conversions.	

P-38 LIGHTNING - SUMMARY OF PRODUCTION AND SERIALS

Model	USAAF Serials	Qty	Remarks
XP-38	37-457	1	ff 27/01/39, crashed 11/02/39
YP-38	39-689/701	13	pre production, ff 17/09/40
P-38	40-744/761	18	first production model, ff 06/41
P-38	40-763/773	11	
XP-38A	40-762	1	experimental pressure cabin
P-332	–	143	RAF Lightning I (AE978-999, AF100-220), ff 08/41, 3 only delivered, remainder to USAAF
P-38D	40-774/809	36	first delivery 07/41
P-38E	41-1983/2097	115	first delivery 10/41
P-38E	41-2100/2120	21	
P-38E	41-2172	1	
P-38E	41-2219	1	
P-38E	41-2221/2292	72	
P-38F	41-2293/2321	29	first delivery 02/42
P-38F	41-2323/2358	36	
P-38F	41-2382/2386	5	
P-38F	41-2388/2392	5	
P-38F	41-7486/7496	11	
P-38F	41-7498/7513	16	
P-38F	41-7516/7524	9	
P-38F	41-7526/7530	5	
P-38F	41-7432/7534	3	
P-38F	41-7536/7538	3	
P-38F	41-7542/7543	2	
P-38F	41-7545/7547	3	
P-38F	41-7551	1	
P-38F-1	41-2322	1	
P-38F-1	41-2359/2361	3	
P-38F-1	41-2387	1	
P-38F-1	41-7484/7485	2	
P-38F-1	41-7497	1	
P-38F-1	41-7514/7515	2	
P-38F-1	41-7525	1	
P-38F-1	41-7535	1	
P-38F-1	41-7539/7541	3	
P-38F-1	41-7544	1	
P-38F-1	41-7548/7550	3	
P-38F-1	41-7552/7680	129	
P-38F-5	42-12567/12666	100	
P-38F-13	43-2035/2063	29	ex RAF Lightning I
P-38F-15	43-2064/2184	121	cancelled RAF order, first with 'combat' flap setting
P-38G-1	42-12687/12766	80	
P-38G-3	42-12787/12798	12	
P-38G-5	42-12799/12866	68	
P-38G-10	42-12870/12966	97	
P-38G-10	42-12987/13066	80	
P-38G-10	42-13127/13266	140	
P-38G-10	42-13327/13557	231	
P-38G-13	43-2185/2358	174	cancelled RAF Lightning II
P-38G-15	43-2359/2558	200	cancelled RAF Lightning II

Model	USAAF Serials	Qty	Remarks
P-38H-1	42-13559	1	first flight 09/42
P-38H-1	42-66502/66726	225	first delivery 03/43
P-38H-5	42-66727/67101	375	
P-38J-1	42-12867/12869	3	P-38J production started 08/43
P-38J-1	42-13560/13566	7	
P-38J-5	42-67102/67311	210	
P-38J-10	42-67402/68191	790	introduced optically flat bulletproof windscreen
P-38J-15	42-103979/104428	450	
P-38J-15	43-28248/29047	800	
P-38J-15	44-23059/23208	150	
P-38J-20	44-23209/23558	350	
P-38J-25	44-23559/23768	210	introduced dive recovery flap
P-38K	42-13558	1	paddle bladed propellers, experimental
XP-38K	41-1983	1	conversion of first P-38E
P-38L-1	44-23769/25058	1290	into service 06/44
P-38L-5	44-25059/27258	2200	
P-38L-5	44-53008/53327	320	
P-38L-5-VN	44-50226/50338	113	built by Vultee, Nashville
P-38M	44-25237	1	prototype converted from P-38L, ff 05/02/45
F-4-1	41-2098/2099	2	photo-recce based on P-38E, delivered 12/41
F-4-1	41-2121/2156	36	
F-4-1	41-2158/2171	14	
F-4-1	41-2173/2218	46	
F-4-1	41-2220	1	
F-4A-1	41-2362/2381	20	based on P-38F
F-5A-1	42-12667/12686	20	based on P-38G
F-5A-2	41-2157	1	based on P-38E
F-5A-3	42-12767/12786	20	based on P-38G-3
F-5A-10	42-12967/12986	20	based on P-38G-10
F-5A-10	42-13067/13126	60	
F-5A-10	42-13267/13326	60	
F-5B-1	42-67312/67401	90	based on P-38J
F-5B-1	42-68192/68301	110	

Conversions

P-38M: 75 from P-38L
F-5C-1: 128 from P-38J-5
XF-5D: 1 (42-12975) from F-5A-10
F-5E-2: 100 from P-38J-15
F-5E-3: 105 from P-38J-25
F-5E-4: 508 from P-38L-1
F-5F-3: unknown number from P-38L-5
F-5G: 63 from P-38L-5
All retained original serial numbers

Note: All Lightnings (except the Vultee built P-38L-5-VN) assembled at Lockheed's Burbank (California) plant. A major modification centre was established at Dallas (Texas) to perform conversions.

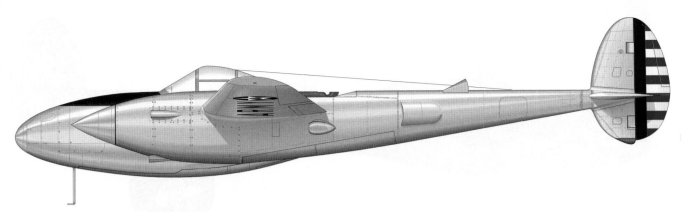

XP-38 prototype 37-457 as it appeared during record breaking flight from California to New York on 11 February 1939, just two weeks after first flight.

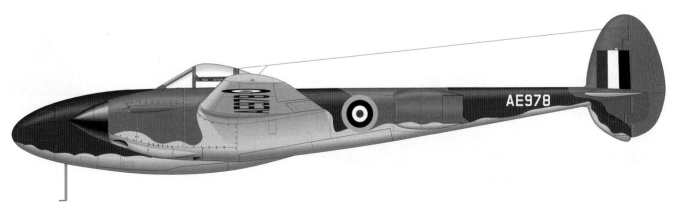

Lockheed YP-38, one of 13 service evaluation aircraft delivered from September 1940.

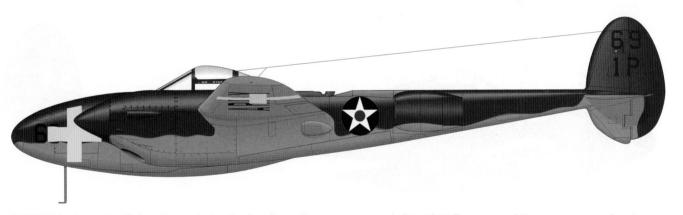

P-38D Lightning of 1st Fighter Group during the Carolina military manoeuvres in late 1941. Temporary white cross on nose denotes aircraft attached to White Force for the exercises.

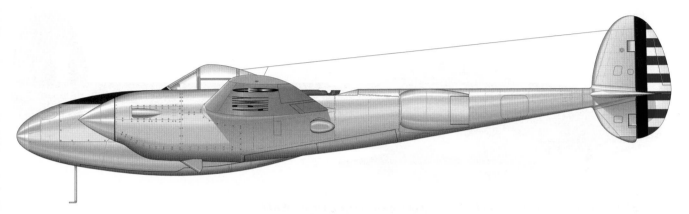

Lightning I AE978 in RAF markings. Only three of order delivered to RAF, remainder taken over by USAAF as P-322. Retained RAF serials in US service. Note lack of turbocharger in top of tail boom.

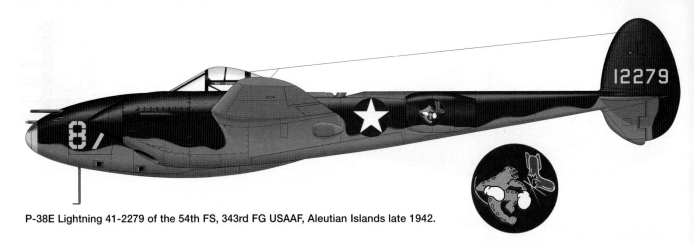

P-38E Lightning 41-2279 of the 54th FS, 343rd FG USAAF, Aleutian Islands late 1942.

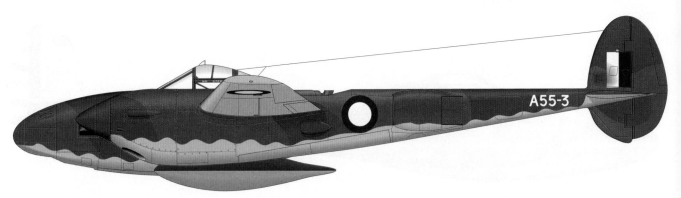

F-4 Lightning A55-3 of No 1 PRU RAAF 1943. Last of three transferred from USAAF.

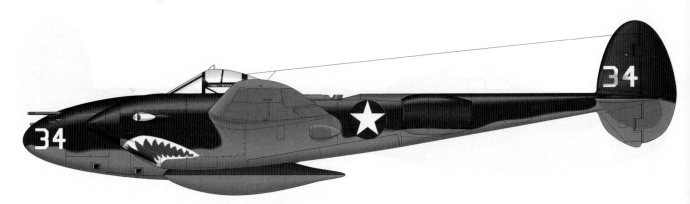

P-38F-5 Lightning 42-12647 of 39th FS, 35th FG USAAF, New Guinea January 1943.

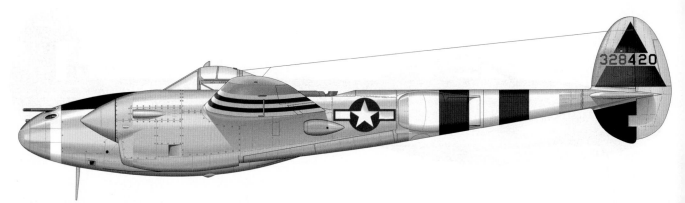

P-38J-15 Lightning 43-28420 of 55th FS, 20th FG USAAF, Kings Cliffe UK June 1944. Note invasion stripes.

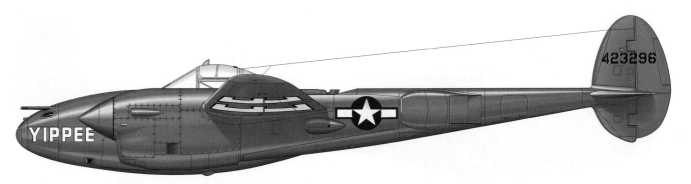

P-38J-20 Lightning 44-23296 'Yippee', the 5,000th Lightning in temporary celebratory colour scheme.

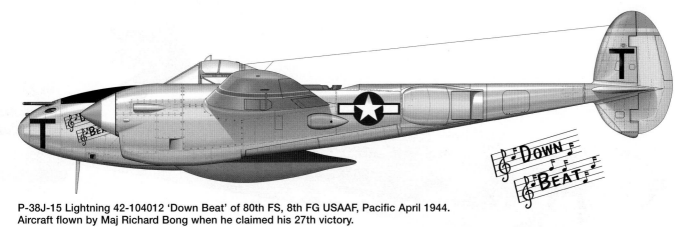

P-38J-15 Lightning 42-104012 'Down Beat' of 80th FS, 8th FG USAAF, Pacific April 1944.
Aircraft flown by Maj Richard Bong when he claimed his 27th victory.

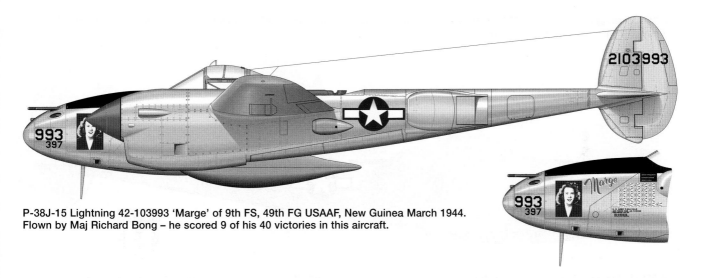

P-38J-15 Lightning 42-103993 'Marge' of 9th FS, 49th FG USAAF, New Guinea March 1944.
Flown by Maj Richard Bong – he scored 9 of his 40 victories in this aircraft.

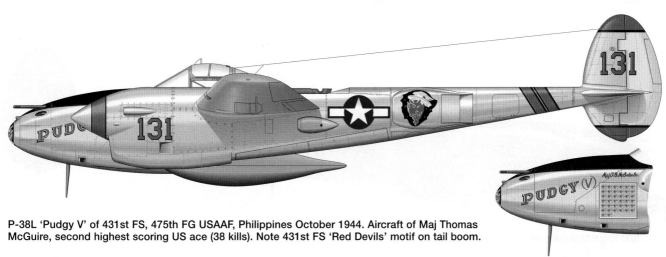

P-38L 'Pudgy V' of 431st FS, 475th FG USAAF, Philippines October 1944. Aircraft of Maj Thomas
McGuire, second highest scoring US ace (38 kills). Note 431st FS 'Red Devils' motif on tail boom.

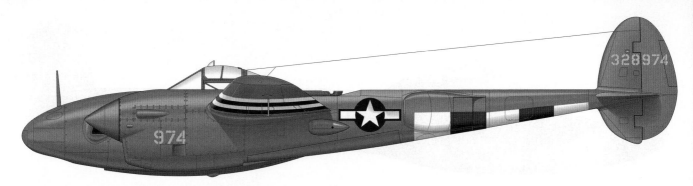

F-5E-2 Lightning (ex P-38J-15) 43-28974 of 31st PRS, 10th PRG USAAF, Europe October 1944.

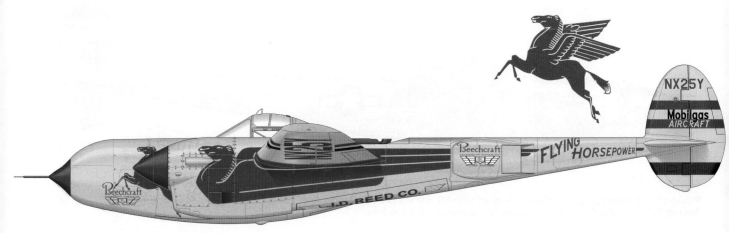

F-5G Lightning (ex P-38L-5 44-53254) NX25Y of J D Reed Co, used as air racer 1947-49. Later N25Y Confederate Air Force, Marvin 'Lefty' Gardner and Lloyd Nolan as racer.

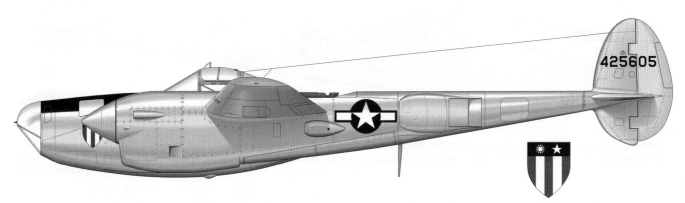

P-38L-5 Lightning Droop Snoot 44-25605, India 1944-45. Modified by Hindustan Aircraft as VIP transport for commander of US forces in China-India-Burma, Maj Gen George Stratemeyer.

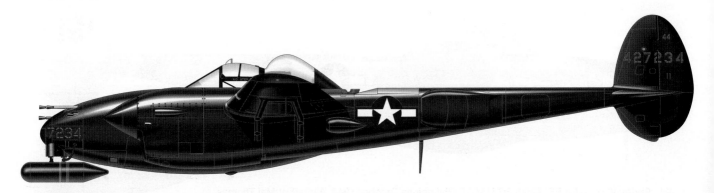

P-38M Night Lightning 44-27234 (ex P-38L-5) used by Lockheed for trials late 1945.

THE ALEUTIAN ISLANDS

In June 1942, Japan staged a diversionary raid on the Aleutian Islands of Attu and Kiska, invading them in an attempt to lure US Navy forces away from the Battle of Midway in the south. Although this attempt failed and the US scored a major victory which proved to be a turning point in the Pacific War, Japan's activities in the Aleutians required attention as its presence there posed a threat to Alaska and potentially to the rest of the USA.

Operations in the Aleutians gave the Lightning its first look at combat, P-38Es equipping the 54th Fighter Squadron (part of the 343rd Fighter Group) of the newly established 11th Air Force. Initially flying from Adak in Alaska, the P-38 was the only fighter capable of operations along the 1,200 miles (1,930km) chain of islands making up the Aleutian Archipelago, usually flying in appalling weather conditions which included dense fog, strong winds and driving rain.

The weather provided the greatest threat to the P-38s, with most of the early losses resulting from this. A 54th FS P-38E recorded the Lightning's first aerial victory of the war on 4 August 1942 when Lt Stan Long downed a Kawanishi H6K *Mavis* flying boat over Dutch Harbour.

The feared serious Japanese threat in the Aleutians never materialised and most of the P-38's operations were ground attack rather than combat with enemy fighters. As time went on the Americans were able to move further up the island chain and Attu was recaptured in May 1943 followed by Kiska in July.

EUROPE, THE MED and AFRICA
Operation Bolero

The build up of US forces in Europe began in July 1942 under the auspices of Operation Bolero, a massive exercise intended to ferry large numbers of USAAF aircraft across the Atlantic to England, from where they would be used in the fight against Germany. Obviously, this was going to be a simpler exercise for the long range bombers and transports than it would be for the relatively short range fighters, even one with reasonably long legs like the Lightning.

The problem was that there was no such thing as external fuel tanks on USAAF aircraft, at least not officially, and the P-38's normal maximum range of about 800 miles (1,290km) on internal fuel was uncomfortably short, even with several stops planned *en route*.

Unofficially – and luckily for the USAAF – some work had been done on fitting drop tanks to the P-38. Several different types had been tested and one aircraft had already flown 2,200 miles (3,540km) non stop with the tanks fitted. Later in 1942 a P-38F would cover 2,900 miles (4,670km) with two 300 USgal (1,135 l) underwing tanks, although the aircraft was lacking armament and was allowed to operate at well above normal maximum weight.

Nevertheless, the concept was viable and Lockheed quickly provided sufficient 165 USgal (625 l) underwing tanks to equip 200 Lightnings for their trans-Atlantic journey and for operations once they arrived in Britain.

The first Lightnings to cross 'The Pond' were the P-38Fs of the 1st Fighter Group, comprising the 27th, 71st and 94th Fighter Squadrons. Two of the squadrons arrived in England in July 1942 but the third unit, the 27th, was held in Iceland until late August for operations against German Focke-Wulf Fw 200 Condors which were patrolling in the area.

On 15 August Lt Elza Shahan and one of the 27th's P-38Fs made history when it and a Curtiss P-40 of the 33rd FS combined to shoot down a Condor over the Atlantic. This was the first *Luftwaffe* aircraft destroyed by the USAAF in World War II and the P-38's second victim after the Aleutians *Mavis*.

Lockheed's outdoor production line at Burbank fairly early in the P-38's life and before mass production began in 1943. Note the RAF Hudsons in the background (Lockheed)

Early production P-38s over the Californian mountains. Far from combat worthy, these aircraft even lacked guns.

The 14th FG (48th, 49th and 50th FS) followed the 1st across the Atlantic in the second half of August, although the 50th remained in Iceland to replace the 27th which moved on to England. The 37th FS subsequently joined the 14th FG to give it its full complement of units.

The P-38s crossed the Atlantic in flights of four, each with a Boeing B-17 'lead ship' to provide navigation for the fighters. The flights were long and difficult and even though the P-38s now had adequate range for the flights, weather and navigation problems posed the greatest hazards.

Operation Bolero eventually saw 178 Lightnings fly to Britain from the USA. Six failed to make it but in all cases the pilots were picked up. Another 656 were transported by sea.

North Africa

Although attached to the USAAF's 8th Air Force in Britain, the Lightnings of the 1st and 14th FGs saw only limited service in that theatre of operations as they were destined for transfer to the 12th Air Force (commanded by General Jimmy Doolittle) to cover the Allied landings in North

Africa – Operation Torch. No contact with the Luftwaffe was made during the two months the aircraft remained in Britain.

A third Fighter Group – the 82nd – comprising the 95th, 96th and 97th Fighter Squadrons arrived in the UK in October 1942 but saw no action before it was also transferred to North Africa. Likewise the 78th FG (82nd, 83rd and 84th Squadrons) which arrived late in 1942 but was immediately sent to North Africa to cover losses sustained by the other three Groups. The 78th subsequently re-equipped with Republic P-47 Thunderbolts.

These transfers meant that the Lightning would play no part in the 8th Air Force's European operations until the second half of 1943.

The 1st and 14th FGs arrived in Tunisia during November 1942 with the 82nd following the next month. Their primary mission was bomber escort but resistance from the Luftwaffe and Italy's Regia Aeronautica was strong and heavy losses were sustained between November 1942 and early 1943. Such was the extent of these losses that not only did the

78th FG have to be sent from Europe to cover them, but the 14th FG was taken off operations and rested for several months.

Morale was low and wasn't helped by Operation Torch's commander, General Dwight Eisenhower's misunderstanding of the proper deployment of the aircraft, which were spread over a vast area of North Africa. Also, there was a vast gap in the experience levels between often seasoned German pilots and the 'wet behind the ears' Americans.

As their experience grew, so did their success and gradually the Lightning pilots were able to give as well as receive punishment. Although losses continued to be a problem, good use was made of the P-38's heavy firepower which was particularly effective against German and Italian transport aircraft.

Against enemy fighters, the Lightning suffered at higher altitudes as both power and manoeuvrability began to wane. Use of the P-38F's 'combat flap' setting helped, meaning the aircraft could just about hold its own in a dogfight at medium and low altitudes.

One such action occurred in early April 1943 when 82nd FG Lightnings shot down 17 Luftwaffe aircraft at a cost of four of their own which fell to the escorting fighters. Shortly afterwards, the 1st FG claimed 16 victories in one action and no fewer than 28 in another. The Lightnings also found useful employment in the ground attack and tactical reconnaissance roles, their firepower and long range providing advantages in these areas.

The P-38s were joined by another Lightning unit in December 1942, the 3rd Photographic Reconnaissance Group commanded by Col Elliot Roosevelt, son of the US President. Equipped with F-4 and F-5As, the 3rd PRG made a significant contribution to the North African campaign in a role that would become increasingly important for the Lightning.

The Mediterranean

With the May 1943 surrender of German and Italian forces in North Africa, the emphasis shifted to the Mediterranean as part of the Allies' plan to retake Europe through what Winston Churchill described as its "soft underbelly".

The first stage of this was the invasion of Sicily, which occurred in early July. The Lightnings of the 1st and 82nd FGs moved to the area where they encountered fierce opposition from both the Luftwaffe and Regia Aeronautica.

Losses were heavy with 17 P-38s shot down in the first week of July

A P-38H with two 1,000lb (454kg) bombs under the centre section. Ground attack and even conventional bombing became an important part of the Lightning's activities, especially in Europe, North Africa and the Mediterranean.

alone. A battle with the *Luftwaffe* at the end of August saw 13 Lightnings lost in return for the destruction of only eight enemy aircraft. This situation gradually improved and by September 1943 and Italy's surrender, the Lightnings were beginning to gain an ascendency in the air. They continued to be used in the ground attack role as well as performing their usual bomber escort missions and were also used to provide cover for British naval operations against Crete in October 1943.

With the surrender of Italy came the establishment of a new Army Air Force, the 15th, which was intended to be part of the Combined Bomber Offensive against Germany, although there was still a considerable amount of fighting to done in Italy as the Germans had occupied Rome at the time of Italy's surrender and weren't removed until June 1944.

The P-38H Lightning began replacing P-38Fs of the 1st, 14th and 82nd Fighter Groups around the time of the Italian surrender, this model offering a theoretically useful increase in power, although due to cooling problems it couldn't be fully utilised at high altitudes. From November 1943 all three groups were transferred to the 15th Air Force and based at the airfields around Foggia. The photo-reconnaissance Lightning units previously with the 12th Air Force were also transferred to the 15th.

The much improved P-38J soon replaced the P-38Hs and the Lightnings of the three 15th AF Fighter Groups were quickly put to work escorting Boeing B-17 Fortress and Consolidated B-24 Liberator bombers to targets in southern Germany, the Balkans and central Europe.

One of the best known of these missions occurred on 10 June 1944 when the 1st and 82nd FGs' Lightnings took part in the attack on the Ploesti oil refineries in Romania. The 1st's aircraft provided top cover for the raid while the 82nd's were used as dive bombers in support of the heavy bombers.

The 1st FG went in ahead of the bombers so as to engage whatever enemy fighters were sent up to meet them. A heavy air battle ensued with one American pilot – Lt Herbert Hatch of the 71st FS – becoming an instant 'ace' by destroying five German fighters in the melee. It was Hatch's first mission!

The Lightnings also flew a number of shuttle missions in which they landed in the Soviet Union to refuel and returned to their Italian bases a day or two later.

One operation in conjunction with the Russians in November 1944 went very wrong. Lightnings from the 82nd FG were briefed to give support to Soviet troops in Yugoslavia, where the situation on the ground was very confused. The Lightnings inadvertently strafed a column of Soviet troops and as there was no communication between ground and air, the Russians had little choice but to send up some Yak fighters in an attempt to drive off the P-38s. In the ensuing air battle, two Lightnings were shot down along with a handful of Yaks before the American aircraft could escape.

By late 1944 the P-38L was in service but the opportunities for air combat had all but disappeared as the *Luftwaffe* became progressively weaker. As a result, the aircraft was used more frequently for ground attack and Droop Snoot navigation and bomb aiming lead ship Lightnings were added to the 15th AF's fleet. Ever increasing loads of bombs and rockets under the Lightnings' wings added to their effectiveness in this role, April 1945 alone seeing aircraft from the 14th FG destroying 111 locomotives as they roamed around Germany, almost at will.

The 15th Air Force's Lightnings also notched up a good record in air-to-air combat, scoring 608 confirmed kills, 123 probables and 343 damaged. On the other side of the ledger, 131 P-38s were lost.

Lightnings over Europe

As discussed earlier, plans to operate the Lightning in Europe were interrupted towards the end of 1942 when the three Groups which had been sent to Britain were instead transferred to North Africa to meet more urgent needs there. A year later, there were sufficient aircraft being manufactured to meet the USAAF's needs in Italy, the Pacific and Europe, with the result that Lightning operations were once again able to begin with the 8th Air Force in England.

Four 8th AF Fighter Groups were equipped with Lightnings. First to arrive was the 55th FG (38th, 338th and 343rd FS) in August 1943, initially equipped with P-38Hs but with the more effective P-38J soon to replace them.

The 55th was joined by the 20th FG (55th, 77th and 79th FS) in late 1943; the 364th FG (383rd, 384th and 385th FS) and the 479th FG (434th, 435th and 436th FS) in the first half of 1944. These were all equipped with P-38Js on formation.

In anticipation of the Allied invasion of Europe, the USAAF established another Air Force – the 9th – in Britain during October 1943. From early in the following year this contained three Fighter Groups equipped with P-38J Lightnings, the 367th, 370th and 474th.

It has been suggested that the Lightning was a failure as an escort fighter in the European Theatre of Operations and didn't find its niche until it was given a new primary role – ground attack – with the 9th Air Force. The aircraft was certainly removed from 8th Air Force service

Photo-reconnaissance was another increasingly important Lightning mission. This is an F-5A taxying out.

fairly quickly with all three of its Fighter Groups relinquishing the P-38 for P-51D/K Mustangs in mid 1944.

Two of the three Lightning equipped Fighter Groups of the 9th AF swapped their Lightnings for Mustangs in early 1945 after using them primarily as ground attack aircraft with only the 474th FG keeping the Lockheed fighter until the end of European hostilities in May 1945.

Although this fairly rapid change in favour of the P-51 does seem to indicate a degree of failure on the part of the Lightning it also emphasises the superb qualities of the Mustang, which combined extraordinary range and high speed with the agility of the single engined fighter it was. The Mustang's qualities naturally made it the preferred fighter to escort the 8th AF's bombers into Germany.

In the meantime the Lightning was hardly a dead loss in the vital role of bomber escort, its long range and other qualities making it more than useful in this role and usually able to hold its own against the *Luftwaffe's* Messerschmitt Bf 109s and Focke-Wulf Fw 190s until the superb Mustang came along in numbers.

Early operations by the P-38Hs of the 55th FG were not entirely satisfactory due to constant engine cooling, turbocharger and engine detonation problems. The early combat record was also of concern. By late 1943 the 55th FG had claimed 18 enemy aircraft destroyed for the loss of 12 of its own, while the recently arrived 20th FG had lost five P-38s without any victories.

As the Mustang arrived in Europe in numbers it rapidly gained dominance, and this in combination with the changing nature of the battle as time went on saw the Lightnings used more often in the ground attack and low altitude fighter sweep roles, continuing these activities through the D-Day landings and for a short time afterwards until the 8th Air Force relinquished its last examples in July 1944.

In the meantime, the two seat Droop Snoot navigation and bomb aiming lead ship Lightnings had begun to appear, leading formations of single seat P-38s on what amounted to normal bombing missions. The first of these occurred in April 1944 when two Lightning squadrons from the 55th FG bombed targets in the St Dizier area from 20,000 feet (6,096m)

carrying one 1,000lb (454kg) bomb and a drop tank. The Group's third Lightning squadron provided cover during the raid.

The concept was regarded as successful, leading to its wider use over the remaining year of the European war, albeit by 9th Air Force aircraft after July 1944. One or two 2,000lb (907kg) bombs could be carried under the Lightning's centre section, the latter equivalent to a typical B-17 load and on missions where range was not a consideration. Pathfinder Lightnings with their Bombing Through Overcast (BTO) radar extended the concept even further.

The Lightning is generally regarded as not being entirely suitable for operations in Europe, warmer climates apparently suiting its qualities more readily. The fact that it was not really wanted in Europe from the second half of 1944 did mean that more aircraft were available for the theatre in which it really shone – the Pacific.

THE PACIFIC

The Pacific was the theatre of operations to which the Lightning was most suited, its long range and firepower quickly establishing it as the major USAAF fighter resource in the area. Compared with the Curtiss P-40 Warhawks and Bell P-39 Airacobras which constituted the USAAF's main fighter forces during 1942, the Lightning offered substantial advantages over both and was generally superior to the Japanese Zero.

The main advantage was the Lightning's superior performance over 20,000 feet (6,096m) where it was faster, climbed at a higher rate and could match the Zero in all manoeuvres except slow speed turns. The advantage increased with the introduction of the later P-38J and L models.

All Allied pilots quickly learned not to dogfight the Zero but instead use a 'hit and run' method of attack, diving in from above and then zoom climbing away, a manoeuvre in which the Lightning was far superior to the Zero. The Lightning's weight of fire also made short work of the lightly constructed Zero which in all but the very last models lacked proper pilot and fuel tank protection.

Finally, the Lightning's two engines made for considerable morale boosting security among its pilots with the loss of one engine to battle damage or mechanical failure not necessarily meaning a dunking in the Pacific Ocean on a typical overwater and long range mission.

Early Operations

The first Lightnings to operate in the Pacific area were not fighters but photo-reconnaissance F-4s of the 8th

With mass production comes the need for a rapid rate of production test flying. Lockheed's Milo Burcham was responsible for much of it. Here he poses with a P-38J. (Lockheed)

Photographic Squadron. Arriving in Australia in April 1942 they were sent to Port Moresby in New Guinea three months later to undertake the vital role of keeping track of the enemy's movements in New Guinea, New Britain and Rabaul. In undertaking these missions, the 8th mapped a significant part of eastern New Guinea and New Britain, providing information that would subsequently prove invaluable to the Allies.

The first combat Lightnings arrived at the RAAF's Amberley base near Brisbane during August 1942 preparatory to moving north. These 30 aircraft belonged to the 35th Fighter Group's 39th Fighter Squadron, part of the 5th Air Force. By September a further 35 had arrived but operations were delayed temporarily while problems with leaking rubber fuel tank cells were sorted. In addition, many of the Lightnings didn't have their gun feeds installed. In order to give the Lightnings the range they would need on combat duties, some 10,000 150 USgal (568 l) drop tanks were ordered from Australian light engineering factories.

The first Lightnings arrived in New Guinea during September 1942 but they weren't able to begin operations until near the end of the year due to technical problems with their turbocharger intercoolers, armament and other areas. These required substantial modifications to the wing leading edges (where the intercoolers were located on early model P-38s), the work carried out in both New Guinea and back in Australia.

The Lightning's first combat in the Pacific was recorded on 18 November 1942, not by 39th FS aircraft but those belonging to the 13th Air Force's 339th FS (part of the 347th FG), based on Guadalcanal to perform bomber escort and anti shipping missions in conjunction with 70th FS P-39 Airacobras. The 339th had received its first P-38s a few days earlier and on this occasion the squadron claimed three Zeros destroyed while escorting 11th Bomb Group Boeing B-17s.

The 39th FS claimed its first Zero on 24 November 1942 during a raid on Lae when a bomb dropped from one of the squadron's P-38s overshot its target and exploded in the water just as an intercepting Zero was passing low over the point. The Zero was downed by the wall of water from the exploding bomb! Unconventional, but the 5th Air Forces first Lightning kill of the Pacific War nevertheless.

A 'proper' kill in more conventional air-to-air combat had to wait for another month, until 27 December. On that day, twelve 39th FS Lightnings were scrambled to intercept a force of

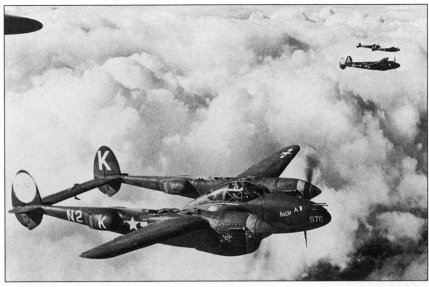
British based P-38Js in the cruise. The 8th Air Force quickly replaced the Lightning with the P-51 Mustang as the preferred escort fighter in Europe.

12 Aichi D3A *Vals*, 31 Nakajima Ki.43 *Oscar* fighters and 12 Zeros heading from Rabaul for a raid on Dobodura. P-40s from the 9th FS joined in the free wheeling dogfight and at the end of it all the P-38 pilots claimed nine enemy aircraft destroyed for no losses.

One of the P-40 pilots involved in that action was a certain Richard Bong, who claimed his first two victories of the war. Bong would shortly be making a name for himself as the top American ace of World War II, flying Lightnings.

Send More Lightnings

The 5th Air Force's commander, General George Kenney, had campaigned long and hard during 1942 for reasonable quantities of Lightnings to be sent to his area of responsibility as he recognised the aircraft's qualities were well suited to the Pacific's needs. Similarly, Maj Gen Millard Harmon of the 13th Air Force (based further east in the Pacific) was constantly asking for Lightnings but like Kenney was told that North Africa and Europe had priority. The problem was exacerbated by the fact that Lightning production didn't really get into its stride until 1943, so supply was limited.

The Pacific eventually got sufficient Lightnings to pretty well satisfy the commanders, one aspect which worked in their favour being the fact that the P-51 Mustang became the preferred escort fighter in Europe, freeing up more Lightnings for the Pacific.

The 5th Air Force's Lightning strength gradually grew during 1943 with F, G and H variants coming along to replace the earlier aircraft which were mainly P-38Es. From 1944, the highly capable P-38J and then L models also became available.

The 49th FG's 9th FS (Richard Bong's unit) changed from P-40s to P-38s in January 1943 and all of this group's squadrons would eventually be equipped with Lightnings. Other units were added as time went on: the 80th FS (8th FG) in March 1943 and in August the 475th FG comprising the 431st, 432nd and 433rd Fighter Squadrons, based in New Guinea. This group resulted from Kenney's pleas for more Lightnings during a visit to Washington DC, the powers-that-be somewhat reluctantly complying. Europe was still the priority, after all.

For Kenney, his ideal combination of aircraft for the Pacific War was the

The P-38J represented a quantum leap for the Lightning with its potential at last being exploited. This is P-38J-20 44-23315.

Similar but not the same: a P-38J-5 (foreground) and a photo-reconnaissance F-5B, the latter based on the 'J'.

B-25 Mitchell medium bomber for strafing, the B-24 Liberator for conventional bombing, the C-47 Skytrain/Dakota transport and the P-38 because of its significant ground attack capabilities as well as its rapidly growing reputation as the premier land based fighter of the region.

The 13th Air Force also added to its list of Lightning units with the formation of the 70th FS (347th FG) and the arrival in 1943 of another significant outfit, the 13th Photo Squadron, flying F-5s and operating from the Solomons. The 347th FG Lightnings often operated in conjunction with US Marine Corps F4U Corsairs as well as the other USAAF and US Navy types such as the F4F Wildcat, P-39 Airacobra and P-40 Warhawk.

All the Lightnings in the area were used for a variety of missions including bomber escort, air defence, ground support and quite often, attacking targets of opportunity on the ground and the water.

They were involved in some significant actions, an early example of which was the Battle of the Bismark Sea at the beginning of March 1943. This battle successfully stopped a Japanese force headed from Rabaul to Lae, the enemy fleet comprising eight transports carrying 6,000 reinforcing troops and eight escorting destroyers. *Oscar* fighters provided air support.

The operation against the convoy was a joint one involving P-38s from the 9th and 39th Fighter Squadrons, B-25 Mitchell, B-17 Fortress and A-20 Havoc bombers and Royal Australian Air Force Beaufighters from Nos 30 and 31 Squadrons. The first day of the battle saw B-17s attack the fleet escorted by Lightnings. One transport ship was sunk.

The scenario developed on the second day with no fewer than 109 aircraft attacking the convoy with the Australian Beaufighters at its the forefront. A raging battle followed which resulted in all the troop ships sunk along with four of the eight destroyers. In the air, numerous claims were made by the P-38 pilots.

Lightning Supreme

Similar battles occurred as the Pacific War progressed with the Lightnings displaying equal aplomb in air-to-air combat and in ground and shipping attack missions. The number of P-38 victories rapidly increased as it stamped its authority on the campaign as the tide inexorably turned against Japan.

Stories of multiple kills in a single sortie were not uncommon, a good example occurring in June 1943 when Lightnings of the 339th Fighter Squadron plus Warhawks and Wildcats intercepted a force of 118 Japanese aircraft heading for Guadalcanal. The air battle which followed resulted in the claimed destruction of no fewer than 49 Zeros and 32 Aichi *Vals*, one P-38 pilot, Lt Murray Schubin, getting six Zeros in this action including four out of five he found himself alone with for a period of 40 minutes. As a result, Schubin became the only P-38 'instant ace' of the Pacific War.

As the war progressed, the P-38s were able to move further northwards along with other US and Allied forces as the Japanese were pushed back. The arrival of the P-38J and L models brought with them extra ground attack capability in the form of rocket projectiles mounted on the 'Christmas Tree' racks under the centre section. Some were also fitted with earlier launching tubes mounted on

the sides of the forward fuselage, therefore freeing the underwing hardpoints to carry drop tanks.

One major operation in which the Lightnings were engaged was the Battle of Leyte Gulf, the opening of the Philippines campaign in late October 1944. Aircraft from the 27th and 49th Fighter Groups took part, based at Tacloban and as such were the first American aircraft on Philippine soil since the US surrender in May 1942. The P-38's pilots were greeted by Generals Kenney and MacArthur, the latter fulfilling his famous promise to return to the Philippines.

By the beginning of 1945 the Lightning was reckoned to be the most numerous aircraft operating in the South-West Pacific area with more than 500 attached to the 5th and 13th Air Forces. As was the case for all Allied fighter pilots in the region, fewer opportunities for air-to-air combat presented themselves over the last year of the war and in 1945 attacks on targets on the ground (and water) became the P-38's major activity.

More P-38s joined the Pacific campaign from early 1945, predominantly the 7th Air Force's 318th FG which also had P-47 Thunderbolts on strength. Photographic reconnaissance activities increased as the Americans neared Japan, the F-5s of the 28th PRS mapping Iwo Jima prior to its invasion and taking over 1,700 photographs in the process.

The 49th FG was selected as the first USAAF fighter unit to be based on the Japanese mainland as part of the occupation force following the surrender. It arrived in early September but by the end of the year the Lightnings were already replaced by Mustangs.

The P-38 was removed from USAAF service with what seemed to some to be indecent haste after the fighting was over. By 1946 it was effectively no longer part of the service's order of battle apart from some P-38M Night Lightnings of the 421st Night Fighter Squadron which were based at Fukuoka in Japan. By March 1946, they too were out of service and heading for the scrapper's yard.

P-38 versus Yamamoto

The P-38 achieved a significant military and psychological victory on 18 April 1943 when 16 aircraft from the 339th FS intercepted and shot down the Mitsubishi G4M *Betty* bomber carrying Admiral Isoroku Yamamoto, who was flying from Rabaul to Bougainville to inspect his forces there.

The interception involved an 870 mile (1,400km) round trip over water and relied heavily on Yamamoto demonstrating his usual strict punctuality

Admiral Isoroku Yamamato, the architect of Pearl Harbour and Japan's other early victories. P-38s from the 339th FS were responsible for his death.

Major Thomas McGuire, second only to Bong.

in the first few months of the war. Perhaps more importantly, he was also a realist who refused to let past glories affect his judgement of things to come. As such he was probably the only Japanese commander who fully appreciated Japan's position by mid 1943 – that is, the battle would inevitably be lost.

Two Aces

The two leading American aces of World War II both flew P-38s for the 5th Air Force in the Pacific. Majors Richard Bong (40 kills) and Thomas McGuire (38) had a kind of 'race' develop between them to see who could gain the most victories, although this was almost entirely at the instigation of McGuire. Their personalities were very different, Bong the quiet country boy and McGuire an "unpleasant man with a large ego", according to one writer.

The fact that Bong was always a few steps ahead in the 'race' was a source of much annoyance to McGuire and he was especially annoyed when General Kenney grounded him when Bong reached 40 kills, so the latter could be properly honoured when he was sent back to the USA. At that stage McGuire had 38 and disobeyed orders in an attempt to catch up. He didn't make it, dying in January 1945 when his 431st FS P-38 stalled at very low altitude while turning hard at low airspeed in pursuit of a Zero.

Neither did Bong survive 1945, although the flying accident which killed him occurred in the USA. Testing a Lockheed P-80 Shooting Star jet fighter in August of that year, the engine failed shortly after takeoff from Burbank and the aircraft crashed.

Richard Bong had a head start on McGuire in their race. As recorded earlier, Bong's first two victories came in late 1942 while flying a 9th FS

P-40. The unit switched to the P-38 in January 1943 and Bong was an ace within a few days of that. His score steadily mounted, reaching 21 by November 1943 when he was sent home on leave. The fact that he returned to the Pacific annoyed Thomas McGuire to a very large extent because to that point he thought he had the field to himself.

Not so – Bong added another 19 victories to his tally during his second tour of duty, in which he was basically allowed to operate as a freelance. General Kenney decided to send him home once and for all once the 40 mark had been reached, despite protests from the pilot.

McGuire opened his account in August 1943 when he shot down two *Oscars* and a *Tony* fighter in his first engagement. Three days later he scored a double and became an ace.

Doubles and triples became a feature of his increasing tally but his desire to beat Bong's score became obsessive to the point that he was disobeying orders and flying when he'd been told not to, and taking unnecessary risks. The odds finally closed on him and he remained two short of his rival's tally at the time of his death.

Although there were many P-38 aces, one pilot who didn't achieve that status in World War II deserves special mention. Charles Lindbergh – the man who had crossed

and sticking to his planned schedule. Access to this information came via Allied intelligence, which had been able to decode messages between Yamamoto and his officers at the front line.

The Admiral's formation comprised two *Bettys* (with Admiral Ugaki in the other) and six escorting Zeros. Of the Lightnings, four were allocated the task of shooting down the *Betty*, the so called 'Killer Flight' comprising pilots Tom Lanphier, Jim McLanahan, Joe Moore and Rex Barber.

True to form, Yamamoto departed exactly on time early on the morning of the 18th while the P-38s headed for the interception point at very low level so as to avoid detection. Yamamoto's formation was spotted on time and on course, the Lightnings then climbing to perform the interception. The escorting Zeros jettisoned their drop tanks when the Lightnings approached, signalling the start of the battle. Three Zeros were shot down as were both *Bettys*, one of them containing Admiral Yamamoto. One Lightning was lost and the mission was claimed a success.

Yamamoto's death was a severe blow to Japan's Pacific campaign as although he had suffered a setback at Midway, he had masterminded the attack on Pearl Harbour and Japan's successes

Major Richard Bong, the USA's top scoring fighter ace.

Thomas McGuire and technical representative Charles Lindbergh at the 475th FG. A civilian, Linbergh managed to talk his way into flying some combat missions in the P-38 and claimed at least one kill!

the Atlantic solo between New York and Paris in 1927 – was sent to the Pacific in mid 1944 as a civilian technical representative. He soon wrangled himself into a position where he flew combat missions despite his civilian status, his justification being that he could gather real life performance statistics for the companies he represented.

As he was a national hero it would have been difficult to refuse Lindbergh his request to fly combat, especially as his argument had some plausibility to it – at least it did the way it was presented! Lindbergh flew his first combat mission with the 35th FS in late June and then transferred to the 475th FG. He then shot down a Mitsubishi Ki.51 *Sonia* single engined light bomber, an aircraft known to be highly manoeuvrable and adept at avoiding interceptor fighters. It is not recorded what the official response to the news of Lindbergh's kill was!

CHINA-BURMA-INDIA

The Lightning saw limited combat service in the China-Burma-India (CBI) theatre despite calls by the local commanders for more to be sent to that part of the world. The 449th FS arrived in China in July 1943 and remained there until the end of the war, while the 80th Fighter Group's 459th FS operated in India-Burma.

The 449th flew mainly ground support missions due to a lack of opportunities for aerial combat while the 459th saw more of the latter as its primary role was to protect the major stores terminals in India and the transport aircraft which flew over the 'Hump' (the Himalayas) to China. Ground support missions were also flown, especially in northern Burma.

A sidelight to CBI P-38 operations was the conversion of P-38Ls to Droop Snoot configuration by India's Hindustan Aircraft. These were used in China for their intended role as navigation and bomb aiming lead ships, although one ended up as a VIP aircraft for Maj Gen George Stratemeyer – overall commander of US forces in the CBI – complete with plush accommodation in the nose instead of the usual bombing equipment.

Photo-reconnaissance Lightnings operated extensively throughout the CBI, F-4s and F-5s serving with several units including the 9th Air Force's 10th and 67th Photographic PRGs; the 3rd and 5th PRGs of the 12th and 15th AFs, respectively; the 15th AF's 154th Weather Reconnaissance Squadron; the 14th AF's 21st PRS; and the 5th AF's 8th PR Group.

FOREIGN USERS

Several nations other than the USA flew Lightnings during and after World War II, although its use was not as extensive as other types such as the P-51 Mustang and P-47 Thunderbolt. Britain's limited use of the Lightning has already been described in the previous chapter. Other foreign operators of the aircraft were:

Australia: Three F-4s were delivered

P-38L-5 44-53015 from the last batch of Lightnings built by Lockheed. Production ended with Japan's surrender but orders had begun to be cancelled earlier in 1945.

An F-5B flying considerably lower than its usual operating altitude. Including conversions, about 1,400 photographic reconnaissance Lightnings were built, indicating the importance of these variants' role.

to the RAAF in 1942-43, transferred from the USAAF's 8th PG based in northern Australia to meet an urgent need for photo-reconnaissance aircraft. The aircraft operated over the islands to the north of Australia but their service lives were relatively short with one withdrawn from service in late 1942 and both the others written off in landing accidents by August 1944.

France: Several Vichy controlled former *Armee de l'Air* units returned to the Allied cause after the invasion of North Africa in November 1942 and one of these – the *Groupe de Reconnaissance* II/3 – began receiving F-4A and then F-5A, C, E, and G Lightnings in November 1943. The group operated in conjunction with USAAF units in Tunisia and subsequently as an independent unit in Italy, Corsica, Sardinia and southern France.

Among its members was famous pilot and author Capt Antoine de Saint Exupery. At 43 he was considered too old for combat flying but was accepted to perform reconnaissance sorties over a part of the world he knew intimately from his pre war flights. He disappeared in July 1944 flying an F-5A on a mission.

China: About 15 Lightnings, mostly F-5s, were supplied to China under Lend-Lease in 1944-45 and operated by the Chinese Nationalist Air Force against Japan. The type was flown by both the Nationalist and Communist forces during the civil war of 1948-49.

Portugal: A single P-38F was impounded by Portugal when it and a second aircraft landed at Lisbon by mistake while flying from Britain to North Africa. The other aircraft's pilot realised the error in time to take off and get away. The impounded Lightning joined others which had also been seized – mainly P-39 Airacobras – in a special fighter unit.

Honduras: A small number of P-38Ls and Bell P-63 Kingcobras were supplied to Honduras by the USA in 1947 as part of a foreign aid package. The survivors served until 1961 after having been used mainly in the training role.

Italy: The largest foreign customer for the Lightning was Italy, which received 50 P-38Js in 1949 following its signing of the North Atlantic Pact. The aircraft were used only briefly and replaced by de Havilland Vampire jets in 1952.

An F-4 in RAAF service. Australia was one of seven countries apart from the USA to operate Lightnings, although in most cases it was only briefly.

A P-39M Night Lightning, all 75 of which were converted from P-38Ls. Although a capable aircraft, it arrived too late to see combat and like other Lightnings was retired from USAAF service soon after World War II ended.

MITSUBISHI
A6M ZERO

All lined up and ... somewhere to go. A6M2 Zeros prepare for departure on another mission early in the Pacific War, a time when the aircraft and its country seemed unbeatable. (via Mike Kerr)

Undoubtedly Japan's most famous combat aircraft, the Mitsubishi A6M *Reisen* (Zero Fighter) came as an unexpected shock for its opponents when it first appeared, offering high performance, long range and unmatched manoeuvrability in a light and relatively low powered airframe. To achieve this in an aircraft designed for carrier operations was itself a considerable feat, but the unpleasant surprise it created for its foes – firstly in China and subsequently in the early stages of the Pacific War – resulted largely from the West's ignorance of Japan's industrial and technological capabilities as much as anything else.

There were many who simply didn't believe that Japan was capable of producing a modern and original combat aircraft like the Zero, basing that opinion on the fact that many earlier projects were licence built foreign designs, or developments of them. While this is true – as is the fact that many Japanese designers learned their skills in the West – the level of expertise in the Japanese aircraft industry quickly developed along with the ability and desire to produce original designs.

By the 1930s these were plentiful and powerplants and armament development proceeded apace with the result that by the time Zero was being developed, Japan's industry was much more advanced and efficient than many other nations chose to believe.

The Zero came to be regarded as just about invincible by the Japanese and was certainly largely unmatched in the Pacific during the opening stages of the conflict. By 1943 it was outclassed by new American naval fighters such as the Grumman Hellcat and Vought Corsair and attempts to improve its capabilities were largely unsuccessful, limited by a relative lack of engine power throughout its career. By the time a notably more powerful version was developed it was too late, with Japan's forces in retreat and its industry in ruins.

Despite this, the Zero remained a substantial force throughout the Pacific War due to its numbers and providing it was flown by a skilled pilot. Unfortunately for Japan, these became more scarce as the war progressed and with the failure of Japanese industry to produce an appropriate successor with performance and armament matching the American fighters, the Zero was forced to soldier on despite its obsolescence.

Reliable production figures for the Zero are difficult to come by, but most informed sources put the figure for single seat A6M1-8 fighter variants at 10,449 manufactured by both Mitsubishi (3,879) and Nakajima (6,570). To this should be added 515 A6M-K two seat fighter trainers built by Dai-Nijuichi and Hitachi, and 327 Nakajima built A6M2-N floatplane variants, bringing the grand total to 11,291.

Japanese Naval Aviation

The Imperial Japanese Navy (INJ) was one of the first to recognise the potential of a shipborne combat aircraft fleet, commissioning its first 'aircraft carrier' – actually a seaplane carrier – as early as 1914. The *Wakayima* was a 4,400 tonne freighter which had been captured in 1905 during the war with Russia and used initially as a transport.

British built and originally named *Lethington*, the ship became a seaplane carrier in 1914 and as such was the first INJ vessel to have a major air capability. In 1920, the *Wakayima* was fitted with a planked deck over the

A captured A6M3 Zero 32 flies in USAAF markings during evaluation. Note the square wingtips of this model.

The Mitsubishi Navy Type 10 carrier fighter first flown in late 1921 and the first product of the company's newly established aircraft manufacturing division.

fo'c'sle for the launching of Sopwith Pups.

The British connections here are indicative of the closeness which had developed between the Imperial Japanese Navy and the Royal Navy in the latter part of the 19th century, from when the two nations were bound by treaty. When the time came for Japan to look closely at naval air power, the obvious thing to do was to turn to Britain for assistance and advice, both of which had previously been forthcoming on other matters of naval equipment, administration and organisation.

An official technical mission comprising 30 British naval officers arrived in Japan in April 1921 and remained there for the next 18 months, advising and training their Japanese counterparts in many aspects of naval flying. Their influence was to have far reaching effects on some philosophical matters, especially one which suggested it was essential to have aircraft with sufficient range to fly from a land base to a fleet at sea so as to offer support. This philosophy loomed large in the INJ's planning throughout the 1920s and '30s and had a direct influence on the specification for what would emerge as the Zero, including an endurance of six to eight hours with external tankage. This resulted in early Zeros having a maximum range of over 1,900 miles (3,060km) with an under-fuselage drop tank. With external fuel only the maximum range was 1,160 miles (1,870km), more than twice that of any contemporary single engined fighter.

Japan is credited with commissioning the world's first aircraft carrier designed from the start for that role, the *Hosho*, launched in November 1921 and put into service in December 1922. The ship was built very quickly and undoubtedly with the considerable help of the British technical mission. There is evidence to suggest that the speed of its construction resulted from the fact that the hull was originally laid down to be an oiler and subsequently adapted, but for the purposes of history, the *Hosho* can be regarded as the world's first purpose built conventional aircraft carrier with full length flight deck, longitudinal arrestor wires and a lift between the flight and lower decks.

Hosho displaced 10,100 tonnes loaded, was 551 feet (168m) in length and could carry up to 26 aircraft. She was relegated to a secondary role in 1933 but returned to the front line with the outbreak of war and was part of Admiral Yamamoto's fleet at Midway. The ship survived the war but was scrapped in 1947.

The Washington Treaty

Like many other nations, Japan's naval growth during the 1920s was shaped by the terms of the Washington Treaty of 1922 which imposed restrictions on tonnage. In Japan's case the so called '5:3:3' ratio applied, restricting the tonnage of battleships, battlecruisers and aircraft carriers to three-fifths that of Britain and the USA. Interestingly, there was no restriction placed on aircraft numbers, which allowed Japan to develop a naval aviation philosophy based around both ship and land based combat aircraft.

The Washington Treaty allowed Japan a capital ship tonnage of 315,000 (with a maximum of ten vessels and no new construction allowed) and 81,000 tons were available to the IJN to establish a carrier force with the displacement of individual units restricted to 27,000 tons although two could be up to 33,000 tons.

At the time of the Washington Treaty, Japan was implementing its '8-8' programme, a plan to equip the IJN with eight new battleships and a similar number of battlecruisers. This treaty meant they couldn't be completed as such and the decision was made to convert two of the more advanced battlecruiser hulls to aircraft carriers. One was damaged beyond repair by an earthquake at Yokosuka ship yard, but the other, the 30,000 tonnes *Akagi*, was completed and commissioned as Japan's second aircraft carrier in March 1927.

The *Kaga* of similar displacement followed in 1928, based on one of the battleship hulls made redundant by the Washington Treaty and the remaining allowable tonnage was filled by the smaller *Ryujo*, commissioned in 1933. The *Ryujo* proved deficient in many areas and this in combination with Japan's desire to establish a worthwhile carrier force with the emphasis on strike capability resulted in firstly the construction of a 'shadow' carrier fleet and secondly the eventual abrogation of the Washington Treaty.

The shadow programme was established as insurance against the relatively small Japanese carrier force imposed by the Treaty being disadvantaged in case of war and resulted in the construction of a number of ships which could be readily converted to aircraft carriers should they be required. The programme went ahead and the carriers were of course required, not by accident but by design as by 1934 Japan had already decided that war in the Pacific was inevitable and plans revolved around that fact.

The shadow programme served two purposes: it disguised Japan's true future intentions and also kept the IJN's official capital ship and aircraft carrier tonnage within the limits imposed by the Washington Treaty, at

Mitsubishi Navy Type 93 land based attack aircraft of 1932. Separate land and ship based fleets were an early part of the Imperial Japanese Navy's air philosophy.

least while Japan gave token recognition to its terms and conditions.

The result was that by the beginning of the Pacific War in December 1941, Japan had 13 commissioned aircraft carriers and seven others which would enter service during 1942.

An Industrial Giant

Mitsubishi was and is one of the world's leading engineering companies, its activities covering a wide variety of fields ranging from motor vehicle manufacture through to aircraft, engines, ships and numerous industrial engineering tasks. It was also involved with Japanese naval aviation from the beginning.

Aviation activities began in May 1920 when the Mitsubishi Shipbuilding and Engineering Co Ltd of Kobe established a new aircraft manufacturing company, Mitsubishi Nainenki Seizo KK or the Mitsubishi Internal Combustion Engine Manufacturing Co, for the manufacture of aircraft and cars. A plant was built at Nagoya with the intention of manufacturing both, but the car idea was unsuccessful and the plant was quickly dedicated to aircraft and aero engine production. Nagoya remained Mitsubishi's primary aircraft plant throughout World War II. It was the largest facility of its type in Japan and was considered to be very modern, incorporating the latest technology of the time.

Mitsubishi's connection with aviation was already established by the time the Nagoya plant opened. Four years earlier, in 1916, the company had begun manufacturing Renault engines under licence and this was quickly followed by a licence to produce Hispano-Suiza engines. From 1920 the aircraft manufacturing part of the Mitsubishi Combine was divided into three separate operations: one providing aircraft for the Navy, one for the Army and one producing civilian types.

The company underwent some name changes over the following years. In May 1928 it became Mitsubishi Kokuki (Mitsubishi Aircraft) and in June 1934 there was a major reorganisation with all of Mitsubishi's activities grouped a single company – Mitsubishi Heavy Industries Ltd – with each individual field of endeavour organised as separate divisions within the overall conglomerate. Aircraft manufacturing activities were performed under the Nagoya Kokuki

(right) Three pre war Mitsubishi aircraft for the Army (top to bottom): Type 87 light bomber (first flown 1926); Type 92 reconnaissance aircraft (1931); and Type 93-1 heavy bomber (1933).

Japan's second aircraft carrier, the Akagi, photographed in 1940 after being fitted with a full length flight deck. Note the port side island. Akagi was commissioned in 1927, modernised in the 1930s and took part in the second Sino-Japanese war of 1937 as well as leading the task force which attacked Pearl Harbour. It was sunk in June 1942.

Seisakusho (Nagoya Aircraft Works) title, itself divided into airframe and engine departments.

The Nagoya Aircraft Works was intimately involved with Japanese naval aviation from the start, and the company's first product was Type 10 carrier fighter first flown in October 1921.

This was the first of three types of carrier borne aircraft developed under a Navy contract and without competition from any other manufacturer. This set of circumstances virtually ensured the success of Mitsubishi's aircraft manufacturing venture. The three types were for operation from the carrier *Hosho* and were a fighter, reconnaissance aircraft and torpedo bomber, all confusingly designated Type 10 by the IJN, a reflection of the

system in use at the time which indicated all three designs were accepted in the 10th year of the Taisho era – 1921 for those more familiar with our Gregorian calendar system.

The Type 10 fighter (company designation 1MF1-5) was first flown in October 1921. Powered by a 300hp (224kW) Mitsubishi Type Hi eight cylinder vee water cooled engine, it was single seat biplane armed with two 7.7mm machine guns. A total of 128 was built between 1921 and 1928.

The Type 10 carrier reconnaissance aircraft followed in January 1922. This was basically a scaled up version of the fighter powered by the same engine but carrying two crew members. Production of this aircraft reached 159 by 1930.

The third Type 10, the torpedo bomber, was a totally different design first flown in 1922 but only 20 were built before the superior Mitsubishi Type 13 replaced it. The Type 10 was interesting in that it was a large single seat triplane powered by a 450hp (335kW) Napier Lion 12-cylinder engine.

The British influence remained in Japanese naval aviation through the design and development of these aircraft. All three were designed by Herbert Smith, previously with Sopwith in England. Smith and seven other British engineers had been hired by Mitsubishi to assist the company in the design and manufacture of military aircraft. The Sopwith influence was apparent in these designs.

The Type 13 carrier attack aircraft was another Smith design, this time a two/three seater biplane powered by either a Napier Lion or similarly rated Mitsubishi vee-12 engine. The first Type 13 was flown in 1923 and production continued into the early 1930s, by which time about 440 had been built.

Development and production of numerous other navy, army and civilian aircraft established Mitsubishi as a major manufacturer during the 1920s and '30s with no fewer than 50 different types being flown, many of them as prototypes only but a healthy number achieving production status. A wide variety of aircraft was produced ranging from basic trainers through general purpose aircraft, fighters, multi engined bombers, survey aircraft and passenger transports.

Monoplane Fighters

As the 1930s progressed, so did the quest for more speed become the driving force behind fighter designers' plans and the only way this was going to be achieved was by adapting a monoplane configuration for design. Mitsubishi was responsible for the Imperial Japanese Navy's first monoplane carrier fighter, the 1MF10 (or 7-Shi), designed by Jiro Horikoshi who would later be responsible for the Zero.

Like many Japanese aircraft designers and engineers, Horikoshi had spent time in the West studying the aeronautical engineering methods employed by European and American manufacturers. He was associated with Curtiss in particular, gleaning ideas about fighter design and construction.

The 1MF10 was built in response to a 1932 requirement for a new fighter and emerged as a stubby single seat monoplane with fixed undercarriage and a 580hp (432kW) Mitsubishi A4 14-cylinder radial engine. Two prototypes were built and flown in 1933 but both crashed, one through structural failure of the fin and the other after entering an unrecoverable flat spin. Although adjudged a failure due to controllability problems and not ordered into production, the 1MF10 was nevertheless regarded as advanced for its day – particularly in its unbraced, box spar cantilever wing design – and was able to achieve a maximum speed of 200mph (321km/h).

Horikoshi applied the lessens learned to his next naval fighter design, the very much more successful Type 96 (service designation A5M), later code named *Claude* by the Allies during the Pacific War. The A5M was designed in 1934 to fill a requirement for a new fighter, although it's important to note that the original specification did not include a requirement to operate from aircraft carriers.

A prototype was flown on 4 February 1935 under the company designation KA-14 powered by a 600hp (447kW) Nakajima Kotobuki 5 nine cylinder radial. The aircraft was of all metal construction with an inverted 'gull' wing, fixed undercarriage, open cockpit and a maximum speed of 280mph (450km/h). After some deliberation, the decision was made to install a 'trousered' fixed undercarriage rather than retractable units in the interests of weight and complexity, while great emphasis was put on weight and drag reduction and controllability.

The inverted gull wing of the first prototype was replaced by a 'straight' wing on the second and subsequent prototypes. Several different engines were fitted to the prototypes during the aircraft's period of testing, inevitably delaying its entry to service. The powerplant finally selected for production A5Ms was the 600hp Kotobuki 2-Kai-1 radial with more powerful engines fitted as production of the aircraft continued.

Mitsubishi's new fighter entered service in early 1937 as the Type 96 Carrier Based Fighter (A5M1), in time to see action in the Sino-Japanese War which started in July of that year. Production by Mitsubishi had ended by 1940 by which time the ASM was obsolescent, but it nevertheless saw some service in the early stages of the Pacific War. Watenabe and Dai-Nijuichi also built A5Ms until 1942 in

A pair of Mitsubishi civilian types of the pre war era: the R-1.2 trainer of the early 1920s (top) and the Hato-type survey aircraft, a one-off from 1936.

the case of fighters and as late as 1944 for the trainer variant. Total production reached 1,094 including three evaluated by the Army in 1935-36 as the Ki-18 and Ki-33.

The A5M was the Imperial Japanese Navy's first operational monoplane fighter, highly manoeuvrable, structurally advanced and a vitally important stepping stone towards Jiro Horikoshi's next project – the Zero.

The Designations Puzzle

At this point it might be convenient to explain the aircraft designation system used by the Imperial Japanese Navy as it applies to the Zero.

The complexity of Japanese aircraft designations resulted in the Allies' decision to allocate a code name to each during World War II, fighters and float planes being given boys' Christian names and most other types (with the exception of trainers), girls' names. The Zero was allocated the code name *Zeke*, although several others were at times temporarily applied to new models when it was at first thought they were different aircraft. Despite allocation of the *Zeke* code name, the term 'Zero' has been almost universally used, then and now.

The Zero's official naval designation was A6M, ordered under the 12-*Shi* programme, the 12th year of Emperor Hirohito's reign. The aircraft was formally defined as the Naval Type 0 Carrier fighter, the '0' indicating the fact that it was accepted for service in the Japanese year 2600, or 1940 under the Gregorian calendar system.

The Japanese name *Reisen* was also applied, this being not a popular name but a contraction of *Rei Sentoki,* which means Zero Fighter. As a result of this combination of Type 0, Zero and *Reisen*, another variation – Zero-Sen – has also found some use.

The A6M designation can be broken down into its components, the 'A' a functional letter meaning carrier borne fighter; the '6' signifying the aircraft was the manufacturer's sixth aircraft built for carrier operations; and the 'M' signifying Mitsubishi.

Individual mark numbers were simply added to the designation, eg A6M2 means the second major variant while specialist variants could be indicated by a dash and another letter, A6M2-K for example indicating the two seat trainer version of the A6M2 family.

Model numbers were also applied as well as sub variants of these, for example the A6M2 Model 11 or Model 21 and the A6M5 Models 52, 52a, 52b and 52c. A description of all the Zero major and minor variants appears in the next chapter.

The prototype Mitsubishi 9-shi (Type 96) monoplane fighter as first flown in February 1935. Note the inverted gull wing, unique to this aircraft.

Towards The Zero

On 19 May 1937, shortly after the Type 96 (A5M) had entered service, the Imperial Japanese Navy issued a preliminary specification for what was called the Navy Experimental 12-*Shi* Carrier Fighter. Issued to Mitsubishi and Nakajima, it was intended as a successor to the A5M and its requirements called for an aircraft far in advance of that fighter and indeed any other carrier fighter in service anywhere in the world.

The specification called for a combination of qualities – notably manoeuvrability with exceptional range and endurance – which usually could not be combined successfully. The lessons learned from combat experience with the A5M in China led to the issue of a revised and even more demanding specification in October 1937, one which Nakajima considered impossible to meet and forced its withdrawal from the competition.

The details of the specification were:

Requirement: a fighter capable of intercepting and destroying enemy attack bombers, and of serving as an escort fighter with combat performance greater than that of enemy interceptors.
Maximum speed: 270kt (311mph/500km/h) at 4000m (13,123ft).
Time to climb: 3,000m (9,842ft) in 3min 30sec.
Takeoff distance: less than 70m

(230ft) with 12m/sec (23kt) wind over deck headwind; less than 175m (574ft) in calm wind.
Landing speed: 60kt (111km/h) or less.
Endurance: 1.5-2.0 hours at normal rated power (maximum continuous) at 3,000m (9,842ft); 6-8 hours with external fuel tank at economical cruising speed; maximum range (with drop tank) 1,685nm (3,120km).
Armament: two Oerlikon type 20mm cannon, two 7.7mm machine guns; provision for two 30kg (66lb) bombs.
Radio: provision for full radio equipment including direction finding equipment.
General equipment: reflector gunsight, oxygen system, engine fire extinguisher, lighting, standard aircraft and engine instruments.
Wing span: less than 12m (39ft 4in).
Manoeuvrability: at least equal to the Navy Type 96 (A5M) Carrier Fighter.
Power loading: less than 5.5lb/hp (1.86kg/kW).

Nakajima's withdrawal from the competition to design and produce this 'impossible' aircraft left Mitsubishi alone to tackle it with its design team led by Jiro Horikoshi, then 34 years old. The problems facing him were enormous as any one of the specification's requirements inevitably compromised several others. The question of reconciling the need for

The production version of the Type 96 (designated A5M) entered service in 1937, in time for the second Sino-Japanese war. The Allies later applied the codename 'Claude' to Japan's first monoplane fighter.

Type 96-2-1s (A5M2a) fighters in service.

manoeuvrability equal to the A5M's while at the same time providing for the space and weight required to meet the endurance/range requirement is indicative of the challenge. This in itself appeared to be beyond the limits of possibility in a single engined fighter – let alone a naval one – in 1937.

A look at the state-of-the-art in naval fighter design elsewhere emphasises the 12-*Shi* specification's advanced nature. Britain's Royal Navy had the Hawker Nimrod biplane with fixed undercarriage, open cockpit and a maximum speed of 196mph (315km/h). The US Navy also had a biplane, the Grumman F3F with retractable undercarriage and enclosed cockpit. Top speed was 231mph (372km/h).

Against this it can be seen just how advanced the new fighter was planned to be, and even its predecessor, the A5M, looked advanced by comparison with these aircraft thanks to its monoplane configuration (albeit with fixed undercarriage) and 252mph (405km/h) maximum speed in production form.

Design Features

Horikoshi and his team set themselves a target of three years from starting work on the new fighter to its entry to service. One year of that was allocated to design work, six months for the construction of the prototype, 12 months for prototype trials and evaluation and a further six months for the building and testing of an initial production batch.

In order to achieve the design aims, the airframe had to be strong yet as light as possible; long span ailerons were required to achieve the necessary rate of roll; the wing area had to be relatively large so as to provide a low wing loading to keep the landing speed down; drag had to be minimised to achieve the required speed (meaning a retractable undercarriage and the weight penalty it carried); the relationship between fuselage length, fin size and yawing moment had to be balanced to provide stability as a gun platform.

What emerged was a clean, uncomplicated shape of all metal construction with the control surfaces fabric covered. Several innovative for the time features were incorporated including a framed sliding canopy with cut down rear fuselage for all-round visibility, the incorporation from the start of provision for a 73imp gal (330 litre) underfuselage drop tank to achieve the necessary range and the armament, which for its day was very

heavy as it included two 20mm cannon as well as a pair of machine guns.

The cannon were mounted one in each wing – just outboard of the inwards retracting main wheels – while the two 7.7mm machine guns were installed on top of the engine cowling with the breaches reachable from the cockpit. The tailwheel was also retractable.

The internal fuel capacity of 115imp gal (525 l) was also large for its time and installed in two wing tanks plus a forward fuselage tank between the engine and cockpit. This capacity was some 35 per cent greater than the contemporary Supermarine Spitfire I.

The quest for weight reduction led to some of the greatest innovation, particularly in the area of structural design. The fuselage centre section was built as an integral part of the wing, which in turn was built around a one piece main spar manufactured from a material called Extra-Super Duralium (ESD). The 12-*Shi* provided the first application for this alloy which had been developed in Japan by the Sumitomo Metals Company. Comprising mainly zinc and chrome, the metal had a tensile strength more than one-third greater than previously used alloys.

The tapered wing featured a subtle application of decreased incidence at the tips, or 'washout'. This had the effect of delaying tip stall, resulting in the ailerons retaining some effectiveness even though the inner wing might be stalled. This provided the opportunity for better manoeuvrability in a dogfight, especially where low speeds and tight turns were involved.

ESD was also used in other parts of the airframe and contributed greatly to Jiro Horikoshi's team being able to achieve most of its design aims. The other side of the ESD coin was its susceptibility to self generating corrosion, although this did not matter so much at the time as the life of a combat aircraft was expected to be relatively short. To facilitate storage and maintenance, the fuselage could be 'broken' just aft of the cockpit.

Other weight saving measures incorporated included the use of a minimal number of fasteners and connecters, while a complete lack of armour protection for the pilot and the aircraft's vital systems also made a major contribution to keeping the weight down. This had not been called for in the Navy's specification and although subsequently criticised by many foreign 'experts', it should be remembered that a lack of armour protection was common in 1937 including in Britain's Spitfire and Hurricane, neither of which gained such protection until it became operationally necessary to do so.

A late production Type 96-2-2 (A5M2b). Note the sliding cockpit canopy.

Whether or not the weight saving programme was successful can be judged by the fact that the prototype weighed in at just 4,380lb (1,987kg), about 950lb (431kg) lighter than the prototype Supermarine Spitfire, itself not exactly a heavyweight.

One of the early decisions which had to be made was the selection of a suitable powerplant. There were basically three choices, none of them regarded as being wholly satisfactory at a time when Japanese engine development was lagging slightly behind the rest of the world. All three options were 14-cylinder, two row air cooled radials, two from Mitsubishi and one from Nakajima.

The 950hp (708kW) Nakajima Sakae 12 (Prosperity) engine then un- der development was favoured by some within the Navy as it offered the best weight/power compromise but as Mitsubishi itself produced two en- gines in the required class, Horikoshi was put under pressure to use one of these.

Producing a maximum 1,070hp (798kW), the Mitsubishi Kinsei 46 (Golden Star) was the most powerful

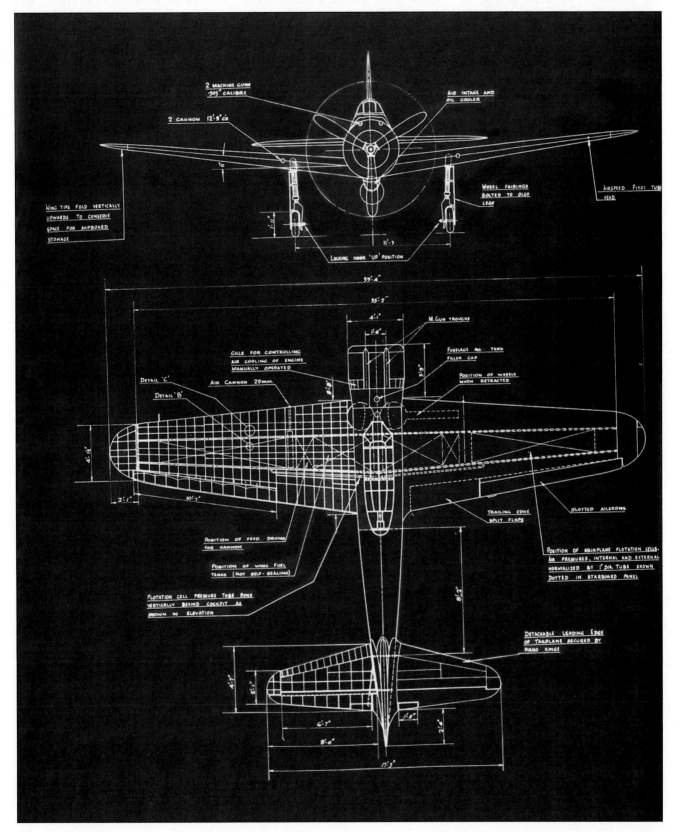

of the alternatives but also the heaviest by a considerable amount. It was therefore decided to go with the least powerful option, the 875hp (652kW) Zuisei 13 (Holy Star) engine which was also in the early stages of development. It was slightly lighter than the Nakajima powerplant and of more compact dimensions than either it or the Kinsei, these factors influencing the decision in its favour despite its relative lack of power at that early stage of development.

The decision to use the Zuisei delighted Mitsubishi, which enjoyed the fact that the new fighter would have airframe and engine designed and built by the same company. Unfortunately, the choice proved to be flawed and all but the first two Zeros would be powered by the Nakajima Sakae.

Plans to install a three bladed constant-speed propeller on the prototype had to be postponed due to development problems and a two bladed variable-pitch unit was substituted.

Philosophical Differences

The development of the Zero was not all plain sailing, with Jiro Horikoshi at one stage having severe doubts that it was possible to combine optimum speed, manoeuvrability, minimal weight and long range in a single design after all.

Horikoshi sought guidance from the Navy, looking for a ruling on which of these characteristics should receive priority. To him, the insistence on severe weight reduction was compromising everything else, especially as the Zuisei engine was still really an unknown quantity such was its early

stage of development and the constant-speed propeller was not developing at the necessary rate and probably wouldn't be available in time for the prototype.

Two different views came from the Navy via two experienced and respected aviators – Lt Cmdr Minoru Genda, Fighter Group Leader, combat leader, tactician and test pilot; and Lt Cmdr Takeo Shibata, a man with similar credentials.

Genda argued the case for manoeuvrability as the most desirable primary characteristic at the expense of speed, range and weight of fire. Shibata's view was the opposite. He was prepared to sacrifice manoeuvrability for speed and especially range as experience in China had shown that the fighters had insufficient range to offer proper protection to the bombers. It is not surprising that no clear decision emerged from these disparate views, although Mitsubishi itself tended to take the Genda line. This left Horikoshi no better off than before and still facing the same problems.

The result was that the 12-*Shi* fighter programme was in a state of limbo for much of 1938 while the Navy tried to decide what it wanted. For a time, the project's future looked threatened as the various points of view were bandied about. Several factions were established in the Navy hierarchy, some wanting a particular characteristic of the new fighter receiving prominence, others wanting another.

Jiro Horikoshi meanwhile returned to his calculations and had another

look his design. After due consideration he decided the requirements could be met – assuming engine and propeller lived up to expectations – and continued with the support of the Navy.

Construction of the three prototypes continued. The first was completed in March 1939 and rolled out from the Nagoya factory on the 19th of the same month. From there, it was dismantled and transported by ox cart in shipping crates the 30 miles (48km) to the Army airfield at Kagamigahara. The tortuous journey over often rough roads took nearly two days to complete and was conducted in great secrecy.

Once at Kagamigahara, the 12-*Shi* was reassembled and briefly flown for the first time on 1 April 1939, a quick hop down the runway being sufficient for the moment. It was flown by Mitsubishi test pilot Katsuzo Shima, who reported nothing more serious than poor braking action, something which would stay with the Zero throughout its life.

Six more flights were recorded over the next 12 days, all of them at low speed with the undercarriage down before the envelope was expanded. Although the aircraft handled satisfactorily, it suffered high engine oil temperatures and a nasty vibration at all times. This was subsequently cured by replacing the two bladed variable pitch propeller with the planned three bladed constant-speed unit. Flight testing of the prototypes is described further in the following chapter.

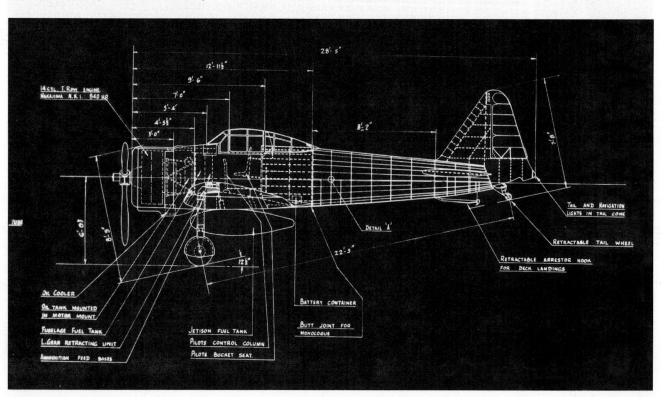

ZERO DEVELOPMENT and VARIANTS

A6M1 ZERO

As discussed in the previous chapter, the unarmed prototype 12-*Shi* fighter first took to the air – a short hop above the runway – on 1 April 1939. The first few flights were conducted at low speeds with the undercarriage locked down and revealed a constant vibration which was at first attributed to the undercarriage being down. The vibration persisted when the undercarriage was up and was quickly traced to the two bladed variable-speed propeller. A three bladed constant-speed unit was fitted and the problem was solved. First flight with the new propeller was on 17 April.

The aircraft's performance envelope was gradually expanded, higher speed tests uncovering a problem with elevator response, considered to be too sensitive. This was solved by the ingenious idea of deliberately incorporating a degree of elasticity into the elevator control cables and torque tubes, meaning they stretched at higher speeds, thus reducing the elevators' sensitivity at that end of the flight regime without sacrificing the proper 'feel' at lower speeds.

By the end of April 1939 sufficient testing had been performed to con-firm the new fighter met or exceeded all of its requirements except that of maximum speed which had been recorded at 265 knots at 9,840ft (305mph/491km/h at 3,000m), five knots short of the specification. This and some minor problems with the still immature Mitsubishi Zuisei 13 engine resulted in an early decision by the Navy that the third prototype and production aircraft would be powered by the 950hp (708kW) Nakajima Sakae 12 engine which offered more power and the promise of greater reliability for a minuscule increase in weight.

By September 1939 the prototype had completed 119 flights and 43hr 26min in the air. It was handed over to the Imperial Japanese Navy at its Oppama Air Base at Yokosuka on the 14th of that month and given its formal military designation: A6M1 Type 0 Carrier Fighter. From now on we'll refer to the aircraft by its A6M designation and the name 'Zero' for convenience, unless circumstances dictate otherwise.

Second Prototype

The second A6M1 – and the last Zero powered by the Zuisei engine – was flown on 18 October 1939 and delivered to Yokosuka for evaluation by the Navy a week later. This aircraft was used for armament trials but had a relatively brief life as it was destroyed in accident on 11 March 1940, killing pilot Masumi Okuyama.

The flight was part of a series of tests intended to analyse propeller response to airspeed changes, resulting from problems with the constant-speed propeller which was proving to be reluctant to quickly change its pitch angle as airspeed rapidly fluctuated, as would be encountered in a combat situation.

A terminal velocity dive was called for and one was successfully completed before the second, fatal one was attempted. Okuyama put the aircraft into 50 degree dive and what appeared to be an engine overspeed was heard, followed by an explosion and disintegration of the aircraft. The pilot fell clear of his aircraft and his parachute opened, but inexplicably, he was then seen to fall clear of the 'chute about 1,000 feet (300m) above the water.

The official explanation for the accident was structural failure caused by elevator flutter following the loss of the mass balance weight on the actuating rod inside the tail cone. The

The prototype A6M1 Zero, first flown on 1 April 1939. This and the second aircraft were the only Zeros powered by the 875hp (652kW) Mitsubishi Zuisei 13 engine.

installation was subsequently strengthened but some were unsure that this was the cause of the crash due to the engine overspeed which was clearly heard by many witnesses on the ground. Failure of the main wing spar due to faulty machining was also put up as a possibility but later ruled out, although it's interesting to note that modified spars were introduced early in the production run and the first few aircraft were limited to just 50 operational flying hours.

The Navy's evaluation of the Zero prototypes was highly successful despite the crash, and the aircraft's capabilities quickly overcame resistance from pilots who were used to biplanes, fixed undercarriages and open cockpits. The same occurred in other countries where pilots were also being subjected to modern retractable undercarriage monoplane fighters for the first time during the latter half of the 1930s.

A6M2 ZERO
A6M2 Model 11

The early decision to install the more powerful Nakajima Sakae 12 engine in the third and subsequent Zeros resulted in this aircraft flying only two months after the second Zuisei powered prototype, on 28 December 1939. Installation of this new engine resulted in the designation A6M2 being applied and transformed the aircraft's performance, making it exceed the Navy's most optimistic expectations. Maximum speed increased by about 25mph (40km/h) and time to height performance was also enhanced.

An example of the first production Zero variant, the A6M2 Model 11. This example belongs to the 12th Kokutai and was photographed over China, during the aircraft's first combat deployment.

The A6M2 featured some external differences to its predecessor including an increase in overall length from 28ft 8in (8.74m) to 29ft 8.7in (9.06m), mainly as a result of redesigned tail surfaces which saw the fin and rudder moved aft and the horizontal surfaces slightly up. This was done to correct a tendency for the aircraft to enter a flat spin under certain circumstances.

Installation of the Sakae engine accounted for some of the length increase and also for a change in the cowling profile. The A6M1's engine had a downdraught carburettor, resulting in the carburettor intake being mounted prominently on top of the cowling. On the A6M2, the Sakae 12's updraught carburettor meant the intake had to be placed on the lower part of the cowling and was fixed on its leading edge immediately below the spinner. The A6M1's large oil cooler on the bottom of the cowling was replaced with a much more compact unit behind the newly located carburettor intake.

Two prototype A6M2 Model 11s were built, followed by 15 pre production and 48 production aircraft. The 'Model 11' nomenclature was applied from the end of July 1940 when the aircraft was accepted into service by the Imperial Japanese Navy Air Force (JNAF) following the completion of carrier trials. The official designation was Navy Type 0 Carrier Fighter Model 11. The Japanese designation system is explained in the previous chapter.

There were some minor running changes to the Model 11 during its relatively brief production life. The exhaust system was modified, there was some redesign of the rear glass panes of the cockpit canopy and the extreme aft fairing was covered in metal (from aircraft number 47) and the cannon apertures in the wings were made flush with the leading edges rather than recessed. A more significant modification was the incorporation of a reinforced rear wing spar from the 22nd aircraft on.

The Model 11 was the first Zero variant to see combat, an initial batch of six of the pre production aircraft sent to China to join the 12th *Rengo Kokutai* (Combined Air Group) in central China for land based combat trials in late July 1940. Most of the Model 11s (including the pre production batch) served in China, the first mission being flown on 19 August when Zeros escorted bombers over the then enormous distance of 930 miles (1,500km). There was no combat on this occasion, that milestone occurring on 13 September when 13 Zeros took on 27 Chinese Polikarpov I-152, I-153 and I-16 fighters with the result that all were shot down for the loss of no Zeros.

The Zero's combat record in China is discussed in more detail in the following chapter, but overall it was responsible for the destruction of 103 Chinese aircraft for only two losses, both to ground fire.

The Nakajima Sakae 21 radial engine as fitted to initial production versions of the Zero.

A6M2 Model 21

The A6M2 Model 21 appeared in the second half of 1940 and it was this version which took part in the Pearl Harbour raid and the other actions which saw Japan dominate the early months of the Pacific War. Of the 3,432 A6M2s built, all but the first 65 were Model 21s. Nakajima began manufacturing the aircraft at its Koizumi (Okawa) plant in November 1941 and this company in fact dominated the A6M2 production tally, building 2,628 as opposed to Mitsubishi's 804.

The main difference between the Model 21 and its predecessor was the incorporation of folding wingtips so the aircraft would fit the standard 36ft 1in (11.0m) deck elevators on Japan's aircraft carriers. With the tips folded about 20 inches (51cm) was removed from each wing, bringing the overall span down to just under 35 feet (10.97m).

Production modifications incorporated in the Model 21 were minor, the most important being installation of a new aileron balance system from the 127th aircraft onwards and the fitting of a ground adjustable aileron trim tab from aircraft number 192. These finally solved ongoing niggling problems with aileron balance and its associated flutter.

The Allies began their system of applying code names to Japanese aircraft during the course of 1942 with *Zeke* given to the Mitsubishi fighter. This was followed by a number to differentiate the variant, the A6M2 Model 21 becoming, for example, the *Zeke* 21.

A6M3 ZERO
A6M3 Model 32

One of the crucial elements in the Zero's ultimate failure to match Allied fighters in combat was its lack of power, especially at altitude. It's interesting to note that no production Zero ever had more than 1,130hp (843kW) at its disposal and from early 1943

An A6M2 on the approach with undercarriage and flaps down. This one seems to be lacking the usual drop tank.

A6M2 MODEL 21 ZERO
Powerplant: One Nakajima NK1C Sakae 12 14-cylinder air cooled radial with single stage/two speed supercharger rated at 940hp (701kW) for takeoff and 950hp (708kW) at 13,780m (4,200m); three bladed Sumitomo constant-speed propeller of 9ft 6in (2.90m) diameter. Internal fuel capacity 115imp gal (525 l) in fuselage and wing tanks; provision for one 73imp gal (330 l) underfuselage drop tank.
Dimensions: Wing span 39ft 4.4in (12.02m); length 29ft 8.7in (9.06m); height 10ft 0in (3.05m); wing area 241.5sq ft (22.44m²); tailplane span 15ft 5in (4.70m).
Weights: Empty 3,770lb (1,710kg); normal loaded 5,313lb (2,410kg); max loaded 6,164lb (2,796kg).
Armament: Two 20mm Type 99 cannon in wings with 60 rounds per guns; two 7.7mm Type 97 machine guns in upper forward fuselage with 500 rounds per gun; provision for two 132lb (60kg) bombs; provision late in war for one 250lb (113kg) or 551lb (250kg) underfuselage bomb for fighter-bomber or suicide missions.
Performance: Max speed 288kt (533km/h) at 14,930ft (4,550m), 245kt (454km/h) at sea level; cruising speed 180kt (333km/h); max climb 3,150ft (960m)/min; time to 19,685ft (6,000m) 7.5min; service ceiling 32,810ft (10,000m); max range (internal fuel) 1,010nm (1,870km), with drop tank 1,675nm (3,102km).

---

was fighting against American fighters with 2,000hp (1,491kW) on tap.

The need for more altitude and climb performance was recognised as the A6M2 Zero was entering service, Nakajima developing its Sakae engine to incorporate a two stage supercharger. Called the Sakae 21, it produced 1,130hp (843kW) for takeoff and although the same diameter as the earlier Sakae 12, was longer due to the supercharger installation and heavier.

The Zero variant powered by this engine was dubbed the A6M3, the first example of which was flown in June 1941. Despite the extra power, the A6M3's performance proved to be

disappointing, the aircraft only slightly faster than the A6M2. In addition, the longer engine resulted in the firewall being moved 8in (20cm) aft, which encroached into the area occupied by the fuselage fuel tank, reducing its capacity by about 18imp gal (82 litres). This, in conjunction with the Sakae 21's higher fuel consumption, had a notably detrimental effect on range and its combat debut in August 1942 on operations in the Solomons and New Guinea was handicapped by this.

The first two A6M3s were flown with standard folding wing tips but the third (flown in January 1942) featured these tips removed and faired over in an attempt to increase speed. This gave the first production A6M3, the Model 32, its distinctive square wing tip shape.

Other changes installed in the Model 32 compared to the A6M2 included the fitting of a propeller of slightly greater diameter, increasing the ammunition for the two 20mm cannon from 60 to 100 rounds per gun and installing some armour protection for the pilot. The cowling shape changed again, being slightly more bulbous and modified to house the carburettor intake in the upper rather than lower lip as the Sakae 21 had a downdraught carburettor. The propeller spinner was also slightly

The A6M2 Model 21 was the Zero variant exclusively involved in all of Japan's battles during the first year of the Pacific War. This example shows its 73imp gal (330 l) drop tank to good advantage.

MITSUBISHI A6M
REISEN *(Zero* Fighter)

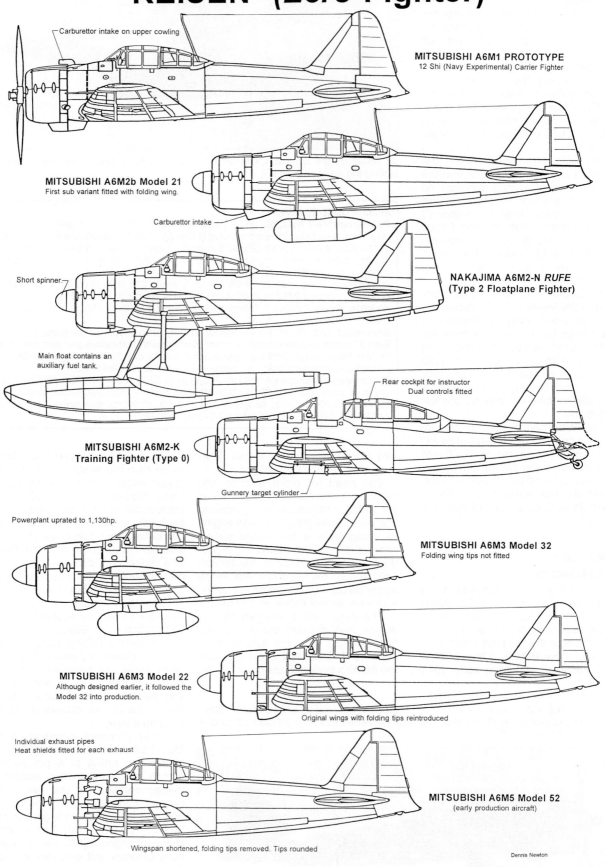

Carburettor intake on upper cowling

MITSUBISHI A6M1 PROTOTYPE
12 Shi (Navy Experimental) Carrier Fighter

MITSUBISHI A6M2b Model 21
First sub variant fitted with folding wing.

Carburettor intake

NAKAJIMA A6M2-N *RUFE*
(Type 2 Floatplane Fighter)

Short spinner

Main float contains an
auxiliary fuel tank.

**MITSUBISHI A6M2-K
Training Fighter (Type 0)**

Rear cockpit for instructor
Dual controls fitted

Gunnery target cylinder

Powerplant uprated to 1,130hp.

MITSUBISHI A6M3 Model 32
Folding wing tips not fitted

MITSUBISHI A6M3 Model 22
Although designed earlier, it followed the
Model 32 into production.

Original wings with folding tips reintroduced

Individual exhaust pipes
Heat shields fitted for each exhaust

MITSUBISHI A6M5 Model 52
(early production aircraft)

Wingspan shortened, folding tips removed. Tips rounded

Dennis Newton

MITSUBISHI A6M
REISEN *(Zero* Fighter)

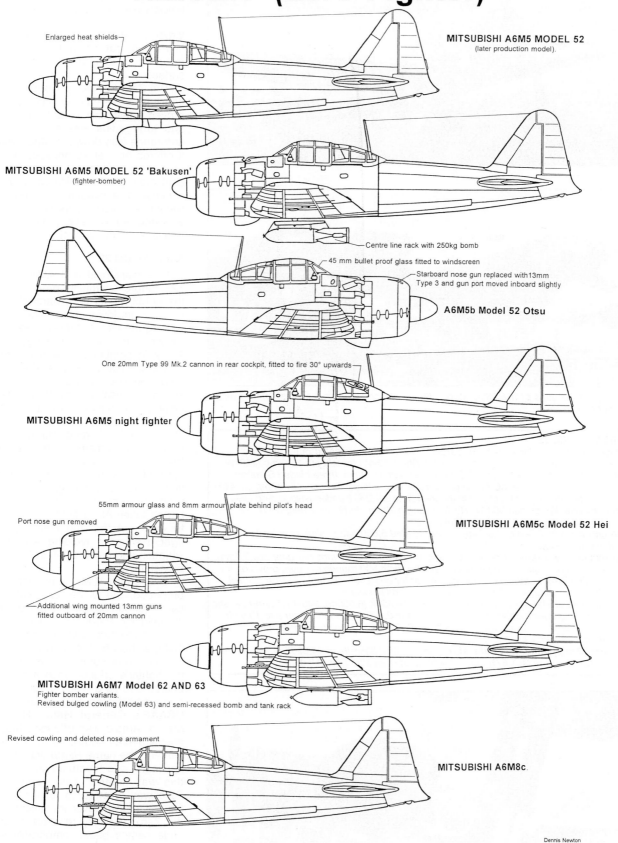

Enlarged heat shields

MITSUBISHI A6M5 MODEL 52
(later production model).

MITSUBISHI A6M5 MODEL 52 'Bakusen'
(fighter-bomber)

Centre line rack with 250kg bomb

45 mm bullet proof glass fitted to windscreen

Starboard nose gun replaced with13mm
Type 3 and gun port moved inboard slightly

A6M5b Model 52 Otsu

One 20mm Type 99 Mk.2 cannon in rear cockpit, fitted to fire 30° upwards

MITSUBISHI A6M5 night fighter

55mm armour glass and 8mm armour plate behind pilot's head

Port nose gun removed

MITSUBISHI A6M5c Model 52 Hei

Additional wing mounted 13mm guns
fitted outboard of 20mm cannon

MITSUBISHI A6M7 Model 62 AND 63
Fighter bomber variants.
Revised bulged cowling (Model 63) and semi-recessed bomb and tank rack

Revised cowling and deleted nose armament

MITSUBISHI A6M8c.

Dennis Newton

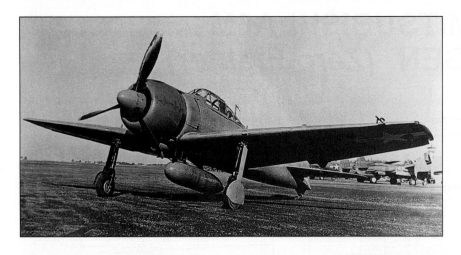

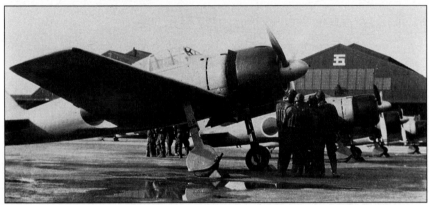

The square wingtips of the A6M3 Model 32 are well shown in this shot of 204th Kokutai aircraft at Iwakuni.

A6M3 MODEL 32
Powerplant: One Nakajima NK1F Sakae 21 14-cylinder air cooled radial with two stage/two speed supercharger rated at 1,130hp (843kW) for takeoff, 1,100hp (820kW) at 9,350ft (2,850m) and 980hp (730kW) at 19,685ft (6,000m); three bladed Sumitomo constant-speed propeller of 10ft 0in (3.05m) diameter. Internal fuel capacity 97imp gal (440 l) in fuselage and wing tanks; provision for one 73imp gal (330 l) underfuselage drop tank.
Dimensions: Wing span 36ft 1in (11.0m); length 29ft 8.7in (9.06m); height 11ft 6in (3.51m); wing area 231.7sq ft (21.52m²).
Weights: Empty 3,984lb (1,807kg); normal loaded 5,609lb (2,544kg); max loaded 5,829lb (2,644kg).
Armament: Two 20mm Type 99 cannon in wings with 100 rounds per gun; two 7.7mm Type 97 machine guns in upper engine cowling with 500 rounds per gun; provision for two 132lb (60kg) bombs; provision late in war for one 250lb (113kg) or 551lb (250kg) bomb under fuselage for fighter-bomber or suicide missions.
Performance: Max speed 294kt (544km/h) at 19,658ft (6,000m), 243kt (450km/h) at sea level; cruising speed 200kt (370km/h); max climb 3,100ft (945m)/min; time to 19,685ft (6,000m) 7.3min; service ceiling 36,253ft (11,050m); max range (with drop tank) 1,284nm (2,328km).
Model 22 supplementary data: Max speed 288kt (533km/h) at 14,930ft (4,550m); max range (with drop tank) 1,677nm (3,106km); wing span 39ft 4.5in (12.00m).

(top left) A captured A6M3 Zero 32 shares space with some Lockheed P-38 Lightnings. This model's main changes were the fitting of the more powerful Sakae 21 engine with two-stage superchargers and clipped wingtips in an attempt to increase speed.

larger and the two cowl mounted machine guns sat within the upper cowl rather than in channels on its top surface.

The Zero 32 was not popular with its pilots. It offered only marginally improved speed, climb and rate of roll and turn radius was slightly worse and range was down. In other words, it offered no real advantages over its predecessor despite nearly 20 per cent more power, which came at the expense of a substantial increase in weight. Additionally, its service entry was delayed for several months due to a lack of powerplants.

A6M3 Model 22

Mitsubishi built 343 A6M3 Model 32s before switching production to the A6M3 Model 22 towards the end of 1942, its lower model number reflecting the fact that it reverted to the longer span, folding tip wings of the A6M2 in combination with the more powerful Sakae 21 engine. The loss of range demonstrated by the Model 32 was compensated for with the installation of an additional 10imp gal (45 l) fuel tank in each outer wing. This restored the Zero's range but the major problem still remained – the fact that the Zero was already being outclassed as a fighter after only one year of war. Even though its manoeuvrability remained unmatched, it hadn't taken Allied fighter pilots long to work out that the best tactic to fight it was by avoiding a dogfight situation and using a 'hit and run' approach instead.

One other A6M3 subvariant was produced, the Model 22a with long barrel cannon providing a higher muzzle velocity. Production of all A6M3 variants reached 903 aircraft to mid 1943, all built by Mitsubishi.

There was some confusion as to the fighter's origins when it first appeared and as a result it was initially codenamed *Hap* in honour of the USAAF's General Henry H 'Hap' Arnold. Arnold was offended that an enemy aircraft should be named after him and the name *Hamp* was quickly applied. It was eventually realised that this was another Zero variant and *Zeke* was reverted to. In the meantime, confusion over identification of the Zero generally resulted in other code names being temporarily allocated, *Ray* and *Ben* among them.

(bottom left) The A6M3 Model 22 reverted to the Model 21's longer span, folding tips as illustrated by these aircraft at Iwakuni.

A6M4 ZERO

A designation applied to two A6M3s modified by the installation of an experimental turbosupercharged version of the Sakae 21 engine in an attempt to improve the Zero's performance at medium and high altitudes, where it was heavily outclassed by American fighters. Major teething problems were experienced and the project was cancelled.

A6M5 ZERO

The most numerous of all Zero versions with some 6,000 built (including about 3,500 by Nakajima), the A6M5 was quickly developed as a temporary expedient pending availability of the Zero's intended replacement, the Mitsubishi A7M *Reppu* (Hurricane). Codenamed 'Sam' by the Allies, the A7M was first flown in May 1944 after three years' development but only eight were built before Japan's surrender following a period of vacillation and indecision by the Navy on the fighter's specification.

That was finally settled towards the end of 1944 by which time it was too late with material shortages, Allied bombing and the December 1944 earthquakes in the Nagoya area taking their toll.

The production version of the A7M would have at last given the Japanese Navy Air Force an aircraft which on paper at least matched the Hellcat, Corsair and Lightning with 2,200hp (1,640kW) available from its Mitsubishi MK9C 18-cylinder radial engine, a maximum speed of 390mph (628km/h) and manoeuvrability which was said to equal that of the Zero.

The problem of finding a more modern replacement for the Zero were exacerbated by delays in the development of another new Navy fighter, the Mitsubishi J2M *Raiden* (Thunderbolt). Intended as a purely land based interceptor, the *Raiden* (codenamed 'Jack') first flew in March 1942 but didn't enter service until late 1943, the problems discovered during prototype testing taking longer to sort out than they should have due to Mitsubishi's preoccupation with building and developing the Zero.

Powered by an 1,800hp (1,342kW) Mitsubishi Kasei 14-cylinder radial, the J2M was capable of 365mph (587km/h) but was plagued by technical troubles throughout its life and only 476 were built, most of them used in the defence of Japan during the latter months of the war. Despite these problems (which included more indecision from the political masters), the *Raiden* was recognised as a good bomber destroyer but like many other Japanese aircraft of the time, it was a case of too little, too late.

The result of this was that the Zero simply *had* to remain in production with all its faults as there was no alternative and the A6M5 was still being built at the time of the capitulation. It combined old and new features but its main (and most limiting characteristic) was that it retained the 1,130hp (843kW) Sakae 21 engine of the A6M3 models, albeit with a new exhaust system in which the earlier exhaust collector ring was replaced with individual 'ejector' stacks to provide a bit of extra thrust. The result was the fastest production Zero with a maximum speed of 351mph (565km/h).

A6M5 Model 52

The initial production model of the A6M5, the Zero 52, combined some of the features of earlier aircraft including the A6M3 Model 32's non folding short span wing (but with rounded rather than square tips and the folding mechanism removed rather than simply faired over), the Model 22's increased fuel capacity, the Model 22a's long barrel cannon and, as mentioned above, the Sakae 21 engine with modified exhaust.

New features incorporated were modified ailerons and flaps and the use of heavier gauge wing skinning which allowed the maximum diving speed to be increased, although a gap remained between the Zero and its American opposition. Armament remained as per the earlier Zeros – two 20mm cannon and two 7.7mm machine guns. Pilot and fuel tank protection remained minimal.

The first Zero with the new wing was the 904th A6M3, first flown in August 1943 and in effect serving as the prototype for the A6M5 series. Service began in October 1943, the

The A6M5 Model 52 was the most produced of all the Zero variants with some 6,000 built by Mitsubishi and Nakajima from August 1943.

The A6M5 Zero was intended as a temporary expedient pending the availability of a more modern replacement. Mitsubishi's failure to do so meant the Zero had to soldier on against increasingly more effective opposition. Two planned replacements were the purely land based J2M Raiden (top) which suffered lengthy delays and the shipborne A7M Reppu (bottom) which never entered service. This is the fourth of only eight A7Ms built, photographed after the war.

new Zero variant proving to be almost a match for the Grumman F6F Hellcat in some areas of combat in experienced hands – it was more manoeuvrable – but it lost out badly in the areas of firepower and durability. Poorly protected and lightly built, the Zero 52 was no match for the American fighter which was more often than not well flown by pilots who were quickly developing their skills and were quickly replaced if lost. By the end of 1943 Japan's supply of experienced, skilled pilots was starting to be stretched.

A6M5a Model 52a

The Zero 52a was an attempt to boost the firepower of the aircraft and further improve its diving capability, something which was becoming more important in combat as the higher the diving speed, the more options a pilot had when it came to breaking off the battle or following his adversary. Further thickening of the wing skinning

increased the maximum diving speed from 410 to 460mph (660 to 740km/h) at the expense of a bit of level speed and extra weight, although even this improved diving performance was still behind that of the American F4U Corsair.

The armament was improved by replacing the cannons' original drum feed mechanism with a belt feed system which allowed an increase in ammunition capacity from 100 to 125 rounds per gun. Deliveries began in March 1944 and 391 of this sub variant was built, all by Mitsubishi.

A6M5b Model 52b

The Zero 52b represented a probably belated attempt to rectify two of the aircraft's major failings – a relative lack of firepower and protection. To help achieve the latter, a 1.75in (44mm) plate of armour glass was installed behind the windscreen and the wing fuel tanks gained the protection of an automatic CO_2 fire extinguisher system. The armament underwent the first change since the Zero was introduced but then only by small measure when one of the two upper cowling 7.7mm machine guns was replaced by a 13.2mm weapon.

The Zero 52b first appeared in combat during the first Battle of Philippine Sea in June 1944, but its debut was inauspicious as it coincided with one of the Imperial Japanese Navy's great defeats, the infamous 'Marianas Turkey Shoot' in which US Navy Hellcats shot down 42 Japanese aircraft for just one loss.

Zero 52b production amounted to about 470 aircraft.

A6M5c Model 52c

First flown in September 1944, the Zero 52c well symbolises the problems facing the Japanese Navy and Japanese industry at the time. The Zero was by now well and truly obsolescent but efforts continued to make the aircraft at least slightly viable in the face of a lack of suitable replacement.

Increased firepower and protection were again the key elements of this variant which for the first time included armour plating to protect the pilot. The armament was considerably changed with two 13.2mm machine guns each with 240 rounds of ammunition added to the wings outboard of the existing cannon and the cowling mounted 7.7mm gun deleted. This left a single 13.2mm weapon in the nose and the total gun complement at five. Provision was also made for underwing ordnance, the 52c capable of carrying up to ten 22lb (10kg) bombs or two 132lb (60kg) rockets.

An attempt was also made to retrieve some of the range performance

The Zero 52 was hampered by a lack of firepower, airframe and pilot protection and performance when compared to its American adversaries. Captured examples such as this were flown against aircraft like the Vought Corsair and Grumman Hellcat.

Development of the Zero 52 continued through several subvariants in attempts to improve the aircraft's combat worthiness, but by then the airframe and powerplant were stretched beyond reasonable limits. Something entirely new was needed.

A6M5 MODEL 52 ZERO
Powerplant: One Nakajima NK1F Sakae 21 14-cylinder air cooled radial with two stage/two speed supercharger rated at 1,130hp (843kW) for takeoff, 1,100hp (820kW) at 9,350ft (2,850m) and 980hp (731kW) at 19,685ft (6,000m); three bladed Sumitomo constant-speed propeller of 10ft 0in (3.05m) diameter. Internal fuel capacity 129imp gal (588 l) in wing and fuselage tanks; provision for 73imp gal (330 l) underfuselage drop tank.
Dimensions: Wing span 36ft 1in (11.0m); length 29ft 11in (9.12m); height 11ft 6in (3.50m); wing area 229.3sq ft (21.3m²).
Weights: Empty 4,136lb (1,876kg); normal loaded 6,025lb (2,733kg); max loaded 6,508lb (2,952kg).
Armament: Two 20mm Type 99 cannon in wings with 100 rounds per gun; two 7.7mm Type 97 machine guns in upper cowling with 500 rounds per gun; provision for two 132lb (60kg) bombs or one underfuselage 250lb (113kg) or 551lb (250kg) bomb.
Performance: Max speed 305kt (565km/h) at 19,685ft (6,000m), cruising speed 200kt (370km/h); max climb 2,805ft (855m)/min; time to 19,685ft (6,000m) 7.0min; service ceiling 36,255ft (11,050m); max range (with drop tank) 1,037nm (1,921km).

---

which had been lost as the aircraft evolved by adding a 31imp gal (140 litre) fuel tank behind the pilot, complete with another first – self sealing protection. This caused centre of gravity problems with the result that the other tanks' capacities had to be reduced, leaving the Zero 52c with an overall internal capacity of 123imp gal (560 l) or only slightly more than the original production A6M2.

The effect of these and previous modifications was that the Zero's airframe and powerplant were now stretched beyond reasonable limits. The 52c was more than 600lb (272kg) heavier than the 52b with obvious penalties in performance.

By now, a new and more powerful engine was urgently needed and designer Jiro Horikoshi's pleas to install the 1,350hp (1,007kW) Mitsubishi Kinsei engine were rejected and installation of the water injected Sakae 31 suggested instead. Problems with the development of that engine precluded its use and the aircraft had to plod on grossly underpowered with the Sakae 21. As a result of all this, the Zero 52c was a failure and only 93 were built.

A6M5d-S Zero

This designation was unofficially applied to some A6M5s of the 302nd Kokutai which was charged with the defence of the home islands, mostly operating at night. These Zeros were modified in the field to incorporate an oblique firing 20mm cannon mounted in the rear fuselage, its barrel projecting outwards and upwards at angles of 30 degrees.

Fighter Bombers

The thought of using the Zero as anything other than a pure fighter almost represented heresy in the minds of those who flew it, but operational necessity dictated that the aircraft be made capable of carrying a bomb for use in the fighter-bomber role. A modified version of the A6M5's drop tank fitting was produced to enable a single 250lb (113kg) or 551lb (250kg) bomb to be carried. This philosophy was subsequently extended when *Kamikaze* suicide missions began in October 1944, the Zeros thus allocated flying to oblivion with a bomb under the fuselage.

A6M6 ZERO

A single prototype of the A6M6c Model 53c was flown in November 1944, based on the Zero 52c and featuring the same armament of three 13.2mm machine guns and two 20mm cannon.

The basis of the 53c was the installation of a water-methanol injection Sakae 31a engine which retained the basic 1,130hp (843kW) rating of the Sakae 21 but theoretically maintained it more readily. The other innovation incorporated was the fitting of self-sealing fuel tanks.

The plan was for the A6M6 to follow the Zero 52 models on the production line but ongoing problems with both the water-methanol system and the new fuel tanks caused the project to be abandoned. The water-methanol metering system was the main culprit, failing repeatedly during testing and for most of the time limiting the available power to a figure below that achieved by the unboosted Sakae 21!

A6M7 ZERO

The final Zero variant to achieve production (albeit limited), the A6M7 Model 63 was developed as a fighter-bomber for operation from Japan's smaller aircraft carriers following the loss of most of its larger ships. Powered by the finally sorted out (to a rea-

The A6M7 Zero 63 was the final variant to achieve production, although this was very limited. It was developed as a fighter-bomber and was manufactured only from May 1945.

MITSUBISHI A6M3
Model 32 *ZERO*

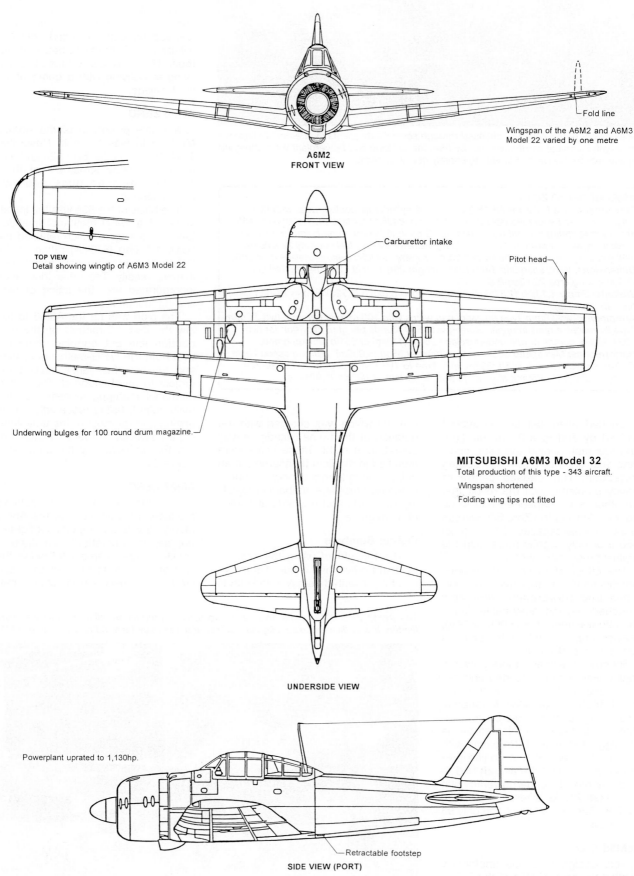

A6M2
FRONT VIEW

Fold line

Wingspan of the A6M2 and A6M3
Model 22 varied by one metre

TOP VIEW
Detail showing wingtip of A6M3 Model 22

Carburettor intake

Pitot head

Underwing bulges for 100 round drum magazine.

MITSUBISHI A6M3 Model 32
Total production of this type - 343 aircraft.

Wingspan shortened

Folding wing tips not fitted

UNDERSIDE VIEW

Powerplant uprated to 1,130hp.

Retractable footstep

SIDE VIEW (PORT)

Dennis Newton

MITSUBISHI A6M5
Model 52 *ZERO*

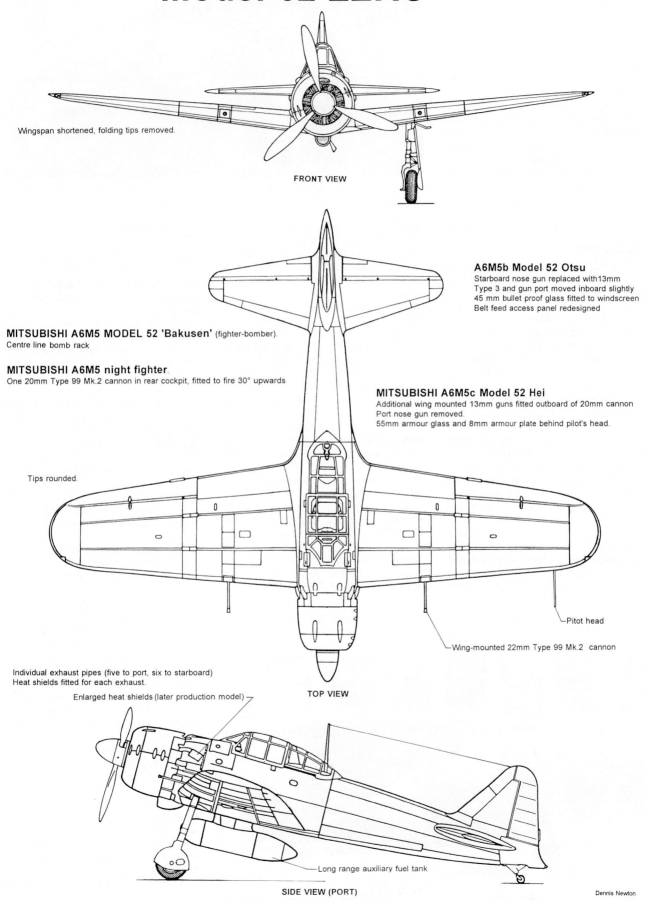

Wingspan shortened, folding tips removed.

FRONT VIEW

A6M5b Model 52 Otsu
Starboard nose gun replaced with13mm
Type 3 and gun port moved inboard slightly
45 mm bullet proof glass fitted to windscreen
Belt feed access panel redesigned

MITSUBISHI A6M5 MODEL 52 'Bakusen' (fighter-bomber).
Centre line bomb rack

MITSUBISHI A6M5 night fighter.
One 20mm Type 99 Mk.2 cannon in rear cockpit, fitted to fire 30° upwards

MITSUBISHI A6M5c Model 52 Hei
Additional wing mounted 13mm guns fitted outboard of 20mm cannon
Port nose gun removed.
55mm armour glass and 8mm armour plate behind pilot's head.

Tips rounded.

Pitot head

Wing-mounted 22mm Type 99 Mk.2 cannon

TOP VIEW

Individual exhaust pipes (five to port, six to starboard)
Heat shields fitted for each exhaust.

Enlarged heat shields (later production model)

Long range auxiliary fuel tank

SIDE VIEW (PORT)

Dennis Newton

sonable extent, anyway) Sakae 31 water-methanol injection engine, the Zero 63 retained the Model 52c's five gun armament, a 551lb (250kg) bomb was carried under the fuselage instead of the normal drop tank and to compensate for this loss of fuel capacity, a 33imp gal (150 l) drop tank could be carried beneath each wing. The tailplane structure was reinforced to cope with the extra weights and stresses involved.

Production of the Zero 63 began in May 1945 and the exact number built is unknown due to the loss of records, but around 150 is a popular estimate.

A6M7 leading particulars: normal loaded weight 6,614lb (3,000kg); max speed 296kt (548km/h) at 20,100ft (6,400m); time to 19,685ft (6,000m) 8.0min; service ceiling 33,400ft (10,180m); max range 820nm (1,518km).

A6M8 ZERO

The A6M8 finally provided the Zero with the more powerful engine it so badly needed but by the time this aircraft appeared it was too late and production was limited to just two prototypes despite orders having been placed for 6,300 more.

Installation of the 1,560hp (1,163kW) Mitsubishi Kinsei 62 14-cylinder radial engine formed the basis of the A6M8 and although this provided only marginally improved performance over the A6M5 it was able to do so while carrying proper pilot and fuel tank protection including an upgraded automatic fire extinguishing system. Continuing problems in developing satisfactory self sealing fuel tanks meant that this feature was not included.

The new engine was larger in diameter than the Sakae and the aircraft's nose profile was changed as a result. This also meant that the upper cowling machine gun had to be deleted,

The A6M2-K was flown mainly by operational units as a conversion trainer for new pilots. Production amounted to 510 by Hitachi and Dai-Nijuichi.

leaving the fixed armament at two 20mm cannon and two 13.2mm machine guns in the wings. The underfuselage bomb and underwing drop tanks capability of the A6M7 was retained.

Designated the A6M8c Model 54c, the first of two prototypes was completed in late April 1945 (after a month's delay following air raid damage to the factory) and was handed over to the Navy in May. The second prototype was delivered in June 1945 and testing revealed satisfaction with the aircraft.

It was given top priority for production but by then it was too late for Japan, whose aircraft manufacturing capacity lay in ruins. Production aircraft would have been designated A6M8 Model 64.

Leading particulars for the A6M8 include: empty weight 4,740lb (2,150kg); normal loaded weight 6,945lb (3,150kg); maximum speed 309kt (773km/h) at 19,685ft (6,000m); time to 19,685ft (6,000m) 6.8min; service ceiling 37,075ft (11,200m).

ZERO TRAINERS

The first Zero two seaters appeared in 1942, these aircraft not intended for training purposes but for armed reconnaissance and command duties in the south-west Pacific. A small number was modified from A6M2 fighters in the field but none were produced new.

The need for a two seat advanced trainer variant of the Zero was subsequently recognised, but not until 1943 when a specification was issued for such an aircraft based on the A6M2 Model 21 airframe and powerplant. Designated the A6M2-K (or Type Zero Training Fighter Model 11 – *Rei Shiki Renshu Sentoki Ichi Ichi Gata*), the two seater was developed by the engineering staff of the Dai-Nijuichi Kaigun Kokoshu (21st Naval Air Depot) at Omura, Kyushu) and the first example was completed in November 1943.

Compared to the fighter, the Zero trainer featured two seats in tandem (with the instructor at the rear), the forward cockpit remaining in the same place as the fighter and the rear seat occupying the space previously housing radio and other equipment. A longer canopy structure with sliding hood covered the rear seat but the student's position in the front was permanently open. The tailwheel was fixed down and had a larger wheel, dual controls were fitted, small strakes were fitted to the upper rear fuselage to improve spin recovery characteristics and in order to save weight the two wing mounted cannon and main wheel covers were removed.

The A6M2-K was accepted into service in early 1944 and production was undertaken by Dai-Nijuichi (238) and Hitachi (272) for a total of 510. Hitachi began producing the aircraft from May 1944.

The A6M2-K was flown mainly by

The A6M2-K trainer was based on the single seat Zero 21 fighter but with two seats in tandem. The front (student's) cockpit was permanently open while the instructor's had a sliding canopy.

operational units basically as a conversion trainer before increasingly inexperienced pilots flew Zeros operationally. It was also used for communications and other general duties but towards the end of the war some were pressed into service as *Kamikaze* aircraft.

Hitachi developed similar two seat version of the more powerful A6M5 Model 52 Zero. Designated A6M5-K, the first was flown in March 1945 but only seven were completed.

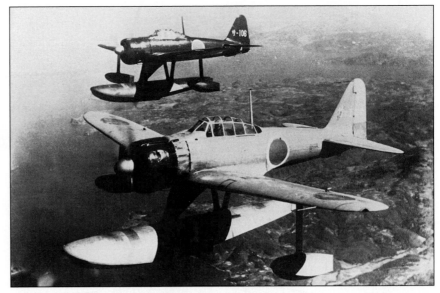

Based on the Zero 21, the A6M2-N 'Rufe' floatplane fighter was intended to support amphibious landing operations in the Pacific.

A6M2-K ZERO
Powerplant: *One Nakajima NK1C Sakae 12 14-cylinder air cooled radial rated at 940hp (701kW) for takeoff and 950hp (708kW) at 13,780ft (4,200m); three bladed Sumitomo constant-speed propeller of 9ft 6in (2.89m) diameter. Fuel capacity 115imp gal (525 l) in wing and fuselage tanks.*
Dimensions: *Wing span 39ft 4.5in (12.00m); length 30ft 0.25in (9.15m); height 11ft 7.2in (3.53m); wing area 241.5sq ft (22.44m²).*
Weights: *Empty 4,010lb (1,819kg); normal loaded 5,146lb (2,334kg); max loaded 5,792lb (2,627kg).*
Armament: *Two 7.7mm Type 97 machine guns in upper cowling; provision for two 132lb (60kg) bombs or one underfuselage 551lb (250kg) bomb for suicide missions.*
Performance: *Max speed 257kt (476km/h) at 13,125ft (4,000m); cruising speed 186kt (344km/h); time to 19,685ft (6,000m) 7.9min; service ceiling 33,400ft (10,180m); range (internal fuel) 745nm (1,380km).*

THE FLOATPLANE FIGHTER

One of the very rare breed of seaplane fighters, the A6M2-N 'Rufe' (as it was called by the Allies) resulted from the issue in September 1940 of a specification for an aircraft capable of providing air support to amphibious landing forces throughout the Pacific in the absence of either carrier or land based fighters, operating from sheltered lagoons and other waterways in the islands. The idea was that the aircraft would 'hold the fort' until permanent airfields were built on these islands.

The specification was originally issued to Kawanishi, which eventually came up with the N1K1 *Kyofu*, but it was realised at an early stage that this advanced design would enter service too late to meet Japan's immediate needs. Instead, it was decided to develop a floatplane fighter derivative of the Zero as an interim measure and as Mitsubishi was fully occupied with other projects, the development and production contracts were given to Nakajima which went on to build 327 A6M2-Ns at its Koizumi plant, alongside standard Zeros.

As indicated by its designation, the Rufe was based on the A6M2, the prototype derived from the Model 11 and all production aircraft from the Model 21 with the exception of the wing, which remained the Model 11's non folding unit.

Modifying the Zero to a floatplane involved removing the undercarriage and all its associated equipment and replacing it with a large central float attached by a forward sloping pylon and aft V-strut plus two smaller outrigger floats mounted by way of single pylons. The arrestor hook was removed and to restore directional stability, a narrow ventral fin was added under the rear fuselage, the rear portion of it being an extension of the rudder.

As no drop tank could be carried, additional fuel was housed within the main float. Armament remained as per the A6M2 – two 20mm cannon in the wings and two 7.7mm machine guns in the upper cowling.

Structurally, the aircraft differed from its wheeled counterpart by incorporating alloys which were less prone to corrosion and the engine mounts and other areas were strengthened to cope with the extra stresses imposed by water operations.

The first Rufe was flown on 8 December 1941, just a matter of hours after the raid on Pearl Harbour. Testing proceeded smoothly and the aircraft was accepted into Navy service in July 1942. The last example was handed over in September 1943.

Although about 60mph (96km/h) slower than the Zero 21, the Rufe still managed a good turn of speed for its type and manoeuvrability was better than expected. The A6M2-N initially served in the Solomons and Aleutians, the former campaign seeing the aircraft briefly unchallenged by the Allies before far superior American fighters removed it from the equation. After that, it was relegated mainly to support and training duties although it did see combat occasionally when there was nothing else available.

At home, the Rufe found some employment late in the war as a last-ditch interceptor, sometimes fitted with night flying equipment.

A6M2-N 'RUFE'
Powerplant: *One Nakajima NK1C Sakae 12 14-cylinder air cooled radial rated at 940hp (701kW) for takeoff and 950hp (708kW) at 13,780ft (4,200m); three bladed Sumitomo constant-speed propeller. Internal fuel capacity 115imp gal (525 l) in wing and fuselage tanks; 71imp gal (325 l) tank in central float.*
Dimensions: *Wing span 39ft 4.4in (12.00m); length 33ft 1.5in (10.10m); height 14ft 1.3in (4.30m); wing area 241.5sq ft (22.44m²).*
Weights: *Empty 4,215lb (1,912kg); normal loaded 5,423lb (2,460kg); max loaded 6,349lb (2,880kg).*
Armament: *Two 20mm Type 99 cannon in wings; two 7.7mm Type 97 machine guns in upper cowling; two 132lb (60kg) bombs.*
Performance: *Max speed 235kt (435km/h) at 16,404ft (5,000m); cruising speed 160kt (296km/h); time to 16,404ft (5,000m) 6.7min; service ceiling 32,808ft (10,000m); range (standard tanks) 620nm (1,148km), with float tank 963nm (1,784km).*

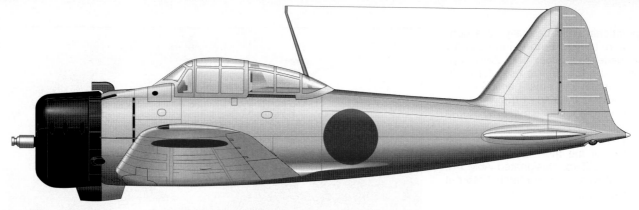

A6M1 Zero prototype at time of first flight, 1 April 1939.

A6M2 Model 11 Zero 3-136 of 12th Rengo Kokutai IJNAF, China May 1941. Aircraft of Kunimori Nakakariya (16 victories).

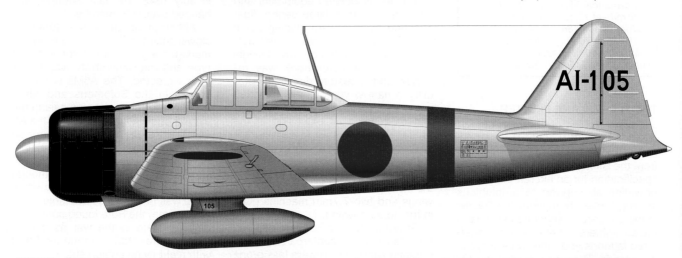

A6M2 Model 21 Zero AI-105 of 1st Koku Sentai IJNAF. Flown from carrier Akagi during attack on Pearl Harbour 7 December 1941.

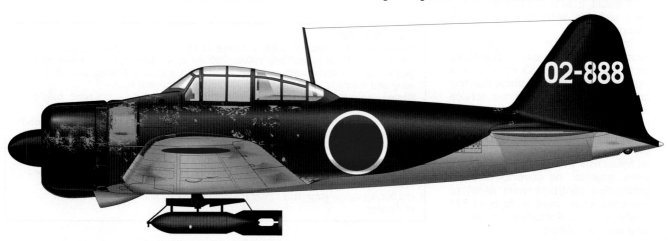

A6M2 Model 21 Zero 02-888 of 201st Kokutai IJNAF, Philippines October 1944. Believed to be one of the aircraft used in the first Kamikaze mission.

A6M2 Model 21 Zero EI-111 of 5th Koku Sentai IJNAF, Battle of Santa Cruz, October 1942. Flown from carrier Shokaku against USS *Enterprise*.

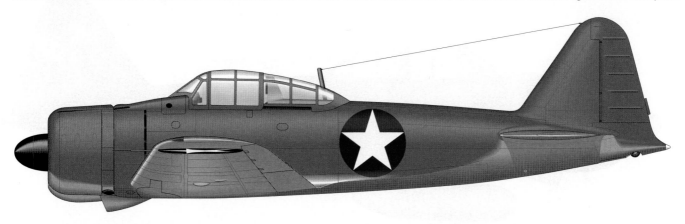

A6M2 Model 21 Zero in US colours September 1942 after capture and repair at NAS North Island, San Diego. Aircraft force landed in Aleutians and recovered by US Navy. This was the first Zero the Allies had the opportunity to examine and flight test.

A6M2 Model 21 Zero BI-12 in RAF markings, Burma. Captured and tested by Allied Tactical Air Intelligence Unit – South East Asia (ATAIU SEA). Note non standard long barrel cannon.

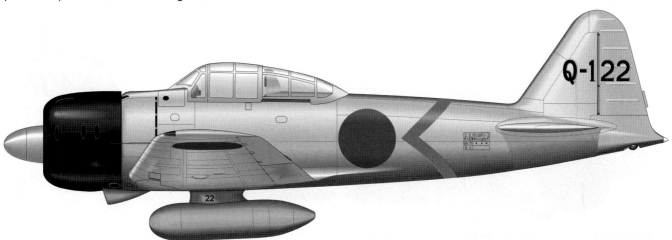

A6M3 Model 32 Zero Q-122 of 2nd Kokutai IJNAF, Rabaul 1942. Markings denote a section leader's aircraft.

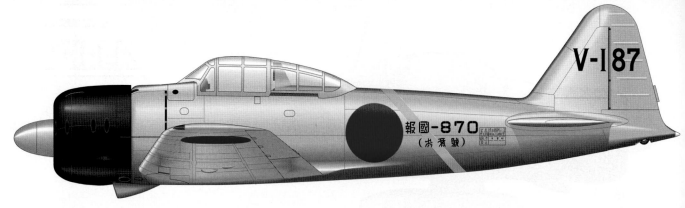

A6M3 Model 32 Zero V-187 of Tainan Naval Air Group, Buna New Guinea early 1943. Presentation aircraft with inscription 'Contributed by Kogen'.

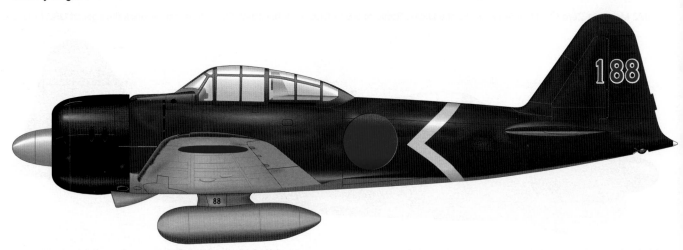

A6M3 Model 22 Zero '188' of 1st Koku Sentai IJNAF, Rabaul early 1943. Aircraft from carrier *Zuikaku* but based at Bougainville. Camouflage green was applied in field over original grey finish.

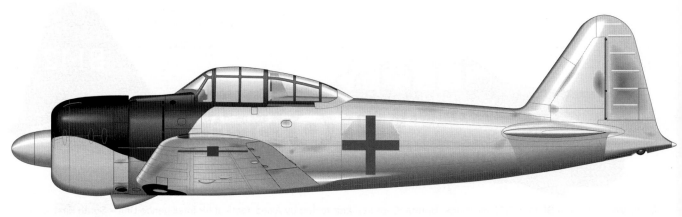

A6M3 Model 22 Zero, Jacquinot Bay New Britain, 1945. Aircraft in official surrender markings.

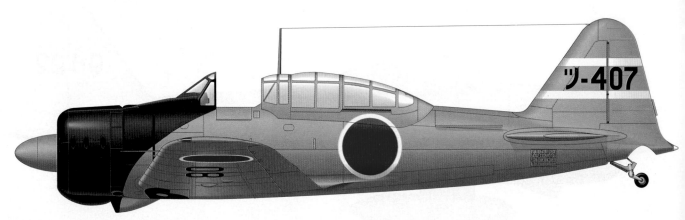

A6M2-K Zero 'TSU'-407 of Tsukuba Kokutai, Japan early 1944.

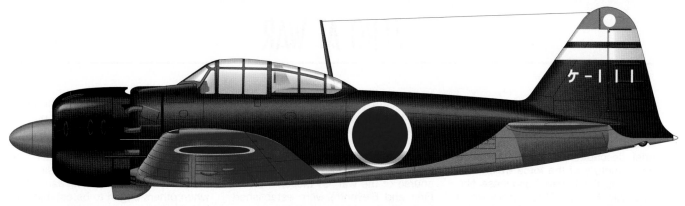

A6M5 Model 52 Zero of Genzan Naval Air Corps at Wonson, Korea mid 1944. Aircraft used for training duties.

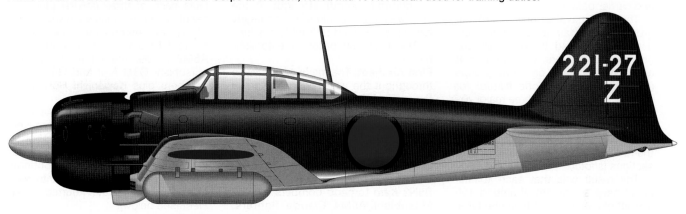

A6M5 Model 52b Zero 221-27 'Z' of 221st Kokutai IJNAF, Kasanohara Air Base 1944.

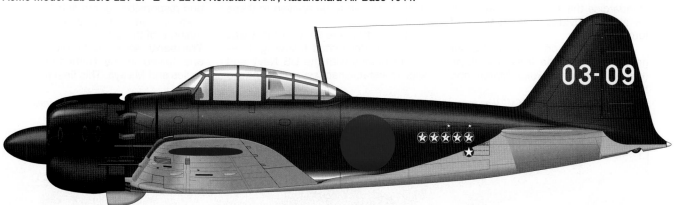

A6M5 Model 52c Zero 03-09 of 303rd Hikotai, 203rd Kokutai IJNAF, Kagoshima Air Base June 1945. Aircraft flown by Takeo Tanizumi who ended war with 18 kills. Markings show five confirmed kills and one probable.

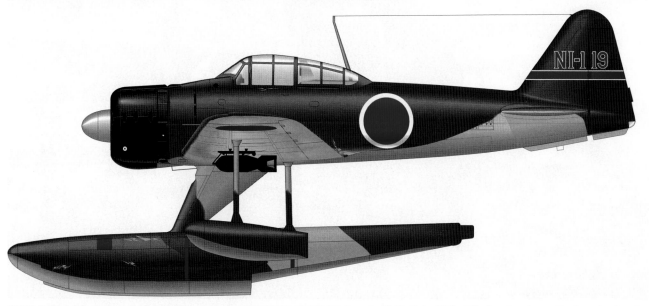

A6M2-N 'Rufe' floatplane fighter of 802nd Kokutai IJNAF, Marshall Islands early 1943. Note 132lb (60kg) underwing anti submarine bombs.

ZERO AT WAR

ORGANISATION

Before beginning a summary of the Zero's combat career, perhaps it would be appropriate to present a brief description of the organisation and structure of the force which employed it, the Imperial Japanese Navy's Air Force. This operated a substantial fleet of aircraft, both land and carrier based.

The basic naval air unit was the air group. Carrier air groups (*hikokitai*) usually comprised three squadrons, one each of fighters, torpedo aircraft and bombers. Land based air groups (*kokutai*) comprised one *hikotai* for each of usually two or three major aircraft types in the group. These were in turn divided into two or three squadrons (*daitai*) of 18 to 27 aircraft, themselves consisting of three aircraft sections (*shotai*).

The result was that each *kokutai* could have a strength of around 150 aircraft of usually more than one type. From 1944 an attempt was made to standardise the size of a squadron at 16 aircraft divided into sections of four aircraft.

Operational control of the air groups lay with the individual fleets (*kantai*), air fleets (*koku kantai*) and area fleets (*homen kantai*). Carrier based aircraft were attached to carrier divisions (*koku sentai*) which normally had two carriers on strength.

The Imperial Japanese Navy had nine operational air fleets during the course of the war. Of these, two (the First and Eleventh) were established by December 1941 and the Navy's total combat aircraft strength at the time was about 3,000 of which nearly half were assigned to front line units.

The fleets (in order of establishment) were:

First Air Fleet: The major carrier force throughout the war, taking part in all the major battles and at the start of hostilities hosting the carriers *Akagi, Kaga, Soryu, Hiryu, Ryujo, Zuikaku* and *Skokaku*. The total air strength of this air fleet in December 1941 comprised 135 A6M2 Zeros, 135 Aichi D3A *Val* dive bombers, 162 Nakajima B5N2 *Kate* torpedo bombers and 22 Mitsubishi A5M4 *Claude* fighters. Note that at this stage the Allied code names still had to be applied to these aircraft.

By late 1943 the First Air Fleet was just about decimated following a series of battles with the US Navy and was re-established as a land based entity, although it remained the combined fleet's main strike force operating from the Mariana Islands, the Philippines and finally Formosa.

Eleventh Air Fleet: A land based air fleet which remained responsible for the entire Pacific area until early 1943 when others began to be established. In late 1941 it comprised three air flotillas each of three *kokutai* plus two seaplane tender units each with about 20 aircraft. Among the total fleet of some 540 aircraft were about 210 A6M2 Zeros, the remainder mainly Mitsubishi G3M *Nell* and G4M *Betty* bombers plus Kawanishi H6K *Mavis* flying boats.

From 1943 the Eleventh Air Fleet was responsible only for eastern New Guinea and the central Pacific but by early 1944 it had been all but destroyed following Japan's continual reversals in battle. The remnants were re-established as the Fourteenth Air Fleet (see below).

Twelfth Air Fleet: Formed in 1943 and responsible for the defence of the north-eastern Pacific area for the remainder of the war.

Thirteenth Air Fleet: Formed in 1943 and based in the Netherlands East Indies and Malaya. This fleet assumed

A Zero that survives. This A6M2 was recovered from New Britain and arrived in Australia in 1974 under the ownership of the Australian War Memorial. A lengthy restoration by the tradesmen at RAAF Wagga was completed in 1988, the fruits of which are shown here.

responsibility for the defence of all of South-East Asia and the south-west Pacific including the Philippines and western New Guinea. In late 1944 the reconstituted First Air Fleet joined the Thirteenth in the Philippines.

Second and Third Air Fleets: Both formed in early 1944 and remained in Japan for the remainder of the war.

Fourteenth Air Fleet: Established in early 1944 from what was left of the Eleventh Air Fleet and responsible for the central Pacific area until it too was virtually destroyed in the first half of 1945.

Fifth and Tenth Air Fleets: Both formed in 1944 and remained in Japan until the end of the war. The Tenth was responsible for providing Naval aircraft and pilots for the *Kamikaze* suicide missions.

FIRST BLOOD

Japan's imperial ambitions had been established and partially put into practice well before the outbreak of the Pacific War in December 1941. More than a decade earlier, in September 1931, Japan had invaded Manchuria and been involved in fighting the Chinese, resulting in the establishment of the puppet state of Manchukuo in Manchuria.

This action precipitated the chain of events which would eventually result in Japan's entry to World War II. In March 1933 Japan was condemned by the League of Nations as an aggressor and left that organisation as a result.

The second Sino-Japanese conflict began in July 1937, Japan using the pretext that its soldiers had been fired upon and immediately occupied Peking. By December 1937 Japan occupied all of northern China despite stout resistance from Chaing Kai-Shek's troops, which were supplied with arms, money and advice by the West. The conflict widened from there, involving (from mid 1940 after the collapse of France) French Indo-China, which it invaded in September 1940.

Within ten months Japan controlled the whole of Indo-China and the first stages of its stated intention to establish "a new order in greater East Asia" were well in place. By now, even the most ardent American and British doubters about Japan's intentions were just about convinced that war with this new power on the world stage was close to inevitable.

Zero Into Action

It was in the second war with China that the Zero earned its first battle honours. One of the features of this conflict was the Imperial Japanese Navy's increasingly long range bombing raids which often meant the bombers were without fighter escort

An early Zero launches from its aircraft carrier. Japan dominated the Pacific War for the first six months, spearheaded by the Imperial Japanese Navy Air Force.

for a substantial period of time. This in turn resulted in mounting bomber losses.

The deployment of an initial batch of six pre production A6M2 Model 11s to the 12th Combined Air Group *(Rengo Kokutai)* in central China at the end of July 1940 for land based combat evaluation trials began the process of reversing this trend and establishing the myth of invincibility that would quickly become part of the Zero's folklore.

Another nine A6M2s were added to the group's strength before operations began. The first mission was flown on 19 August 1940 when 12 Zeros escorted 51 bombers over the then enormous distance of 930 miles (1,500km) during a raid on Chungking, the capital of Nationalist China. There was no combat on that occasion but it was not long before the Zero scored its first kill.

On 13 September, 13 Zeros took on 27 Chinese Polikarpov I-152, I-153 and I-16 fighters near Chungking, the ten minute battle resulting in the destruction of the entire Chinese force for the loss of no Zeros. Wnt Off Koshiro Yashimata became Japan's first Zero 'ace' as a result of this action after claiming five victories. Of interest is the fact that the Japanese pilots could claim only 22 kills from this action as two of the Chinese aircraft had collided and three others were abandoned by their pilots as soon as combat was joined!

Other air battles followed over the next few months in which more Chinese aircraft were downed but these became rarer as it didn't take long for the Chinese to learn to avoid combat with the Zeros wherever possible, and this was usually rigidly adhered to.

The 12th *Rengo Kokutai's* Zeros were joined by aircraft operated by the 14th in mid 1941, the two units between them flying 507 sorties during the course of their tours of duty and claiming the destruction of 103 Chinese aircraft. Zero losses in air-to-air combat were ... zero. The two A6M2s which did go down were both lost as a result of ground fire, and the first of them was not until May 1941.

It was the Zero's combat debut in China which began the Zero myth. Stories of a new Japanese 'super-fighter' began to leak out. They failed to take into account the fact that Chinese opposition to the aircraft was minimal, but it certainly was far superior to anything it was likely to encounter in that conflict. Its exceptional range and manoeuvrability were certainly major attributes and the overwhelming success enjoyed by Japanese forces generally in the opening months of the Pacific War added to the Zero's reputation.

Most important was Japan's own belief in its new fighter. Extending that thought brought them great comfort when planning the battles ahead.

Of greater significance to the history of the near future in the Pacific

A6M2 Model 11s of the 12th Rengo Kokutai over China in May 1941. It was in this theatre that the Zero's myth of invincibility developed.

A6M2 Zeros prepare for departure from the carrier Akagi *on the early morning of 7 December 1941. Next stop, Pearl Harbour.*

was that which the Zero symbolised during its Chinese campaign – the mobility and ambition of Japan, both of which would shortly combine with devastating results in Hawaii, the Philippines, Malaya, Singapore and elsewhere.

Claire Chennault, a former US Army Air Corps officer and commander of the American Volunteer Group in China – the 'Flying Tigers', an organisation intended to help the Chinese Air Force in its battles against the Japanese – kept the powers-that-be in Washington DC and London informed about the Zero and Japan's activities in China generally. Chennault prepared combat reports and even a tactical plan to deal with the new fighter.

These reports fell on largely deaf ears because few believed (or wanted to believe) them, with the Japanese military organisation and its equipment generally being regarded as inferior. Britain, for example steadfastly believed that the very ordinary Brewster Buffalo fighter was adequate to defend its interests in the Far East. The events of early 1942 quickly proved this to be tragically wrong.

THE 'HAWAIIAN OPERATION'

By 1941 the improved Zero A6M2 Model 21 was in service and Japan's military plans were well in place. From September of that year, Japan began deploying its forces in the Pacific and South-East Asia in readiness for the now inevitable battles, despite ongoing negotiations with the USA.

The IJN's Zeros were spread among the six aircraft carriers which would provide the springboard for the raid on Pearl Harbour while land based units were moved to French Indo-China for operations on the Malayan Peninsula and to Formosa for use against the Americans in the Philippines.

The total force of Zeros in late 1941 stood at about 340 including reserves, meaning that if the 135 aircraft aboard the carriers are taken into account, there weren't a lot of others to be spread over a very wide area of operations.

The task force allocated the job of attacking the US Navy base at Pearl Harbour on the Hawaiian Island of Oahu secretly left Hikotappu Bay, at Iturup in the southern Kuriles, on 26 November 1941, travelling to Hawaii

by a seldom used route (because of frequent severe storms) and observing radio silence all the way. By early December the fleet was near the point from which the attack would be launched, about 230 miles (370km) away.

The task force was commanded by Vice-Admiral Chuichi Nagumo who in turn acted under the orders of the architect of the raid, Admiral Irosoku Yamamoto, commander of the High Fleet. It comprised six of the First Air Fleet's seven aircraft carriers (*Soryu, Kaga, Akagi, Hiryu, Zuikaku* and *Shokaku*) along with 17 escorting warships. Between them, the carriers had some 432 aircraft on board of which three-quarters were used in the raids flown against Pearl Harbour.

Bomber's eye view of American ships at Pearl Harbour with exploding bombs clearly visible.

Tora! Tora! Tora!

It is well known the attack on the morning of 7 December 1941 achieved complete surprise and the destruction of a substantial part of the US Navy's Pacific Fleet including several battleships. Of great significance is the fact that the two American aircraft carriers normally based at Pearl Harbour (*Lexington* and *Enterprise*) were not in port at the time and escaped. This

A view of Ford Island during the Japanese attack on Pearl Harbour with 'Battleship Row' clearly visible and the ships neatly lined up for the attackers.

alone helped ensure that Japan would be defeated in the long run.

The element of surprise was aided by an administrative problem at the Japanese Embassy in Washington, which had been unable to decode and deliver the message containing Japan's declaration of war on the USA before the attack began. This was not the intention, but this "day of shame" – as the US Government described it – provided Americans with even more anger than they might otherwise have had.

The raid on Pearl Harbour was conducted in two waves. The first departed the carriers at 6.00am local time and arrived over the target at 7.55am. It comprised 100 Nakajima B5Ns carrying either torpedoes or bombs, 40 Aichi D3As armed with bombs and 42 Zeros commanded by Lt Cdr Shigeru Itaya from the *Akagi's* air group, a total of 182 aircraft. Overall, the operation was led by Lt Cdr Mitsuop Fuchido.

The Zeros' role was to not only protect the strike aircraft but also to strafe ground installations, airfields and anti aircraft gun positions. The element of surprise brought with it little resistance and only one Zero was lost.

The second wave arrived over Pearl Harbour at 8.40am, this force comprising 171 aircraft – 54 B5Ns, 81 D3As and 36 Zeros. By now fully alerted, the Americans this time offered more resistance and six Zeros were lost in air-to-air combat to US fighters, although Zero pilots claimed the destruction of 12 enemy aircraft in the air and 30 more on the ground.

The attack was a complete success for the Japanese force and left the US Navy's Pacific Fleet in a state of disarray for several months, allowing Japanese amphibious landings in the South-West Pacific area to go ahead virtually unopposed.

The final tally of US losses was substantial: The battleships *Arizona* and *Oklahoma* plus the target ship *Utah* and the minelayer *Oglala* sunk; the battleships *California*, *Nevada* and *West Virginia* seriously damaged but not listed as sunk only because they lay in shallow water; the battleships *Tennessee*, *Maryland* and *Pennsylvania*, the cruisers *Helena*, *Raleigh* and *Honolulu*, the destroyers *Cassin*, *Downes* and *Shaw* plus other smaller vessels assessed as severely damaged; 188 aircraft from the Hickman, Wheeler and Ewa airfields destroyed or damaged on the ground; ammunition dumps, fuel dumps and other ground installations destroyed; 2,330 killed and 1,347 wounded.

Japanese losses were considerably lighter: 29 aircraft (including some which fell overboard while attempting to land after the raid) and 64 personnel dead or missing.

Another takeoff to another target, but Japan's early superiority would not last beyond the middle of 1942.

MASTERS OF THE PACIFIC

The Japanese attack on Pearl Harbour heralded a period of six months during which the country's ambitions were to a large extent fulfilled as a series of assaults on various parts of South-East Asia and the Pacific resulted in a string of victories.

The Philippines, Hong Kong and Malaya were attacked almost simultaneously with the Pearl Harbour assault and by the end of the year Guam, Wake Island and Hong Kong had all fallen while Burma was in the midst of invasion. In January 1942 Manila was taken and the Dutch East Indies occupied; in February Rangoon (and the rest of Burma fell), as did Singapore, and Australia's northernmost city, Darwin, was bombed for the first time.

In March it was the turn of Batavia to succumb followed by Lashio in April, Mandalay in May and in the same month, US General Jonothan Wainwright surrendered all his forces in the Philippines.

The Imperial Japanese Navy's First Air Fleet played a major role in several of these battles, starting shortly after Pearl Harbour when the carriers *Hiryu* and *Soryu* were despatched to Wake Island where the Zeros quickly disposed of the US Navy Grumman Wildcat fighters which were opposing the Japanese landings there.

These two carriers then returned to Japan but were shortly sailing again in company with the *Akagi* and *Kaga* to support operations in New Britain, New Ireland and other activities in the South-West Pacific.

It was from these carriers that Darwin was attacked with such devastation on 19 February 1942 by a total of 187 aircraft including 36 Zeros. They shot down eight out of 11 USAAF Curtiss P-40s which just happened to be at Darwin at the time for the loss of only one Japanese fighter. The P-40s were the only serious air defence available. Two more P-40s were destroyed on the ground along with numerous other aircraft. Shipping in Darwin Harbour was sunk, port facilities destroyed, both the RAAF and civilian airfields were attacked – as was the city itself – and at least 243 people were killed.

A second raid on Darwin was carried out later in the same morning, this time by land based Mitsubishi

A6M2s of the 3rd Kokutai on Timor in early 1942.

An A6M2 departs the carrier Zakaku in October 1942. This first major production variant of the Zero carried a substantial burden during the first year of the Pacific War.

GM3 *Nell* and GM4 *Betty* bombers of the IJN's Eleventh Air Fleet based at Ambon and Kendari. They finished off the job started by the first attacking group, leaving Darwin temporarily out of action as major base. Darwin was bombed a total of 64 times between then and November 1943 and other points across the top end of Australia were also attacked.

In March 1942, the Japanese task force began a fortnight of operations

Wnt Off Hiroyoshi Nishizawa, Japan's leading ace of the war with 87 victories, all scored in Zeros. His first kill was recorded over New Guinea in early 1942 and increased rapidly. In August 1942 he shot down six American aircraft in a single action. In October 1944 Nishizawa was selected to provide an escort for the first Kamikaze attack but he survived for only one more day, killed when the transport aircraft in which he was flying was shot down.

in the Indian Ocean, the carrier based aircraft sinking the British carrier *Hermes* and two cruisers. Air-to-air operations resulted in the Zeros destroying six Fairey Swordfish biplane torpedo bombers, 15 Hawker Sea Hurricanes and four Fairey Fulmars for the loss of just one Zero.

In the first six months of Japan's war, there is little doubt that the Zero was the world's prime naval fighter, but its advantage began to diminish after that as more capable Allied fighters became available and the Zero failed to be developed further.

From The Land

In the meantime, land based Zeros also contributed significantly to Japanese successes, their long range time and time again proving to be an invaluable asset.

Operating from French Indo-China initially, the Zeros made short work of the Brewster Buffalos defending Malaya and were also effective against the Hurricanes over Singapore, the first victories against the British fighter being recorded on 21 January 1942 when five Hurricanes were destroyed without loss.

The Philippines campaign began only hours after the attack on Pearl Harbour with bombers escorted by Zeros flying all the way from Formosa and conducting telling strikes against the US air bases at Clark and Iba, destroying numerous Boeing B-17 bombers and most of the American fighter force in the process and for minimal losses. On the second day of the Philippines campaign, the Zeros shot down 11 Curtiss P-40s and 12 hopelessly outclassed Seversky P-35s for the loss of six of their own.

The Dutch East Indies was next, the Zeros of the 3rd *Kokutai* and *Tainan Kokutai* (both part of the Elev-

enth Air Fleet's 23rd *Koku Sentai*) disposed of a numerically superior British, American and Dutch fighter force in a campaign which ended in early March 1942. The Zeros operated from Borneo and Celebes in this action and after the end of Dutch resistance on Java, they operated from there against Australian and American forces in New Guinea, especially around the strategically vital town of Port Moresby.

So far, it had been very one sided, but that would shortly change. Combat experience had already shown up some weaknesses in the Zero. Altitude performance was less than spectacular, as was its ability to dive away at high speed. A lack of robustness was of concern, likewise the lack of proper protection for the pilot and the aircraft's vital systems, especially the fuel tanks.

Combat against the Philippines based B-17s had revealed the Zero's vulnerability against well directed fifty-calibre machine guns, while its own armament of one 20mm cannon with only 60 rounds of ammunition in the A6M2 and rifle calibre machine guns meant a weakness in the area of general firepower, especially when dealing with a large aircraft such as the B-17.

EXAMINING THE MYTH

While the myth of the Zero grew, so did the need for the Allies to capture one, examine it and unlock its secrets. The opportunity finally came in early June 1942 when Japan conducted diversionary attacks on the Aleutian Islands during the Battle of Midway. The A6M2 of Petty Officer Tadayoshi

Japan's second highest scoring ace was Lt Tetsuzo Iwamoto, who notched up 80 kills of which 14 were in China. Iwamoto survived the war.

An A6M2 departs Rabaul in early 1943. This major Japanese base was in effect put out of action by bombing, meaning that Allied forces did not have to mount a potentially expensive seaborne invasion.

Koga developed engine trouble during the raid and made a forced landing on Akutan Island.

Koga landed wheels down but the aircraft ran into marshy ground and overturned, killing the pilot. The inaccessibility of the crash site meant that the Americans at first gave little thought to recovering the aircraft, but a US Navy team went to the site five weeks later and discovered the Zero was not badly damaged. It was subsequently removed and sent by ship to the US Navy facility at San Diego, where it was repaired in readiness for flight evaluation. The work was completed in October 1942.

The Zero was then test flown and data gathered, before it was pitted against several US fighters for a direct comparison. These were the Bell P-39D Airacobra, North American P-51 Mustang (an early model with Allison engine), Curtiss P-40F Warhawk (with Packard-Merlin engine), Grumman F4F-4 Wildcat and Vought F4U-1 Corsair. Of note during the

The captured A6M2 in flight. It flew against several US types for comparative purposes and much of the Zero 'myth' was exploded as a result.

The first Zero captured by the Allies, an A6M2. It is pictured here at San Diego where it was restored to airworthiness for evaluation against US fighters.

Lockheed P-38F: able to engage or disengage combat with the Zero at will.

tests was the relative unreliability of several of the American aircraft, whereas the Zero appears not to have missed a beat!

The results of these comparisons are reproduced below and first appeared in *Zero Fighter* by Robert C Mikesh. This is acknowledged as the source of the information.

P-38F Lightning v Zero 21

To begin this test, both ships took off in formation on a prearranged signal. The Zero left the ground first and was about 300ft in the air before the P-38F was airborne. The Zero reached 5,000ft about 5sec ahead of the Lightning. From an indicated airspeed (IAS) of 200mph the Lightning accelerated away from the Zero in straight and level flight quite rapidly. The Zero was superior to the P-38 in manoeuvrability at speeds below 300mph.

The planes returned to formation at 5,000ft, then separated slightly as both ships reduced to their best respective climbing speeds. Upon signal the climb was started to 10,000ft. Again the Zero was slightly superior in straight climbs, reaching 10,000ft about 4sec ahead of the P-38. Comparable acceleration and turns were tried with the same results.

From 15,000 to 20,000ft the two

were about equal, again comparable acceleration, speeds and manoeuvrability were tried with similar results as before.

In the climb from 15,000 to 20,000ft the P-38 started gaining at about 18,200ft. At 20,000ft the P-38 was superior to the Zero in all manoeuvres except slow speed turns. This advantage was maintained by the P-38 at all altitudes above 20,000ft.

One manoeuvre in which the P-38 was superior to the Zero was a high speed reversal. It was impossible for the Zero to follow the P-38 in this manoeuvre at speeds above 300mph.

The test continued to 25,000 and 30,000ft. Due to the superior speed and climb of the P-38F at these altitudes, it could outmanoeuvre the Zero by using these two advantages. The Zero was still superior in low speed turns.

P-39D Airacobra v Zero 21

Takeoff was accomplished in formation on signal to initiate a climb from sea level to 5,000ft. The P-39D was drawing 3000rpm and 70in manifold pressure on takeoff when the engine started to detonate, so manifold pressure was reduced to 52in. The Airacobra left the ground first and arrived at 5,000ft just as the Zero was passing 4,000ft. This manifold pressure of 52in could be maintained to 4,500ft.

At 5,000ft from a cruising speed of 230mph indicated air speed, the P-39 had a marked acceleration away from the Zero. Climbing from 5,000 to 10,000ft at the respective best climbing speeds, the P-39 reached 10,000ft approximately 10sec before the Zero. At 10,000ft from a cruising speed of 220mph, the Airacobra still accelerated away from the Zero rapidly. Climbing from 10,000 to 15,000ft, both aircraft maintained equal rates of climb to 12,500ft. Above this altitude the Zero walked away from the P-39.

In the climb from 15,000 to 20,000ft the Zero immediately took the advantage and left the Airacobra. The climb from 20,000 to 25,000ft was not completed as the Airacobra was running low on fuel.

On a straight climb to altitude from takeoff under the same conditions as before, the Airacobra maintained the advantage until reaching 14,800ft. Above this altitude the P-39 was left behind, reaching 25,000ft approximately 5min behind the Zero. At 25,000ft from a cruising speed of 180mph IAS, the Zero accelerated away from the P-39 for three ship lengths. This lead was maintained by the Zero for 1° minutes and it took the P-39 another 30sec to gain a lead of one ship length.

Bell P-39D: inferior to the Zero except at low altitudes.

North American P-51: more than a match for the Zero under most circumstances, even the earlier model with the Allison engine.

P-51 Mustang v Zero 21

The P-51 was drawing 3000rpm and 43in manifold pressure for its takeoff and climb to 5,000ft. The low manifold pressure was due to the setting on the automatic manifold pressure regulator [on this early Allison powered example]. The Zero left the ground and reached its best climb speed approximately 6sec before the P-51. However, the P-51 accelerated sharply away from the Zero at 5,000ft from a cruising speed of 250mph IAS.

The climb from 5,000 to 10,000ft and 10,000 to 15,000ft produced the same results, having the Zero accelerate away from the P-51 in rate of climb. At 10,000ft from a cruising speed of 250mph IAS, the Mustang again moved sharply away from the Zero, and at 15,000ft from a cruising speed of 240mph IAS the P-51 had the advantage over the Zero, but slightly slower than at 5,000ft and 10,000ft.

The P-51 could dive away from the Zero at any time. During this test, the P-51's powerplant failed to operate properly above 15,000ft so the comparison was not continued above this altitude.

P-40F Warhawk v Zero 21

These tests were not completed as it was found impossible to obtain maximum engine operation.

F4F-4 Wildcat v Zero 21

The Zero was superior to the F4F-4 in speed and climb at all altitudes above 1,000ft and was superior in service ceiling and range. Close to sea level, the two were equal in level speed. In a dive, the two were equal with the exception that the Zero's engine cut out in pushovers. There was no comparison between the turning circles of the two aircraft due to the relative wing loadings and resultant low stalling speed of the Zero.

F4U-1 Corsair v Zero 21

The Zero with its 950hp engine was by far inferior to the heavier 1,850hp F4U-1 in level and diving speeds at all altitudes. It fell short in climbs starting at sea level and also above 20,000ft. Between 5,000 and 19,000ft the situation varied. With slightly more than the normal fighter load, which may be distributed to give equal range and gun power, the Zero was slightly superior in average maximum rate of climb.

This superiority became negligible at altitudes where carburettor air temperatures in the F4U were down to normal; close to the blower shift points it was more noticeable. However, the Zero could not stay with the Corsair in high speed climbs. The superiority of the F4U at 30,000ft was very evident, and would persist when carrying heavier loads.

Curtiss P-40F: test aborted due to engine problems.

Grumman F4F: no match for the Zero in any aspect.

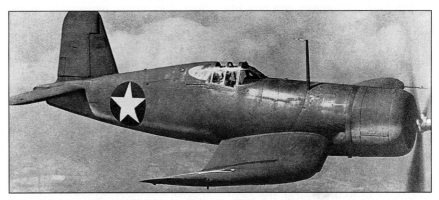

Vought F4U-1: superior to the Zero almost everywhere.

The Zero's nemesis in the Pacific, the Grumman Hellcat. (US Navy)

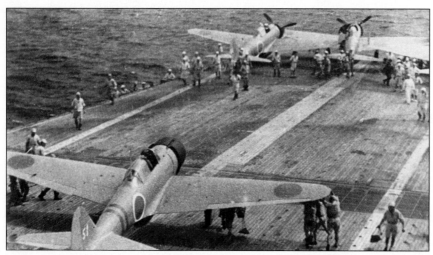

A6M2 Zeros aboard the carrier Zuikaku *during the Battle of the Coral Sea in May 1942. This battle marked Japan's first reversal of the war.*

Later Comparisons

Several more Zeros fell into Allied hands during the course of the war and comparisons between the later A6M5 Model 52, the Grumman F6F Hellcat and a later model F4U-1D Corsair go a long way towards explaining the decline of the Zero from 1943. A new and much more powerful aircraft was really needed to combat the American types but none was forthcoming in numbers.

The Zero 52's speed and rate of climb capabilities were markedly inferior to the Corsair, except in initial climbing. The Zero's rate of roll was equal at speeds below 230mph and inferior above that due to high control forces. Below 200mph the Zero's manoeuvrability could not be matched by the Corsair, although the latter could briefly stay with the Zero at just over 200mph. Acceleration in dives was roughly the same initially but the Corsair quickly accelerated away after that.

Compared to the Hellcat, the Zero 52 climbed faster up to about 9,000ft but the two aircraft were equal at

14,000ft and the Hellcat pulled away after that. The Hellcat was substantially faster at all altitudes, the margin increasing with height until it reached 75mph at 25,000ft. Comparative manoeuvrability was similar to that of the Corsair.

REVERSALS and RETREAT

The Coral Sea

Having achieved its initial objectives – including occupation of the Dutch East Indies with its oil and Malaya with its tin and rubber – Japan now attempted to put into action the second part of its plans. These involved increasing its sphere of influence to include Midway, the Gilbert Islands, the Ellis Islands, Fiji, New Caledonia, the Solomons, Papua and Port Moresby in south-eastern New Guinea.

The Aleutian Islands were also on the list, these and Midway intended to provide northern and eastern defence against operations aimed at Japan itself. The April 1942 Doolittle raid on Tokyo by a force of B-25 bombers

which had been launched from an aircraft carrier had come as something of a shock to the Japanese, who had until then considered their homeland to be immune to attack.

Port Moresby and the southern Solomons islands of Tulagi and Guadalcanal were vital to Japan if its aims were to be fulfilled. From Port Moresby, Australia was within easy reach. There had already been heavy fighting on the ground and in the air in New Guinea but in early May 1942 an invasion force was stopped following a major sea battle.

The Battle of the Coral Sea marked Japan's first reversal of the war and was also significant in that it was the first naval battle in history in which the opposing fleets never saw each other. It was conducted entirely by the two fleets' aircraft.

The battle was carried out over two days – May 7 and 8, 1942 – with the torpedo bombers from each fleet predominant, each trying to take out the other's major warships, especially the aircraft carriers. The fighters attempted to establish air superiority so as to give their strike aircraft an easier run to the targets, the Zeros taking on mainly Grumman Wildcats from the US carriers.

Despite the superiority of the Zero as a pure fighter, it is considered that the Wildcats eventually gained the advantage due to their ability to absorb punishment and the employment of much better tactics.

On the water, the battle was considered a draw in terms of damage inflicted but it was an Allied victory if the full implications are taken into account. The US Navy lost the carrier *Lexington* but not before its crew was able to be taken off, and the *Yorktown* was damaged. The Japanese escort carrier *Shoho* was sunk and the *Skokaku* was damaged to the extent that it had to return to Japan for repairs. Japanese aircraft losses reached 43 compared to the Americans' 33.

The important thing about the battle of the Coral Sea was that it forced postponement (and then cancellation) of the invasion of Port Moresby. This in turn made Australia's position considerably more comfortable but of equal importance at the time was the knowledge that at last, Japan had not achieved one of its major objectives.

Midway

The Battle of Midway on 3-7 June 1942 was probably *the* turning point of the Pacific War. Despite losses on both sides, the battle was very much an American victory and afterwards, the Japanese were almost constantly being pushed back from whence they came.

The Japanese plan was to capture

A6M2s and 3s of the First Naval Air Corps on Bougainville in November 1943. By then, the tide had well and truly turned against Japan.

Midway and attack and destroy the American fleet which Admiral Yamamoto (who was personally in charge of the operation) felt would be forced to challenge the Japanese actions. Yamamoto was correct in this assumption and based his confidence in the plan on the fact that his force was superior to the Americans'.

The Japanese fleet comprised 11 battleships and four aircraft carriers (the *Akagi*, *Hiryu*, *Soryu* and *Kaga*) plus smaller vessels while the Americans fielded no battleships and only three carriers – the *Enterprise*, *Hornet* and *Yorktown*, of which the latter was still carrying damage sustained in the Coral Sea battle, although some quick repairs had been carried out. The US force was commanded by Admiral Chester Nimitz.

Although the Americans had a numerically inferior force, what they did have in their advantage was an extensive knowledge of the Japanese cypher. This had been in use for three months and had been cracked by the Americans. It was well overdue for changing, but almost unbelievably, remained in place due to an administrative problem within the Japanese bureaucracy! Nimitz's use of this advantage was skilful and decisive, while indecision by the Japanese fleet commander Admiral Nagumo (who was also the Pearl Harbour commander) contributed to Japan's defeat.

The battle of Midway was an epic tussle spread over five days. At the end of it the US Navy had lost the *Yorktown* and 150 carrier aircraft but the Japanese lost all four carriers to American dive and torpedo bombers plus 234 aircraft including 72 A6M2 Zeros.

For Japan, the defeat at Midway marked the point where it no longer controlled the seas of the Pacific Ocean.

Associated with the Midway adventure was Japan's diversionary attack against the Aleutians which involved the carriers *Junyo*, *Zuiho* and *Ryujo*. This campaign was successful with the islands of Attu and Kiska being occupied. It was during this operation that the first A6M2 Zero was obtained by Allies and subsequently evaluated, as described earlier in this chapter. The Americans regained control of the Aleutians in 1943.

Guadalcanal

Despite its defeat at Midway, Japan's ambitions in the Solomons and New Guinea remained intact and New Guinea operations continued with the aim of taking Port Moresby. Having been prevented from taking Moresby from the sea, an overland assault from the north was begun instead.

The Battle of Santa Cruz was part of the Solomons campaign and specifically the battle for Guadalcanal. These shots were taken aboard the carrier Skokaku *on 26 October 1942, with Zeros departing to attack the USS* Enterprise.

It was at this point that the Allies decided to go on the offensive with intention of driving the Japanese out of New Guinea and to retake the island of Guadalcanal at the southern end of the Solomons group. This combined air, land and sea assault was the first of the many 'island hopping' operations which was eventually see Japan pushed back to the north.

The Solomons campaign began on 7 August 1942 but Japan was

Admiral Yamamoto waves his pilots off from Rabaul on 14 April 1943. The day before, Allied intelligence had intercepted and decoded a message detailing his travel plans. Four days later he was dead, the aircraft in which he was travelling shot down by USAAF P-38s.

A sign of the times: a captured A6M3 Model 32 is evaluated by the USAAF.

hampered from the start as it had no aircraft carriers in the area and until they arrived had to rely on aircraft based on Rabaul – 870 miles (1,400km) away – to oppose the American landings on Guadalcanal. This stretched even the Zeros' very long range to the limit, not to mention their pilots' physical endurance. Despite this, the Zeros put up a strong showing and were basically holding their own until the Americans established Henderson Field on Guadalcanal.

The battle for Guadalcanal was not finally resolved until February 1943 when the last Japanese were forced to evacuate after repeated attempts to land reinforcements. The campaign was expensive for both sides with Japan losing the one carrier, the *Ryujo*, and the US Navy two, the *Wasp and Hornet*.

Decline and fall: a Zero (top) is examined by Australian servicemen in Brisbane; and US troops look over A6M2 at an abandoned Japanese base. Note the folding wingtips. (via Mike Kerr)

The Zeros therefore operated from both land and sea and the battle saw the debut of the new A6M3 variant with its more powerful Sakae 21 engine with two stage supercharger and clipped wings. This proved to be a disappointment as its performance was only slightly superior to the A6M2 and its higher fuel consumption resulted in reduced range, a critical factor in operations over the Solomons and New Guinea.

Continued Setbacks

By early 1943 Japan had well and truly lost the initiative with the Allied forces beginning their inexorable push north. Landings in New Guinea started in June 1943 followed by Bougainville in November. 1944 saw the greatest gains made with New Guinea, Saipan, Guam, the Marianas (from which the USAAF launched its B-29 attacks on Japan) and the Philippines all being taken back. Elsewhere – including India, Burma and China – the Japanese Army Air Force and Japanese ground forces were suffering similar setbacks and reduced effectiveness.

US Navy aerial strength increased considerably in 1943 with the arrival in large scale service of the Vought Corsair and Grumman Hellcat, while Japan suffered a major loss in April 1943 when the aircraft in which Admiral Yamamoto was travelling was intercepted and shot down by USAAF P-38 Lightnings. This incident is discussed in more detail in the Lightning section of this book.

The entry of the A6M5 Zero into service in late 1943 coincided with the start of the serious decline of all Japan's services including the Navy and Army Air Forces. Intended as an interim solution pending the availability of new designs the A6M5 turned out to be the most produced of all the Zero models and remained in production until the end of the war as no successor was successfully developed.

Philippines Disasters

Another crucial battle in the Pacific War occurred on 19-20 June 1944, the first of two Battles of the Philippine Sea. These were the last major naval battles between the opposing forces, the first involving nine Japanese carriers carrying 225 A6M5 Zeros (plus a similar number of other types) between them and 15 US carriers which had a total of 443 Grumman F6F Hellcats on board. For the USA this was a prelude to taking the Mariana Islands of Guam, Tinian and Saipan and then the liberation of the Philippines; for Japan it was a last chance to prevent that.

The Japanese began the battle by launching an attack on the US fleet by aircraft from its carriers but these were intercepted by American Hellcats before reaching their targets. The battle which followed went down in military history as the infamous 'Marianas Turkey Shoot' in which 42 Japanese aircraft were shot down for the loss of just one Hellcat.

Subsequent attacks were also easily dealt with by the American fighters and at the end of it all the Japanese force had only 20 bombers and 25 Zeros remaining out of the original 450. This left the Americans with complete air superiority which they used to systematically pick off the Japanese carriers with little or no resistance before they could escape. The final tally was three carriers sunk, the *Hiyo*, *Skokaku* and *Taiho*, plus other vessels damaged.

US landings on the three Mariana Islands went ahead successfully.

Desperation: A6M2 fighters and A6M2-K trainers lined up at Genzan before departing on a Kamikaze mission.

The second battle of the Philippine Sea in October 1944 was the last occasion on which Zeros were flown into combat from the deck of an aircraft carrier. US landings began in the Philippines on the 20th of the month and Japan made a last ditch attempt to repulse them using four carriers, the *Chitose*, *Zuiho*, *Zuikaku* and *Chiyodo*.

On board these carriers were just 52 Zeros to take on 565 Hellcats aboard 17 US carriers. An unsuccessful strike was made on 24 October and the following day the 13 surviving Zeros made that last sortie and all were quickly disposed of. In addition, all four carriers were sunk and Japan's position as a major naval force in the Pacific effectively ended.

Divine Wind

The Zero's last hurrahs in World War II revolved around defending the homelands against USAAF B-29 bombers in conjunction with other naval and Army Air Force types, and its use in *Kamikaze* suicide missions.

This desperate measure involved Japanese pilots deliberately flying their aircraft into enemy ships in an effort to sink them, and although some success was achieved there is no doubt that regardless of its noble intentions, *Kamikaze* was a total waste of human and material resources in the face of desperation.

Kamikaze means 'Divine Wind' in Japanese and comes from the storms that wrecked the fleets of Kublai Khan in 1281 and saved Japan from invasion.

The effect of the Kamikaze could be quite devastating, witness the USS Saratoga *during the Iwo Jima bombardment.*

Numerous aircraft types were used in *Kamikaze* attacks and the Zero was prominent among them with about 330 used in this manner during the Philippines campaign (of which half hit their intended targets) and many more after that. A *Kamikaze* Zero normally had a 551lb (250lb) bomb attached to its underside in the place where the drop tank was previously carried.

The first *Kamikaze* attacks were made during the Battle of the Philippines in October 1944 and there was some success with several USN carriers and others ships sunk or damaged as a result. The technique was subsequently used in the defence of Okinawa and Iwo Jima and other locations close to Japan but could never prevent the course of the war and its result changing.

The Japanese regarded *Kamikaze* as a spiritual experience and a great honour as it afforded the 'victim' the opportunity to die bravely and to control his own destiny. Despite this, it's interesting to note that have been numerous reports of pilots being forced to participate in these suicide missions, those who were presumably less spiritually inclined than the others.

To most in the West, it was simply a question of needless waste, symbolic of nothing more than the setting of the once Rising Sun.

A remarkable photograph showing a Kamikaze Zero at the point of impact. The ship is the USS Missouri, *operating off Okinawa.*